✳ ✳ ✳ ✳ ✳ ✳ ✳ ✳ ✳ ✳

DANCING
IN THE
DRAGON'S DEN

*Rekindling
the Creative Fire
in Your Shadow*

ROSANNE BANE

NICOLAS-HAYS, INC.
YORK BEACH, MAINE

This book is dedicated to my "guardian angels":
Fishy, who taught me to believe what others couldn't see,
Black Wolf, who taught me to hunt for beauty and hope,
And the Dragon in My Eyes, who taught me to dance.

First published in 1999 by
NICOLAS HAYS, INC.
P.O. Box 2039
York Beach, ME 03910-2039

Distributed to the trade by
SAMUEL WEISER, INC.
P.O. Box 612 York Beach, ME 03910-0612
www.weiserbooks.com

Typeset in 11 point English Serif
PRINTED IN THE UNITED STATES OF AMERICA
VG
06 05 04 03 02 01 00 99
7 6 5 4 3 2 1

*The paper used in this publication meets the
minimum requirements of the American National
Standard for Permanence of Paper for Printed Library
Materials Z39.48-1984.*

The following publishers have generously given
permission to use material from copyrighted
works: From "The Child and the Shadow" by
Ursula K. Le Guin. Copyright 1975 by
Ursula K. Le Guin. First appeared in the
Quarterly Journal of the Library of Congress 32;
reprinted by permission of the author and the
author's agent, Virginia Kidd. From *What's My
Type? Use the Enneagram System of Nine
Personality Types to Discover Your Best Self* (San
Francisco: HarperSanFrancisco, 1992) and *My
Best Self: Using the Enneagram to Free the Soul*
(San Francisco: HarperSanFrancisco, 1993) by
Kathy Hurley and Ted Dobson. Used with
permission. From January (formerly Janet)
Kiefer at StoryPerformances, P.O. Box 9330,
Richmond Heights, MO 63117; 314-647-1070.
Used with permission.

Library of Congress Cataloging-in-Publication Data

Bane, Rosanne.
    Dancing in the dragon's den : rekindling the creative fire in
your shadow / Rosanne Bane.
        p. cm.
    Includes bibliographical references and index.
    ISBN 0-89254-047-8 (pbk. : alk. paper)
    1. Shadow (Psychoanalysis) 2. Creative ability. 3. Creative
thinking. I. Title.
BF175.5.S55B35 1999
153.3'5–dc21
                                   99-31855
                                   CIP

Contents

Foreword

The greatest sin is the unlived life.
THOMAS MERTON

As Rosanne Bane makes clear in the following pages, there are tremendous personal benefits to realizing and integrating our shadow. One of the first results, when you begin the fateful work of shadow integration, is a release and increase of energy. This makes sense. As we take back our disowned pieces, we are released from the typical pretense and posturing necessary to conceal what we have found unacceptable about ourselves. This is a relief, a refund from energy reserves that we are now free to spend in other ways. What we once believed were debts are now assets. What are we to do with this windfall? Rosanne Bane is gently insistent in her suggestion: invest this energy in self-expression.

Dancing in the Dragon's Den is about releasing the creative factor embedded in the human shadow. What a marvelous recognition by Ms. Bane, what a useful notion to put into practice: "To express your creativity, embrace your shadow; to embrace your shadow, express your creativity."

What is the shadow? The shadow is an alter ego that lives just beyond the sphere of our conscious awareness. To negotiate our way through earthly pursuits, we need an ego identity, an "I." What doesn't fit our ego-ideal, the idealized sense of self that we each have shaped by family and culture, becomes shadow.

Having a shadow is the price we each pay for being part of a family and a culture. In exchange for the benefits and power of civilized society, we are asked to suppress or eliminate those supposedly antisocial, inferior, or unacceptable qualities. It is tribute paid to the civilizing process, a sacrifice made as part of our social contract.

The repression is an honest mistake—a necessary, unavoidable mistake—that occupies the first half of life for many of us. Certainly, there are pieces of our fullest potential that need censorship; but much of the editing we do is careless and expedient, without the benefit of experience. My friend, poet and author Robert Bly, calls the shadow "the long bag we drag behind us. We spend our life until we're twenty deciding what parts of ourselves to put in the bag," Bly says, "and we spend the rest of our lives trying to get them out again."

Because our shadow is an affront to the self-concept we have created, we have little tolerance whenever we catch a glimpse of it. This is the challenge of shadow work. However, it is quite easy to see another's shadow. Others can usually see us as we are. Here lies the irony of the shadow game: In making these distinctions, we haven't really fooled anyone but ourselves. We originally agreed to make a shadow in order to adapt, to win love and approval from others. As it turns out, most everyone can see that the emperor-ego has no clothes. Only polite social grace refrains from mentioning the truth that we are all of a piece, ego and shadow.

Dancing in the Dragon's Den is the first book to specifically address the relationship between shadow and creativity, providing an extensive treasury of specific, practical answers on how to integrate the shadow. Rosanne Bane focuses with persistent intelligence on the shadow imperative that drives self-expression. As you work your way through these chapters, it will become increasingly evident that the shadow is a messenger who brings the good news of the treasures hidden in the depths, who carries the creative vision that has been growing in the darkness. Ms. Bane, like the Buddhist precept, reminds us that we should never try to get rid of our demons; in fact, we cannot get rid of negative energies. They are the very substance of enlightenment, waiting to be transformed and expressed.

We live in a perfectly imperfect world. It falls to each one of us to take on our share of human imperfection. Probably the best contribution one could make to the world would be to integrate our own shadow, to lift our personal piece of the burden off the world.

Though we may have cut ourselves off from our own life force by cutting our world in half, by creating dualisms of this and that, good and bad, ego and shadow, we cannot deny that the shadow has a vital function, which becomes more apparent as we move through life: shadow gives counterpoint to our idealism; it drives us to re-unify and become whole; it challenges us to give creative expression—to live the unlived life. As British analyst and author Liz Greene observes, "The shadow is both the awful thing that needs redemption, and the suffering redeemer who can provide it."

—JEREMIAH ABRAMS
Fairfax, California

Acknowledgments

As far as I can see, the main reasons to read the acknowledgments in any book are to

1. look for your own name
2. look for the name of someone you recognize
3. discover something about the writer and/or the writer's creative process

It's my intention that you will be able to accomplish all three of these purposes.

First, I want to thank you for picking up this book. So let's do that. Write your name in the blank coming up. (This is just the first of many short exercises that can make this book more powerful for you.)

First and foremost, thanks to you, _____. When you read and respond to this book, you complete the cycle. When you complete the circuit, it becomes possible for the energy of this book to flow from me to you. If you use that energy to further your own creativity and someone else responds to you, the cycle goes on. That is, after all, how this book got started in the first place, by someone as "ordinary" as you. You are one of the important people who make all the effort of bringing this book into being worthwhile. And for that I am truly grateful. If ever we meet in person, please let me know who you are so I can shake your hand and thank you again.

Now, I'm going to thank a lot of other people, some of whom you might recognize, all of whom I need to recognize.

To Lois, my mom, thanks for life and all the love. You have an amazingly generous spirit.

To Al, Art, and Chuck, my three dads, thanks for showing so many different ways the masculine can manifest. The different kinds of love and support you all have given me is beyond measure.

To Horton, Russell, and Glendeen, my siblings, thanks for your love and support, but far more important, thanks for all the squabbles of childhood and adolescence. The way we have aggravated and irritated each other over the years has been the "sacred grit" that led to each of us becoming the unique pearls we are.

Special thanks to Glendeen for sharing your artistic energy, enthusiasm, and encouragement. The year we lived together as adults helped me understand a lot about the twelve years we lived together as children. And thanks for showing me how to play while taking artistic risks during that year.

To Claudia, my heart-sister and the best friend I ever hope to have, thanks from the depths of my heart. You have seen more of my shadow and creativity than anyone else. The dance our shadows perform together at times continues to challenge us both to become our personal best. The dance our egos perform is pure joy at times. And the dance our spirits share is the promise of the best that is yet to be.

To Jeremiah Abrams, profound thanks for the introduction—to this book and to this work. We don't always know how far the effects of our actions and ideas will reach, but I hope you will recognize with pride some of what you taught me in my writing and my teaching.

To Linda Star Wolf, my heartfelt thanks. You have carried my white shadow with grace, humor, and love. I'm ready to take it back now with what I hope will be equal grace and humor and what I know is equal love.

To all my fellow Breathworkers (roughly in order of appearance): Claudia, Rob B., Cathy W., Laura U., Lynn A., Glen B., Tom A., Melissa B., Joan J., Gwen O., Bill H., Jeanne H., Cas M., Michelle C., Steve W., Gordy S., Mike U., Sherre H-T., Lisa L., Nita E., Sandy W., Terri D., Karen C., Tom B., Ron P., Ilga C., Maureen O., Lori S., Bobbie M., Jayne W., Nancy H., Carmen S., Kris E., and Nancy R., a whole community of love and gratitude. We have shared our shadows, light and dark, with each other and supported each other on the journey of becoming who we are meant to be. Your presence on this journey means more to me than you may be able to imagine. Thank you, one and all, for being my partners. Good journey to us all.

To my students, especially those who had enough confidence in me and enough courage in themselves to begin exploring the connections between creativity and shadow, deepest thanks. You helped me refine the concepts and fine-tune the exercises. Your enthusiasm and presence in the Explore Creativity and Shadow/Dancing in the Dragon's Den classes helped keep the book alive when publishing hopes looked bleak. Call me anytime you want help keeping your creative dreams alive.

No book is written in isolation, although it can feel that way at times. I am indebted to all the authors I've ever read and all the teachers and mentors I've ever had. And I am grateful for the wonderful professionals I've been blessed to work with during this long book project.

Thanks first to Anne Buchanan, my therapist. You helped me transform the image of the dragon from a threat to a promise. Your continuing support empowered me to give birth to my dreams.

Thanks to Val Olson, my coach. You helped me translate the promise and the dream into reality. I probably could have written this book without you, but I doubt I could have done it on time or as well without your gentle challenges and intriguing inquiries.

A good agent is a jewel beyond price. Thanks to Scott Edelstein for being that kind of agent. I'm grateful for the matter-of-fact way you kept me informed about the inevitable rejections and always offered encouragement along with calm reality checks. May every writer be blessed with a solid, trustworthy representative like you.

To Betty Christiansen, my first editor. Thanks for your enthusiasm and insight. Your willingness to participate in this process as both a student and an editor brought depth and wisdom to your editorial comments, which strengthened the book.

Thanks Michael Kelberer, former publisher of *The Phoenix*, for giving me opportunities to discover I could write nonfiction and challenging me to always ask myself how I could improve that writing.

And finally, thanks to Jim K., my ex-husband, for being a scoundrel. If you had been a boring goody two-shoes like me, I might never have moved to Minneapolis, met the people I've met, and started the journey I'm on. Let's trust that all is forgiven for both of us. Maybe with enough time and distance we can see how all our acts, even the ones we regret, are Divinely orchestrated.

Prologue

If you've ever had an urge to create something and gotten started, only to stop for one reason or another, this book is for and about you. Or if you've had the desire but never started, maybe because you doubt you can be creative or because you think creativity is reserved for special people, this is for and about you too. The desire to create is a creative beginning.

We all have some part of our creativity that's waiting to be expressed. Maybe it's the sunsets you've never painted, the pots you've never thrown, the buildings you've never designed. Maybe it's the blank page, the blank canvas, the blank stage, the unyielding lump of clay or marble or emotion that you've stared at for hours, knowing you want to do something with it but not knowing what. Maybe it's the life you've never fully lived.

This book is about that.

Some people think they've never had a yearning to be creative. They've been taught to believe they're not creative. They have been taught a lie. The life force is creative energy. To live is to create. To live fully is to create fully. To deny or restrict creativity is to deny and restrict life.

Most of the people who believe they aren't creative won't read this book, and that's sad because it's for and about them too. This book is especially for those of us who were taught that we aren't artistic because we couldn't draw in grade school or act in high school or write in college, but still hold a spark of hope that we might have some hidden talent.

This book is for all of us who are both attracted to and a little afraid of our own creativity.

The first thing we must know is that we are not alone. Look around; the next person you see either struggles with this dilemma or has given up the struggle by unconsciously blocking his or her creativity and, as a result, struggles with the surrender. It makes no difference whether that person is a successful, recognized artist or a hopeful unknown or someone who has given up any hope of being artistic. We all struggle with our desire to create fully—and thus live fully—and with our fear of what will happen if we do.

The second thing to know is that this struggle is perfectly natural. We have good reasons to be both attracted to and afraid of our creativity.

There is only one journey. Going inside yourself.
RAINER MARIA RILKE

In the more than ten years that I've taught writing and creativity, I've seen the pure joy that occurs when a student discovers that he or she is creative, that's it's okay to be creative, and that however he or she expresses that creativity is acceptable, even desirable. I've also seen students falter although I thought they had tremendous promise. I've come to recognize that faltering is part of the cycle of living a creative life. Some of those students have persevered, allowing themselves to struggle and fail and struggle some more and eventually succeed. Others quit. I've come to see that quitting is also part of the cycle. We all quit at some time, and we can unquit at any time.

Quitting is not an act of cowardice or laziness. It is a reasonable response to a real threat. How can creativity be a threat, and if it is, how can we hope to express our creativity fully? That's what this book is about.

We don't often talk about the threat our creativity holds for us. We talk about how being in the creative flow is a blissful state. All the books, tapes, and seminars that tell us how to be more creative at work, in our relationships, and in our art assume we want to be more creative and promise we will be if we'll just learn a new set of techniques. We do need to learn techniques and develop our craft, but it usually isn't lack of knowledge that keeps us from being as fully creative as we yearn to be. It is our fear.

We're so busy telling ourselves how wonderful it is to be creative that we conveniently forget to mention, even to ourselves, "By the way, I'm afraid of this creativity. I'm not just afraid that I won't be able to do this or that I'll be criticized or rejected, I'm afraid I don't want to do this at all. When I open up and explore my creativity, I scare myself."

We don't want to give up the joy of creativity, and even if we did, our creative urges would not be ignored. We don't want to go back, yet an unnamed fear keeps us from going on. We are blocked, not just in our art but in our lives.

The only truly satisfactory solution is to acknowledge the shadow of fear that accompanies the joy of creative expression and then, as Susan Jeffers says in her marvelous book of that title, "feel the fear and do it anyway."

In *The Artist's Way*, Julia Cameron writes, "When we open ourselves to exploring our creativity, we open ourselves to God: good orderly direction." This is true because, as Cameron explains,

> Art is an act of tuning in and dropping down the well. It is as though all the stories, painting, music, performances in the world live just under the surface of our normal consciousness. Like an underground river, they flow through us as a stream of ideas that we can tap down into. As artists, we drop down the well into that stream. We hear what's down there and we act on it—more like taking dictation than anything fancy having to do with art.

Herein lies the source of both our joy and our fear. What Cameron describes as "dropping down the well" is the process of exploring our unconscious, hidden self. Not only do we open ourselves to God when we open ourselves to our creativity, we open ourselves to our unconscious as well.

The "underground river" is the stream of the unconscious. It is a flow of ideas and inspiration from a divine source that we can access through our subconscious or unconscious mind. In Jungian terms, our personal unconscious connects us to the collective unconscious. In spiritual terms, our Higher Self connects us to the Higher Power and our creativity connects us to the Creator. However we describe it, what I have observed in my own life and in the lives of my students and friends is that opening ourselves to our creativity requires opening ourselves to our own unconscious.

The problem is that the unconscious is unpredictable. Sometimes I've dropped down the well and discovered an idea for the next scene in my novel. Sometimes I've dropped down the well and discovered old resentments I needed to address in my personal life.

You are never given a wish without also being given the power to make it true. You may have to work for it, however.
RICHARD BACH
Illusions

The unconscious holds energy and inspiration for creative expression. It also holds our shadow-self, what Carl Jung described as the person we have no wish to be. In the process of opening ourselves to our creativity, we open ourselves to this shadow, the denied and repressed parts of ourselves. No wonder we're afraid.

We're afraid that to be creative we will have to become everything we don't want to be. We're afraid that the myth of the dysfunctional, ego-centric artist is true and that being a great artist necessarily means being a rotten human being. But dysfunctional artists are not creative because of their egoism; they are creative in spite of it. The uncomfortable truth is that there are ways to be truly and deeply creative without behaving as a rotten human being, but not without acknowledging our potential to be a rotten human being. We don't have to become the person we have no wish to be; we have to acknowledge that we *already are* that person.

To be truly creative, we need to be aware of the difference between acting out and acting on. Jung called this distinction "taking moral action," which means acknowledging our dark inclinations as part of our human heritage, rather than pretending we don't have any, and then relying on our highest values to choose how we will act on what we find in the deepest parts of ourselves. Those who don't consciously act on their shadow will unconsciously act it out. If you don't own your shadow, it will own you.

To deny the dark potential is to deny an enormous part of ourselves. It takes a great deal of energy, energy that is diverted from creative expression. It is to deny that we are truly, fully human and to deny the depths of our humanity that makes our creativity meaningful.

Echoing both Cameron's image of the unconscious as a well and Jung's comment that the shadow is 90 percent gold, Joyce Sequichie Hifler writes about our fears of tapping the depths of our soul in *A Cherokee Feast of Days*:

> Giving up robs us of drawing up gold from our own depths. Imagine having a well, a very deep well, that is topped off with several feet of tainted water. But deeper down, the water, the *a ma,'* is clear, and down even further it is a spring, a spring that bubbles cold and pure through deposits of gold. Should we give

The gift turned inward, unable to be given, becomes a heavy burden, even sometimes a kind of poison. It is as though the flow of life were backed up.

MAY SARTON

up because of what we saw in the beginning? Or would we want to tap the depths and clear away the polluted water and get down to the very best? If it is true that we only know five percent of who and what we are—then, it is possible that we have untapped depths, where our being is pure and free of contamination. Should we give up such a rich experience because of what we have seen on the surface?

With knowledge, commitment, and reliable support, we can let go of the surface life of spending our energy repressing our shadow—and our creativity along with it—and become fully alive, fully creative, fully moral and human. We can walk through our fears to claim our larger Selves on the other side.

This book is about how to do that.

ONE

RECOGNIZING YOUR CREATIVITY, SEEING YOUR SHADOW

✳ ✳ ✳ ✳ ✳ ✳ ✳ ✳ ✳ ✳

CHAPTER 1

Into the Dragon's Den

THE DRAGON IS A POWERFUL SYMBOL in both Eastern and Western mythology. For the Chinese, dragons bring good fortune and
were once the exclusive sign of the emperor. For westerners, dragons
are darker and more dangerous. Our legends describe fire-breathing
dragons guarding golden treasure hidden deep underground.

When I first started working with the dragon as a metaphor, I saw it
only as a harbinger of darkness and destruction. My journey of discovery began fifteen years ago, when I received an invitation from my psyche. Perhaps *summons* would be a better word because it was the call to
begin the spiritual work of acknowledging and integrating my shadow,
the parts of myself I had disowned and cast aside.

It was no coincidence that I also received an invitation to explore my
creativity at the same time. My interest in writing then was, to a large
extent, an attempt to lose myself in the flow long enough to forget the
misery of going through a divorce I didn't want. I wrote powerful, dark
stories during that time of my life, and that was no coincidence either.

Most of the stories I wrote then disturbed my family and friends.
They scared even me, and, at the same time, they amazed me. I recognized that the emotionally disabled characters I wrote about were thin
disguises of myself. But I didn't know that the value of these stories lay
in the process of writing them. I thought I was writing them for publication or at least for my friends to read and respond to. But they were
painful to read, almost impossible to respond to, and nowhere close to
being ready for publication. I didn't know it yet, but my creative flow
was in service to the spiritual and psychological work I needed to do.

Unfortunately, I didn't have a safe place to do that psychospiritual work. My family and friends didn't know how to respond to the shadowy, draconic aspects slipping out from behind my goody two-shoes persona. With the best of intentions and the worst of effects, they encouraged me to not think such dark thoughts. In response, I cut myself off from them, certain that if my writing was too hard to talk about, then what I was feeling and thinking was unquestionably too horrible to speak aloud.

I didn't have resources or awareness. I didn't know who I could talk to. What my shadow brought up was too shameful for me to acknowledge. I didn't see my unconscious as a well that I could learn to draw pure water from; it was a slimy, black dungeon, and my shadow was a dragon haunting me from its depths. I was lost in depression, which I now see was sheer exhaustion from the effort it took to repress my shadow. In despair, I attempted suicide.

In an attempt to do away with my shadow, I nearly did away with all of me. I learned a dangerous, hard lesson: we aren't supposed to do away with our shadows. We can't. We can't cut off our shadows without cutting and mortally wounding ourselves.

In the years that followed, I knew I wanted to write, but the images came in floods that I didn't have the word craft to keep pace with, interspersed with long droughts when I felt bereft of inspiration. I feared any sign of the depression returning, and yet I had learned to associate the energy of writing with the energy of pushing the depression away. I thought that if I felt too good, I wouldn't have the inclination to write or material to write about, and if I felt too bad, I wouldn't be able to do anything at all. I spent so much energy shoring up the levees against my shadow, I had no time or inclination to trust the joy of floating down the river.

The psyche, our Higher Self, yearns for wholeness and works through synchronicity (meaningful coincidences). I was eventually given resources and awareness. I found a community that encouraged me to restore my faith in the God of my understanding, and I regained my emotional and spiritual footing. I "lucked into" a job writing for and editing a newspaper that addressed the ideas and issues I was most interested in. Later, someone insisted I accept the offer to attend, free of charge, a workshop led by Jacquelyn Small, author and pioneer in transpersonal psychology. I was on a journey back to my hidden self,

Perhaps all the dragons of our lives are princesses who are only waiting to see us once beautiful and brave. Perhaps everything terrible is in its deepest being something helpless that wants help from us.
RAINER MARIA RILKE

and the workshop introduced me to traveling companions. I found a safe container for and a loving community to support my shadow work, this time with understanding and compassion. My psyche had sent me another invitation. Perhaps my Higher Self recognized I had finally learned enough spiritual manners to RSVP appropriately to this one.

Once I thought the dragon was a symbol of my depression and therefore something I needed to conquer. Gradually, I realized that my "dragon-self" held years of repressed anger, and—although I didn't want to burn anyone to a crisp—that dragon-self was the source of important insight and power. First I acknowledged that aspect of myself, then I learned to accept and eventually even embrace my shadowy dragon-self. And just as in the legends, the dragon had a treasure horde to share with me.

It does not do to leave a dragon out of your calculations, if you live near him.

J. R. R. TOLKIEN
The Hobbit

Today, with a safe place and supporting friends, most ventures into the dragon's den—into the depths of my hidden self—are still frightening or uncomfortable. The difference is that now I know the journey has a higher purpose. I've learned that it is possible to repress the shadow—but only at tremendous cost to the totality of the psyche. I've learned that when I allow my shadow out of the self-imposed dungeon, I do experience fear, but I'm always given the gifts of creative energy and insight. I've learned to trust outcomes to a Higher Power, to trust the wisdom of my Higher Self, and even to trust my shadow to deliver the gold it holds. Fifteen years ago I could never have foreseen the day when I would willingly enter the dragon's den and learn to dance with joy there.

It is my privilege and my joy to share what I've learned to guide others in discovering that creativity and shadow rise together from the unconscious. I've watched with love and awe as others descended into the depths of their unconscious and returned with creative insights and energy that are gifts not only to themselves but to everyone they come into contact with.

Many of us are surprised, awed, or shocked at what comes out of ourselves when we create. Michael, a former publisher finally pursuing his dream of being a writer, started a free-form writing exercise that became, to his surprise, the beginning of a murder mystery. He was surprised by how it felt to write the grisly details of the murder scene and shocked that such images came from his own mind.

Paul, struggling with his Ph.D. dissertation in English, wrote, just for fun, a first-person narrative explaining why the main character is a hit man. When I offered to read it, his manner told me that, more than hearing what I thought of the story, he wanted (and feared) to know what I thought of *him*. Did I think he was weird or strange or bad for writing such a dark story?

The surprise at what we create is sometimes so uncomfortable, we cover it by denying that what we've done really is artistic. I often see fear in students' eyes and hear apologies in their voices when they talk about a new project or medium they're exploring. "I know it's not art," Sandy confessed, "but I like romance novels, and I thought I might try writing one," as if writing a romance novel isn't a project of worth and so Sandy had the freedom to try.

When Judy shyly showed the greeting cards she embossed and colored by hand, she insisted before anyone else could comment, "It's not much. The woman who showed me how does so much better," as if to say with pride and awe, "I did this! Isn't it great!" would tempt the gods to punish her for hubris.

This misplaced humility is a common shadow aspect in people exploring their creativity. It is, I'm certain, a behavior we have learned to protect ourselves; so it is something we can unlearn when we realize we don't need to protect ourselves in this way any longer. But until we realize that, we are afraid.

In her book *Source Imagery*, Sandra G. Shuman asks: "Why is the fear so prevalent? What is its cause? The need to depreciate our originality, to tear down what we have made in our own and others' eyes, is almost compulsive. It's as if we must steadfastly keep something hidden from view, something bad and disgusting that being creative exposes to the public eye. What is this negative feeling or projection all about?"

It is about our shadow and its connections to our creativity. No wonder we've repressed our full creative potential. To express our full potential, we must consciously work with our shadow, which can be frightening. It's often a struggle. Yet if we don't work with our shadow consciously, we pay the price of diminished creativity, and we expose ourselves and others to unconscious shadow outbursts anyway.

Creativity and shadow are inexorably intertwined. Some people think craziness is a prerequisite for an artist, while others see artistic en-

> *This [the unconscious] is the source of all creativity, but it needs heroic courage to do battle with these forces and to wrest from them the treasures hard to attain.*
>
> CARL JUNG

deavor as a safety valve that allows an individual to avoid madness. But shadow is not insanity, although sustained resistance to the psyche's call to integrate shadow may look like insanity, and the struggle to acknowledge and integrate shadow sometimes feels like losing your grip. Creating is much more than an avoidance technique or a coping mechanism. And integrating the shadow is much more than a way to break through blocks, although that would be reason enough for many people to undertake it.

Jung said the shadow is 90 percent gold. As difficult as it may be to recognize at first, the shadow—your shadow—holds a tremendous gift, a saving grace you need to be fully creative and fully alive. We don't have to be Christian to recognize the wisdom of Jesus' words: "If you bring forth what is inside you, what is inside you will save you, but if you fail to bring forth what is inside you, what is inside you will destroy you."

As you work through this book, you will find, as I and my students have found, that creative work and shadow work are both spiritual issues and that both your creative nature and your shadow are truly 90 percent gold. You may be uncomfortable when you first venture into the depths of your full Self, but I know that you, too, can discover the joy of dancing in your own dragon's den.

The future belongs to those who believe in the beauty of their dreams.
ELEANOR ROOSEVELT

What to Expect

Exploring your shadow and your creativity is not the work of an evening or two. Plan on reading and responding to one chapter of this book per week.

I've discovered, usually to my chagrin, that reading, writing, or teaching about the shadow often invokes my own shadow. Shadow is a faithful companion, always willing to give me a new lesson. My ego is not always so compliant, and I frequently struggle to accept the lesson my shadow offers. I suspect you'll have similar experiences, so I recommend you take this process slowly. Always be gentle with yourself. One chapter a week is plenty.

Another reason not to rush is that tapping blocked creative energy can cause your interest and imagination to outstrip your skill. Patience is vital. So is accepting mistakes as part of the process.

Don't worry if, in one week, you don't assimilate all the concepts and completely resolve the creativity and shadow issues that arise in response to a chapter. It's likely that you'll complete this book one chapter at a time, then return to various lessons from time to time. Each time you return, the experiences will be different because you will be different.

The first part of the book, "Recognizing Your Creativity, Seeing Your Shadow," will give you a map of the dragon's den in the form of background information about what your shadow is and how it is connected to your creativity. The second part of the book, "Embracing Your Shadow, Expressing Your Creativity," will lead you through the process of using the energy and insight of your shadow to rekindle your creative fire. There are exercises at the end of each chapter, and you'll find that the first part of the book prepares you for the experiential work of the second part.

It's important to find safe places and people to support you as you do this creative and shadow work. I'll discuss this in greater detail as we go along. For now, know that when you get to the experiential work of the second part of this book, you will want and need people who love you for yourself and who are willing to support you as you move through unfamiliar territory. Your support network will probably include both friends and professionals. Part of what can surface as you explore your shadow and creativity is old, old pain that has been stuffed away for years, even decades. These issues can be the raw material for significant psychological growth. Get seasoned guides, including a good therapist you can count on.

One important source of support is the stories of others who have made the journey into unfamiliar territory before you. You'll find those in the third part of the book, "Surrendering to the Creative Shadow Process," which presents insights my former students and I have gained from exploring the depths of our creativity and our shadows. It begins with a retelling of two myths of descent—the story of Inanna, a goddess who descends into the underworld to visit her sister Ereshkigal, and the story of Persephone, who is dragged unwillingly into the underworld. Aided by observations drawn from Clarissa Pinkola Estés's audiocassette *Creative Fire,* you'll discover that both myths have rich insights about the connections between creativity and shadow. Combined with real-life stories of others who've made the descent into the dragon's den, these myths will help you understand why it is important to stop

The truth is, everything is contained in the self. The creative power of this entire universe lies inside every one of us. The divine principle that creates and sustains this world pulsates within us as our own self.
SWAMI MUKTANANDA

resisting your own descent and begin the often difficult, but always rewarding, journey inward. When you want a little extra support as you work through chapters 7 through 11, you may want to skip ahead to the stories in chapters 12 and 13.

I've been enlightened by Carl Jung's explanations of the shadow and its functions in our psyche as I explored the connections between shadow and creativity. I'll refer to Jung and other writers from time to time, but this book isn't strictly Jungian. You don't need to agree with—or even know about—Jung's theories to apply the ideas and exercises in this book.

Practices That Lead to Personal Insights

The exercises at the end of each chapter will give you ample opportunities to experience what the chapter's concepts mean to you. Each exercise has a number of possible "correct" responses; any answer that gives you personal insight is right. Often it is our ego's need to be correct that gets in the way of surprising, and therefore useful, responses. Try to set aside your ego's desire to be right. We'll try a number of different approaches to perform an end run on the ego so you can see what your sometimes elusive and less articulate shadow has to say.

Read through all the exercises and select about half of them to work through. I strongly recommend you do at least one of the exercises you'd really rather avoid. But if there's one that terrifies you, make sure your support network is available before exploring it, or, if you don't feel safely supported, postpone that exercise. Again, be gentle with yourself. Use your own judgment. Only you can tell how much emotional stretching will be healthy and when you should stop so you don't tear spiritual ligaments.

But don't worry, the exercises are not going to be excruciating. Some of them are meant to be fun, even downright silly. Be sure to do some of these too. Go ahead, have a little fun.

In the search for ways to get our egos to take a break long enough to gain insight to our shadows, exercises that allow us to free-associate are often useful. A technique my students and I find particularly useful is freewriting, which Natalie Goldberg describes in *Writing Down the Bones*. Basically, freewriting is writing without stopping and without

The creation of something new is not accomplished by the intellect but by the play instinct acting from inner necessity. The creative mind plays with the objects it loves.
CARL JUNG

fretting about your spelling or punctuation or phrasing (which is, of course, your ego trying to be right again). The trick is to keep writing, keep your hand moving, even if you have to write "I don't know what to write" over and over. Eventually, your internal editor will get so bored with writing "I don't know what to write" that it will give up and go away, and then you'll be free to risk writing something unexpected.

If you are already doing some kind of journaling, continue the practice. If you aren't, establish a time when you can be alone and uninterrupted for about twenty minutes every day. I recommend writing first thing in the morning. When you first wake, your brain waves are slower and you're closer to your unconscious. You'll remember your dreams, and dreams are a significant way your Higher Self communicates with you. If you can't or won't journal in the morning, pick another time of day, preferably a time when you're able to relax and open your awareness to your unconscious by simply sitting quietly for a few minutes. Be consistent in your timing so your unconscious will know when to expect you to listen.

Don't get hung up in thinking you need to write great prose; you don't even need to write at all. If writing feels too cerebral, or when the words seem flat or won't come at all, drawing is an alternative way to fill the journal. *Everyone's Mandala Coloring Book* by Monique Mandali is a great place to start playing with colors and design in a healing, insight-producing way.

My own journals would never qualify as great prose; they can best be described as pages of petty complaints and seemingly unimportant detail interrupted by occasional flashes of insight. But the surest way I've found to get those flashes of insight is by sitting down every day to write or draw whatever comes to my mind without censoring it or trying to be clever. Goldberg calls it freewriting; Cameron calls it doing morning pages. In *Becoming a Writer*, Dorothea Brande calls it effortless writing, "when the unconscious is in the ascendant." Whatever you call it, your unconscious will quickly learn that you're open to receiving messages at this time. By regularly using writing and drawing to listen to your unconscious, you'll reap amazing benefits.

Another practice that works very well for most people is guided imagery or guided visualization. At the end of each chapter, you'll find directions for a different inner journey. It is impossible to read the visu-

We do not write in order to be understood, we write in order to understand.
CECIL DAY-LEWIS

alization instructions from the book and take the journey at the same time. I lead students in guided imagery often, and I've found I simply cannot have the experience they do. I suggest you either read the instructions onto a tape and play it back for yourself or have a friend read the instructions to you. At the very least, read the guided imagery to yourself and close your eyes at the end of each paragraph to picture what has been suggested.

Check the Mixed Media listing in the resource directory at the end of this book if you'd like to order a CD recording of these *Dancing in the Dragon's Den* guided imageries. There are other guided imagery recordings listed in the resource directory, and although not all of them address creativity or shadow directly, you may find many of them helpful.

Some people prefer not to receive suggestions while making an inner journey. With or without guidance, quiet time spent in contemplation or meditation will support you in this creative shadow exploration. I recommend a regular practice, daily if you can fit it into your schedule.

I've just suggested that you read one chapter of this book every week, do about half the exercises at the end of each chapter, freewrite or draw every day, and practice meditation regularly. I've also suggested you think about developing a support network. What have I left out? Oh yes, in the midst of all this extra work, do make time to play. Despite predictions to the contrary, the Puritan work ethic is not dead. For most American adults, play is part of the shadow; we're responsible, serious adults who don't have time for frivolities. When we undertake creative or shadow work, it is essential that we remember creative and shadow play as well. Many spiritual traditions pay homage to the Trickster or the Sacred Clown, recognizing humor's value in the midst of the serious business of spiritual growth. Just ten minutes a day will do wonders, although I recommend setting up an hour of playtime once a week or more. Make time to have fun with your creativity and your shadow.

When playing with your shadow there will, of course, be some inclinations you don't want to act out even though you do acknowledge their existence. That's no reason to ignore the many harmless desires we can make room for. For many women who do too much caretaking, this may be as simple as taking an hour to do what you want for a change. For many men, it may be nurturing yourself instead of being dependent on a woman to take care of your emotional needs. Man or

I don't warn you against action. I just want to cheer you up by saying that nervous, empty, continually willing action is sterile and the faster you run and accomplish a lot of useless things, the more you are dead.
BRENDA UELAND
If You Want to Write

woman, you may very well be surprised at the sudden surge of creative juice you feel shortly after you've raided your partner's supply of bubble bath or stuck your tongue out at your boss's back or thrown darts at a picture of that family member who always gets your goat. You'll find suggestions for creative and shadow playtime activities throughout the book. For now, just plan on making time for some of those forbidden joys.

I recognize that what I'm suggesting is a sizable time commitment in what is probably an already over-busy life. Please bear in mind that the rewards of exploring your shadow are no less than the full, free expression of your creativity and spirituality. This book will lead you through a major transformation if you allow it. Making time for yourself is the first step in allowing yourself to make the changes your spirit cries out for.

Will you give yourself five hours a week to have the life you've always wanted? How about three hours a week just to check it out? If not, perhaps it's best to put this book on the shelf until you're willing to give yourself and the world the gift of your own life. Remember, your psyche has its own wisdom and its own timing. If now isn't the time, now isn't the time. There is no need to judge or rationalize; when it's time, it's time.

If you're ready, let's begin.

Shadow-work is the initiatory phase of making a whole of ourselves.
JEREMIAH ABRAMS

CHAPTER 2

Mapping the Psyche

Introducing Ourselves

WHEN I TEACH A CLASS, I always begin with introductions. Sometimes I ask participants to find a partner to interview and then introduce to the group. Sometimes I ask participants to introduce themselves, telling us a little about how they express their creativity and why they decided to take the class. When I teach Dancing in the Dragon's Den classes, I ask participants to introduce themselves in a more structured way. I ask each person to complete the phrase "I am _____" three different ways.

How would you complete the phrase "I am _____"?

Nearly everyone begins by giving their name. Many people's answers reflect the roles they play at work: "I'm a grade school teacher" or "I'm an attorney." These things are easy to reveal about ourselves. Many people's answers reflect their relationships: "I am a mother of three" or "I am a father, son, and brother" or "I am going through a divorce." These, too, are natural responses, the kinds of information we expect to hear when someone is introduced.

Surprisingly, for groups of people taking a creativity class, many participants complete the phrase without mentioning their creativity. Only a few say, "I am a writer," or "I am a photographer," or "I'm a dancer." This happens, I think, because we don't believe we can claim to be something unless we're getting paid to do it.

When we've gone around the circle once, giving everyone a chance to say, "I am _____" three times, I ask participants to complete the phrase "I express my creativity _____" three different ways. I usually go first, to give an example. "I express my creativity through my teaching. I express my creativity when I color with markers and oil pastels. I express my creativity when I write."

I can tell this is a little less comfortable because people want to give explanations, not just fill in the blank. For example, Bob will start, "I guess I express my creativity when I, let's see, well you could say I express it in my photography even though I haven't sold any of my pictures or anything, but I have taken a couple of classes and they said I've got some really nice ones." Some people get so uncomfortable with this simple question, they give up: "I don't know. I guess I cook and that's about it." I wait and if the person indicates she or he is done, I coax another response. "Didn't you say you're a parent? That's the most creative thing a human being can do!" That usually brings a smile and admission that maybe that *is* creative, and the other thing he or she likes to do is . . .

How do you express your creativity? Don't give up until you have three responses.

Then we go around the circle a third time, this time completing the phrase "I am *not* _____." For example, I always start with, "I'm not one of those women who has a fit just because she broke a nail." For some people, saying what they're not feels like the kind of protest that prompted Shakespeare to write, "Methinks the lady doth protest too much." Others find this introduction feels like a backward affirmation. After all, when we're asked to define ourselves by what we're not, what usually occurs to us is something we have consciously chosen not to be. Try it yourself to see how it feels to you. Who aren't you? What ways would you complete "I am *not* _____"?

We Are Our Ego

Most people are fairly comfortable finding three ways to answer "I am" statements even if the structure seems a little strange. This is because we're accustomed to providing this kind of information when we introduce ourselves—information about our ego-selves. But the other two statements ("I express my creativity" and "I am *not*") require that we give information about our creative-selves and our shadow-selves. We don't usually do that.

By ego-self I mean the person you usually see yourself as. We could make defining the ego confusing, but it doesn't have to be. Your ego is simply the person most people, including you, see you as most of the

If the Angel deigns to come it will be because you have convinced her, not by tears, but by your humble resolve to be always beginning: to be a beginner.

RAINER MARIA RILKE

time. If we didn't have an idea of how we usually are, we could never say something like "I just wasn't myself today."

If you stop to think about it, you can acknowledge that, while you usually define yourself in terms of who you are when you're conscious, a part of you is unconscious. You have dreams every night; even if you don't remember them, you have them. You can recall memories you weren't aware you had. For example, if I suggest you think about grade school and the desk you had, you'll start to remember the wooden lid, the books inside, maybe even a specific book or the scent of crayons, the taste of paste, or the way you and your friends used to spread Elmer's glue on your palm to peel off when it dried. Chances are, you are probably remembering some specific memory from your grade school experience that you weren't aware of before you started reading this paragraph. Clearly, you have memories stored in what is called your unconscious.

Carl Jung called the ego the center of consciousness, so we represent our conscious self as a circle with the ego as the center. At least part of what we call our unconscious can be called to consciousness the way you just recalled a memory of grade school, so I draw the line separating the conscious and unconscious parts of the self with a wavy, indistinct line.

It's never too late to be what you might have been.
ANON

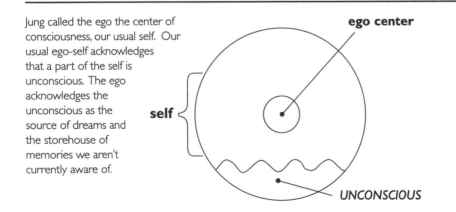

Jung called the ego the center of consciousness, our usual self. Our usual ego-self acknowledges that a part of the self is unconscious. The ego acknowledges the unconscious as the source of dreams and the storehouse of memories we aren't currently aware of.

ego center

self

UNCONSCIOUS

But the unconscious is much larger than the ego usually acknowledges. Our dreams are often so surprising that during our waking moments we can't imagine that we could think up the characters and story lines in our dreams. Remember the old saying about humans using only 5 to 10 percent of their brain capacity? Most of what you've learned in your life you are not now consciously aware of. How could you be? I suspect it's not that we necessarily lose our memories as we age; it's just that we have so much more to forget. But since your ego doesn't like to admit that there is so much more to you than your ego-definition, you probably don't think about this often.

A more realistic picture is that the ego is a bubble of self-consciousness floating in a sea of unconscious.

The unconscious wants truth. It ceases to speak to those who want something else more than truth.

ADRIENNE RICH

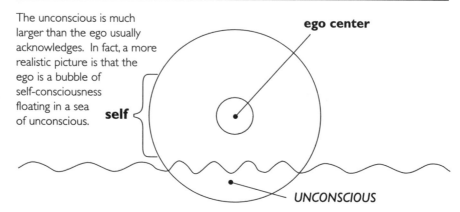

The unconscious is much larger than the ego usually acknowledges. In fact, a more realistic picture is that the ego is a bubble of self-consciousness floating in a sea of unconscious.

ego center

self

UNCONSCIOUS

We Are Ego and More

Your ego may not want to think about it, but you have undoubtedly had experiences that filled you with awe and made you aware that there is more to you than you usually think yourself to be. These experiences are sometimes called "peak" or "flow" or even mystical or religious experiences. You know what it's like. It's when you're writing and the words form effortlessly into exactly the right image, sometimes without conscious volition. Or when you're painting and the brush takes on a life of its own. You experience it when you're dancing and your spirit and body move as one, without strain, in beauty and joy. Or when you take your camera out during a walk and the light is perfect and you know exactly how you want to compose a shot. It is an effortless, ecstatic way of being in the act of creation that all artists yearn for. Sometimes we strive for it, struggling to re-create a peak experience, but that rarely works because it is an act of being and not something you can will yourself to do on command, although you can learn to move more easily and intentionally into that way of being.

In all these experiences, there is a sense of effortless doing that reflects your inner being. There is often the sense that time is altered or just doesn't matter. In a peak experience, we feel fully alive and focused. It's not that we're happy; it's that we are filled with joy even when we aren't quite sure what to do next. We feel profoundly connected. The petty concerns of our ordinary ego-self take a backseat to the something larger we are creating. We lose ourselves, but we lose ourselves in our selves, or more properly, in our larger Selves. A mystical, flow experience like this gives us a profound knowing that our Essence, our True Self, our Higher Self, is much more than our usual ego-self.

It's like channeling. Something kicks in. When you're in the zone, you don't know where it comes from, but it's like being in the eye of a storm–you're calm, but all these things are primed.
ROBIN WILLIAMS

Occasionally, we have a sense that we are more than we usually think ourselves to be. These experiences are sometimes called "peak" or "flow" or mystical or religious experiences. We have a profound knowing that our Essence or Higher Self or True Self is much more than our usual ego-self.

This Self is made up of both conscious and unconscious. The ego-self is only part of this larger Self. All of the Self that the ego has not identified as part of its ego-ideal (the shaded area) is shadow, the unowned parts of the Self, the Self the ego has no wish to be.

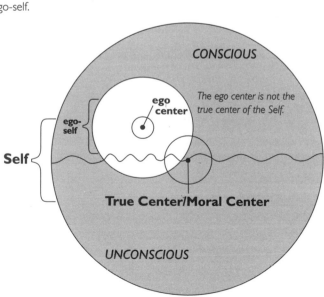

This larger Self is made up of both conscious and unconscious. The ego-self is only part of the Self. Notice that the ego is still the center of the ego-self, but it is not the center of the Self. Some Jungians picture the ego as separate from the Self, but I prefer to see the ego as part of the Self.

John A. Sanford, an Episcopal priest and Jungian analyst, supported this view in an interview with D. Patrick Miller for *The Sun*. Sanford said, "What distinguishes Jungian psychology from practically all other psychologies is the idea that there are two centers of the personality. The ego is the center of consciousness; the Self is the center of the total personality, which includes consciousness, the unconscious *and* the ego. The Self is both the whole and the center. The ego is a self-contained little circle off the center, but contained within the whole. So the ego might best be described as the lesser center of the personality; the Self is the greatest center."

The Self contains all human potential. George Bernard Shaw was aware of his larger Self when he said, "Nothing human is alien to me." All possible human characteristics and traits are contained in the larger Self. Just because we have repressed and denied certain characteristics that don't fit our definition of what a good person should be or what we believe we are capable of doesn't mean these characteristics leave us. They are outside the ego's definition of self, but they remain part of the larger Self—in the shadow. The simplest definition of the shadow Jung offered was that it is the person we have no wish to be. The smaller self, the ego-self, is the person we wish to be; shadow contains all the denied elements of the Self. Everything outside the smaller circle of the ego-self is the shadow. (Jungians divide what is outside the ego-ideal into several concepts—anima and animus as well as shadow. For our purposes, the simpler perspective is sufficient.)

The shadow is nearly all of the unconscious and those parts of the conscious that the ego-self has not claimed. It may seem strange that part of the shadow is the unclaimed consciousness. Sometimes called the "white shadow" or "light shadow," these are the positive characteristics that we feel too small, too petty, too ordinary to claim. We may want them, or think we should want them, but we also fear them and deny they are part of who we are.

Jung referred to the center of the larger Self as the Creative Center. We can see creative expression as ever-expanding circles that come from the Creative Center or True Center and encompass part of the

In reality the psyche . . . reaches so far beyond the boundaries of consciousness that the latter could easily be compared to an island in the ocean. Whereas the island is small and narrow, the ocean is immensely wide and deep and contains a life infinitely surpassing, in kind and degree, anything known on the island.

CARL JUNG

ego and part of the shadow. Seeing creative expression this way explains why we sometimes feel reluctant to claim our creativity—much of it lies outside our usual definition of who we are. Jung also referred to the Creative Center of the larger Self as the Moral Center, which holds our values and principles and enables us to make moral choices.

Jung called the center of this larger Self the Creative Center. Creative expression can be seen as ever-expanding circles that come from the Creative Center and encompass part of the ego and part of the shadow.

Notice that more creativity lies within the shadow than within the ego. To be fully creative is to be fully your Self. It is to be as accepting of unconscious as of conscious awareness, as accepting of shadow as of ego.

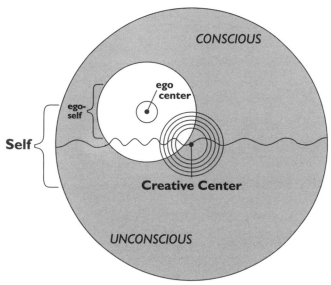

As you work through this book, you'll discover that expanding your creativity will also expand your awareness of your True Self. To be fully creative is to be fully your Self. It is to be as accepting of unconscious as of conscious awareness, as accepting of shadow as of ego. That is an enormous task. It is the task of a lifetime—your lifetime.

✍ Exercise: Over Your Shoulder

The simplest definition of your shadow is that it is the person you usually aren't. So let's start by getting clear about who we usually are. Make a list of the words that describe the kind of person you usually are. All of us have moments of generosity that motivate us to drop a couple of bucks in the Salvation Army's Christmas bucket and moments of self-interest that motivate us to ignore that ringing phone in order to sink into a hot tub or a hot movie, but what kind of person are you usually—generous or self-interested? All of us have changing moods, but some of us are routinely angry or fearful. Is there an emotion you feel most of the time? Describe the person you usually are. For example, part of the list I made when describing myself is

> *intelligent*
> *intuitive*
> *creative*
> *good communicator*
> *kind*
> *compassionate*
> *focused, even absent-minded*
> *a ham*
> *entertaining*
> *competitive*
> *resentful*

You may want to start your list, think about it, and then come back to it in a day or two. Make your list as complete as you can, but include only the traits you usually exhibit. If you feel funny about making this list, notice what you're thinking or remembering. Were you often told not to brag about yourself or not to think about yourself so much? Just remember that and keep making your list.

When you've completed your list, ask a few friends to name five to ten characteristics they would use to describe you. If these characteristics are on your list, put a star next to them. If your friend comes up with a trait you hadn't thought about, add it to the list and put a star next to it. Because we're often different people in different circumstances, and we want this list to be as complete as possible, you may want to ask a few co-workers or family members to describe you too.

We can easily forgive a child who is afraid of the dark; the real tragedy of life is when men are afraid of the light.

PLATO

This list describes who you usually are; that is, it describes the ego-self you show the world. Since every human being has the potential to be all traits, by definition, the traits not on your ego list are those of your shadow-self. To get a glimpse of some of the traits in your shadow, next to each ego characteristic, list its opposite. For example, to my ego list, I add as shadow traits

intelligent	*stupid*
intuitive	*sensory*
creative	*destructive*
good communicator	*poor communicator*
kind	*cruel*
compassionate	*unthinking or mean*
focused, even	*focused on people and things*
absent-minded	*outside of myself*
a ham	*shy*
entertaining	*dull*
competitive	*cooperative*
resentful	*honest about my anger*

Notice that although all the traits on my shadow list are what my ego has decided I don't want to be (because for some reason these traits threaten my existence), these traits aren't necessarily, objectively negative. For example, while I value creativity, the Hindu pantheon recognizes the necessity of destruction. On the same note, the traits on my ego list aren't necessarily positive, either. They are simply the traits I decided years ago I wanted to show the world.

Only you can decide whether the words on the right-hand side truly describe your shadow. It may take you a while to know for sure. For now, just know that these are possible characteristics of your shadow. For me, it is true that my shadow is often less intelligent, unable to communicate clearly, cruel or unthinking, shy or dull. I also hold cooperativeness in my shadow, possibly because my ego-self believes I need to be competitive to survive. And I don't usually feel safe expressing my anger honestly and directly.

Remember, these lists were written by you, not carved in stone by God. This may be your first glimpse of your other self, your shadow. Be gentle. Don't use the list to elevate or denigrate yourself. Just notice what's there.

Inspiration may be a form of superconsciousness, or perhaps of subconsciousness— I wouldn't know. But I am sure it is the antithesis of self-consciousness.
AARON COPLAND

Guided Imagery Instruction

As valuable as it is to understand concepts like ego and shadow intellectually, sometimes the most powerful understanding occurs
when we pause to explore the images and metaphors that arise
spontaneously from our unconscious mind. Guided imagery or
visualization is one way to make the inner journey of discovery. I
usually call this inner journey guided imagery rather than guided
visualization because not everyone "sees" something during the
exercise. Don't assume you aren't doing something right or that
it's not working just because you aren't seeing some kind of mental movie in Technicolor with digitally enhanced Surround Sound
effects. Some people do see flashes of color or symbols. Some people can picture themselves in another place or time. Some people
have a feeling sense or an emotional response or what seems to be
an inexplicable body response. I once imagined detailed scenes,
then for a while I had more kinesthetic responses, usually involun-
tary twitching. This was unnerving at first, but I learned to welcome it as a sign that I was processing information at a cellular
level. Trust that whatever response you have is right for you now.
With practice, your guided imagery experiences will become increasingly vivid.

As mentioned in chapter 1, either record the instructions for
this guided imagery on a tape and play them back when you're able
to relax or ask a friend to read them to you. Having a friend read
the instructions maintains the element of surprise, but make sure
you feel comfortable having this person observe you; you don't
want to feel inhibited and distracted during the guided imagery.
Play soothing music in the background either while you're recording the instructions or while your friend reads them to you.

Whoever is reading the instructions should pause between the
sentences. To be effective, the pause should feel quite long for the
speaker. The speaker should pause even longer between paragraphs.

Be sure you've chosen a place and time where you'll be comfortable and uninterrupted. Wear loose, comfortable clothes and have
a blanket handy in case you become chilled as your body slows.
Turn the phone ringer off and ask your family not to disturb you
or, better yet, invite them to join you.

*Even though we
are not responsible
for the way we
are and feel,
we have to take
responsibility for
the way we act.*
EDWARD C.
WHITMONT
The Symbolic Quest

You'll want to record your impressions when you've finished with the guided imagery. Have drawing paper and crayons, colored pencils, magic markers, glitter paint, oil pastels (my favorite), or modeling clay available. Even if you don't feel you are a great visual artist, rely on nonverbal media right after the imagery. Speaking or writing too soon will bring you back to your usual ways of thinking before you've had a chance to complete the experience. Some people also want to write their impressions after drawing or sculpting, so have pen and writing paper available too.

❋ *Guided Imagery*

Find a place and time when you can be relaxed and uninterrupted. Lie or sit comfortably and begin to relax. Close your eyes. Take several deep breaths, noticing and following the breath in and out of your body.

Consciously tighten the muscles in your feet and ankles. Notice the tension. . . . Feel the tension in all the muscles in your feet. . . . Hold the tension as long as you like . . . holding it until you're ready to let it go with a sigh. . . . Take a deep breath and notice how it feels to let go, to feel the warm relaxation in your feet. . . .

Now, consciously tighten the muscles in your calves and knees. Notice the tension. . . . Feel the tension in your calves and knees. . . . Hold the tension . . . until you're ready to let it go with a sigh. . . . Take a deep breath and notice how good it feels to let your calves and your knees relax and go slack. . . .

Consciously tighten the muscles in your thighs, buttocks, and pelvis. Notice the tension. . . . Feel the tension in your thighs and buttocks and pelvis. . . . Hold the tension . . . until you're ready to let it go with a sigh. . . . Take a deep breath and notice how good it feels to let the lower half of your body relax more and more with each breath you take. . . .

Take another deep breath and consciously tighten the muscles in your stomach, chest, and back. Feel the tension in your torso. . . . Notice what it feels like to hold tension in this part of your body. . . . Hold that tension . . . until you're ready to let it go with a sigh. . . . Take a deep, slow breath and notice how good it feels to breathe all the way down to your belly . . . how good it feels to let your belly go soft and round with each breath. . . .

Now, consciously tighten your hands into fists. Feel the tension move

The shadow cannot be eliminated. It becomes pathological only when we assume that we do not have it; because then it has us.
EDWARD C. WHITMONT
The Symbolic Quest

from your hands to your wrists, your forearms, elbows, upper arms, into your shoulders and the base of your neck. . . . Notice that tension, what it feels like . . . holding it until you're ready to let it go with a sigh. . . . Take a deep breath and notice how good it feels to let any remaining tension ooze out of your fingertips. . . . Notice how good it feels to let your shoulders drop and let your arms relax more and more. . . .

Now, consciously tighten the muscles in your jaw and neck; scrunch up the muscles around your eyes and forehead. . . . Notice the tension in your face and neck . . . holding it until you're ready to let it go with a sigh. . . . Notice how good it feels to let your whole body become more and more relaxed . . . more and more relaxed with every breath. . . .

Continue to breathe deeply. If worries or thoughts about other things come to you, simply remind yourself, "Not this, not now," set the thought aside, and return your attention to your breathing. Allow your breath to assume a slow, natural rhythm.

Experience your whole body now as relaxed . . . your mind as quiet and still . . . your emotions as calm and clear . . . your spirit as peaceful and serene. . . .

From this place of inner serenity, harmony, and relaxation, begin to allow images to occur in your mind. . . . Imagine you are floating in a golden sea. . . . The waves rock gently beneath you, supporting you completely. . . . The sun shines on your face and body. . . . You are completely safe and comfortable. . . . Any discomfort or worry you have falls away from you into the sea. . . .

Floating here in the golden sea, you are exactly the person you want to be. . . . Your body is how you wish it to be. . . . Your personality is how you wish it to be. . . . Your actions and behaviors are those you want to have. . . . Anything that you once disliked about yourself has fallen away into the sea and even the memory of it has faded. . . .

(pause for a minute or two)

The sun above you gives you everything you need. . . . You are completely content to float in the sea beneath the sun. . . .

(pause for at least two minutes)

As the day progresses, the sun begins to set. . . . Without becoming too bright or too hot, the sun moves closer to you as it dips toward the sea. . . . You feel yourself drawn toward the sun, the source of all you need, and so you begin to gently paddle your hands and kick your feet to move through the sea to the setting sun. . . .

Whether the shadow becomes our friend or our enemy depends largely upon ourselves. The shadow becomes hostile only when it is ignored or misunderstood.

MARIE-LOUISE VON FRANZ
Meeting the Shadow

As your feet and legs begin to shine in the red-gold glow of the sunset, you realize the sea you are floating in and the sun setting in it are all inside a huge bubble. . . . The sun isn't setting on the western horizon; it is setting in the center of the sea, in the center of the bubble. . . . You realize the sea is the sea of your unconscious. . . . Your body is your ego. . . . And the sun is your Creative Center. . . .

As your body floats in the center of the bubble, enveloped in the light and warmth of your Creative Center, you realize you are more than this body. . . . You feel your awareness swell to include the sun and the sea, the entire bubble. . . . For now, you are aware of the totality of your Higher Self. . . . All things are possible to you now. . . . All creative expression is yours. . . . All shadow expression is yours too, and you know in your Center how to act in ways that reflect a higher understanding. . . .

(pause for at least three minutes)

Gradually, you feel your awareness return to your ego-body. . . . Your ego drifts from the Center, but not as far away as you were when you began. . . .

Gradually return your attention to your physical body. . . . When you are ready to return to this room, gently touch your fingers to the floor or the sides of your chair. Slowly open your eyes.

When you're ready, draw a picture of yourself as the bubble or draw the colors or images that stand out in your mind. After drawing, write a few notes if there is anything else you want to be sure to remember.

In every adult, there lurks a child–an eternal child, something that is always becoming, is never completed, and calls for unceasing care, attention, and education. That is the part of the human personality which wants to develop and become whole.

CARL JUNG

● Creative Shadow Play

For your creative shadow play this week, make a collage of the different aspects of your Self. Making a collage is a great way to play with images without feeling inadequate about your ability to draw. I started making collages when I assigned them to my students in a class called Return to Your Creative Center. I probably did an adequate job of what adult-education experts call "modeling the behavior." My students felt safer and more at ease with me absorbed in my own collage; after all, who feels comfortable creating "art" when the teacher is watching over your shoulder? But the real lesson for me was that what I recommended to my students was exactly what I needed to do myself.

Making my first collage was astounding. I loved it! I loved the process, I loved the product. I had just collected a bunch of pictures that seemed interesting and ended up with a collection where every element and its placement was significant. I had found a way to put myself on paper and say, "This is who I am." Without thinking about it consciously, I put images that represented part of my shadow in the lower left-hand corner. Surrounded by the other aspects I saw in myself, my shadow didn't seem so bad. Instead of seeing myself as all good or all bad, I had a visual image that put my shadow-self into perspective.

I've made many collages since that first one. Collage making is a powerful process my students and I love, so I make it part of nearly every class I teach. I have four collages in my office and seven or eight in my bedroom, and the person I share a house with is starting to suggest I refrain from making more because she's not sure where we'll hang them. But each time I make a collage, I have so much fun and receive such powerful insights, I doubt I'll ever stop.

For this week's shadow playtime, collect images and phrases that represent aspects of yourself or that simply appeal to you. You can find images in magazines, greeting cards, photos, calendars, catalogs, and your own artwork. Include images of your interests, your dreams, your spiritual-self, your creative-self, your shadow-self. Collage your Self.

Many people are surprised by how wonderful their collages turn out. I suggest making your collage on foam board, which is a quarter-inch of foam sandwiched between two pieces of poster board. Foam board can easily be mounted on or leaned against a wall, so you can appreciate your collage and let it continue to influence you for months. Most art or office supply stores have foam board in a variety of colors.

Once you've gathered images, use a glue stick or rubber cement to glue them to the foam board. There is no wrong way to make a collage. Many of my students have felt apprehensive about making a collage, afraid theirs wouldn't "turn out right." But I've never seen anyone make a collage who wasn't delighted with the results. You may want to work fast and surprise yourself with what images you use and how you arrange them. Or you may want to work slowly, playing with possibilities and relishing the process.

When you've finished, you'll know far better than anyone else what the significance of the elements are. Still, other people's im-

Art is not just ornamental, an enhancement of life, but a path in itself, a way out of the predictable and conventional, a map to self-discovery

GABRIELLE ROTH

pressions can give you valuable information. Show your collage to those people you trust to treat it—and you—with respect. Often, but not always, there is a progression in a collage from lower left to upper right. The elements in the lower left often represent aspects of yourself you are leaving behind, and the elements in the upper right represent those aspects you are moving toward.

⊙ **EXERCISE CHOICES**

1. Find Your Fairy-Tale Psyche. Find Hans Christian Andersen's story "The Shadow" in appendix A, then continue these instructions after you've finished reading the story.

You might notice that the figures in "The Shadow" are not well-rounded characters. As in Jungian dream analysis, where each figure in a dream represents a different aspect of the dreamer, the characters in Andersen's story stand for aspects of the reader's psyche. Consider what aspects of you are shown in the story. What part of you is like the learned young man? How? What part of you is like the shadow? How? What part of you is like the beautiful woman in the house across the street? The princess who marries the shadow? Freewrite your responses. Remember, you don't have to know the answer before you begin to write; write about what you do know, what you suspect, what might be true. Think *as* you write, not *before*.

After you've thought about how these figures apply to you personally, read Ursula K. Le Guin's explanation and interpretation of Andersen's story in her essay "The Child and the Shadow," also in appendix A. Do you agree with Le Guin's interpretation?

2. Freewrite. Complete one of the following statements (depending on your gender) in as many ways as you can in five or ten minutes. Freewrite this list—repeat a response if you need to, but keep your hand moving; don't stop writing. The point is not to record what is objectively true, but to free-associate and see what pops up.

For women: "Good girls don't _____."
For men: "Big boys don't _____."

You'll probably find a host of ideas your parents and other authority figures gave you when you were growing up. Those people

In your longing for your giant self lies your goodness; and that longing is in all of you.
KAHLIL GIBRAN
The Prophet

may have long since changed their opinions, but you still carry these ideas at some level of consciousness. You can use this information about what is appropriate for someone of your gender as a map that defines the borders of your ego-self and hence outlines your shadow.

3. Freewrite Again. Repeat exercise 2, this time completing the statement about children of the complementary (sometimes called opposite) gender. Or list as many responses as you can to one of these statements:

For women: "Men are all _____."
For men: "Women are so _____."

Again, you'll discover a wealth of information about the human potential you've kept hidden in your shadow since most women put what is characteristically "male" in their shadow and most men put what is typically "female" in theirs.

4. Remember the Flow. Remember the last time you had a peak creative or spiritual experience, when you felt immersed in the flow. We've all had them, and yet we all experience them slightly differently. Don't worry that your experience doesn't qualify somehow; just remember a time when you lost track of time and your usual concerns because you were so into the flow of creating or perceiving something.

Make a few notes as you remember the details of the experience. What were you doing when you started? What happened to move you into the flow? Were there significant elements—place, time, people, props—that moved you into the flow or that temporarily blocked your ability to move into the flow? How did you feel during the experience? How did you experience time? How did you feel afterward? What pulled you out of the flow? How did you feel about that? Did you produce anything tangible?

Think about what, if anything, you can do to reproduce the sense of being in a peak experience. We can't have a peak experience on demand, but if we keep ourselves constantly busy, we can block opportunities. Keep a block of time open this week for the possibility of a peak experience. Take a long walk or a hot bath, drive in the country, visit a sacred space, or sit awhile in your favorite creative place.

The source of all creation is pure consciousness . . . pure potentiality seeking expression from the unmanifest to the manifest. And when we realize that our true Self is one of pure potentiality, we align with the power that manifests everything in the universe.

DEEPAK CHOPRA
The Seven Spiritual Laws of Success

5. Begin a Dream Journal. One way to get glimpses into the sea of unconscious your ego-self floats in is to pay attention to your dreams. Keep a notebook and pen beside your bed—this is a symbol of your intention to remember and pay attention to your dreams. You can also speak this intention aloud before you go to sleep: "I will remember my dreams tonight." These symbolic acts do wonders for improving your memory.

If you wake in the night, record in your notebook just a few words that will jog your memory in the morning. In the morning, take ten or fifteen minutes (in addition to or as part of a morning writing practice) to record the main images from your dreams. You don't have to record every detail, but you can if you wish. Then skip a line and write possible interpretations of your dreams. Don't worry about being right, just write.

You can talk to friends or refer to books about the meanings of dream symbols, but remember that your interpretations are always the most significant ones. After all, the images came from your unconscious.

6. Make a Done List. Most of us have too many "to do" lists. Instead, make a list of all the creative things you have done in your life. Be sure to include the cup-on-a-string project you did at day camp and the Mother's Day gifts you made in school or in youth groups (Boy Scouts, Girl Scouts, Camp Fire Girls, whatever). Include all the projects you've started, even if you haven't finished them yet. Include decorating your home, work projects you did with a flair instead of by rote, training your puppy, raising children, all the meals you cooked, all the creative projects large and small.

It may take days, even weeks, to remember and list all your creative experiences. Whenever you remember something, find the list and add to it. (Yes, you can include writing the list itself.)

7. Make a "To Be" List. List the qualities of the ideal you. Write "The Ideal Me" or "The Me I Want to Be" or simply "To Be" at the top of the page. Describe the person you want to be. Be sure to include the qualities you already have as well as the ones you're aspiring to. If you want, put a check mark or a gold star next to the qualities you already possess.

Whatever we try to control does have control over us and our life.

MELODY BEATTIE
The Language of Letting Go

8. Enter Psyche's Coloring Contest. Color the unlabeled map of the psyche below, or draw and color your own map of your psyche. What color is your ego? What color(s) is your expanding Creative Center? What color is your dark shadow, your light shadow?

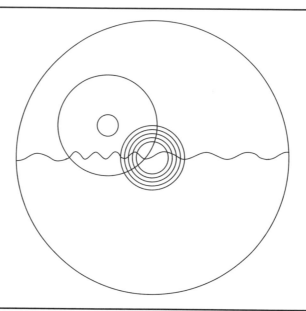

9. Draw the Treasure Chest. Use music or candles or deep breathing to create a quiet, meditative state. Recall the guided imagery presented earlier and how you felt while doing it. Close your eyes and remember that golden sea of your unconscious. Now imagine what lies beneath its surface. . . .

When you're ready, draw a treasure chest at the bottom of this sea. What hidden treasures await your exploration? Or draw the whole sea of your unconscious, complete with treasure chest, undersea dwellers who can help you, sea monsters that might frighten you, or any other images that are meaningful to you.

CHAPTER 3

Mining Psyche's Gold

Shadow Is What We Aren't

BY ITS VERY NATURE, shadow is something that eludes direct examination. No one can turn around fast enough to see all of his or her shadow, either figuratively or literally. But, just as atomic physicists can identify quarks and leptons by the trails they leave behind in a particle accelerator, we can trace our shadow by the trail it leaves in our lives.

Early in the process of identifying my shadow, I would have described that trail as a wake of destruction. This is pretty normal; most of us begin with an adversarial attitude toward our shadow-selves. After all, it contains all the traits our ego denied. But Carl Jung insisted the shadow is 90 percent gold. I've learned to believe him.

Ninety percent gold or not, we have no wish to be our shadow. Yet it is the self we must acknowledge to become fully individualized, which Jung considered the goal of human existence. What Jung called individualization I call being fully, clearly, creatively yourself, being able to enter and remain in the creative flow. It is learning to recognize that your ego isn't your True Center and that you are much larger than your ego-self.

Jung stated that forming a shadow was a necessary part of forming an ego, which is the ideal self. In other words, as we grow from infancy and childhood through adolescence to young adulthood, we constantly make decisions about the kind of person we want—or need—to be. These choices are based on the responses of our parents, siblings, friends, teachers, and other people of influence. As we make these choices, we are also choosing what kind of person we won't be.

For example, if Betsy's mom scolds her every time she makes noise and runs around the house, Betsy may become a quiet, refined little girl to gain her mother's approval. Or she may become a loud person in a re-bellious response to her mother's criticism. She may be the kind of person who annoys others for fun or the kind of person who appears to be respectful but hums and mutters under her breath constantly. What kind of person Betsy decides to be depends on a host of factors we can't begin to identify here. Whatever Betsy decides about the kind of person she wants to be, she will also decide what kind of person she's not going to be. Whatever she decides she's not going to be is still a possibility, but one that she won't (usually) act on. This becomes part of Betsy's shadow, the person Betsy has no wish to be.

In *A Little Book on the Human Shadow,* Robert Bly observes that all humans beings are born with what he calls 360 degrees of potential energy and personality aspects. All behaviors and personality quirks are possible to us, but our parents, who hold the power of life and death for an infant and young child, say things like, "We don't scream at the table in this family, do we?" So we disown that aspect of ourselves. We tell ourselves, "I'm not the kind of person who would do anything like that," and that potential part of us goes into what Bly calls the shadow bag. The process of forming the ego, of deciding which aspects are acceptable to show the world, necessarily means forming the shadow, deciding which aspects will be disowned and hidden.

The ego decides what is safe to reveal and what must be denied and repressed because it is the ego's job to preserve the individual. Human children cannot survive without adults to care for them, and the first job a child's ego must perform is to find ways to get needs met without alienating the people who provide for him or her. The rules and mores of the child's caregivers determine in part what kinds of behavior goes into the child's shadow.

Parents do not necessarily harm children by influencing them to form a shadow. Forming a shadow is a completely normal and necessary part of being a civilized human being. We wouldn't want to live with people, for example, whose parents didn't teach them to use a toilet and not take whatever they wanted whenever they wanted. Although all of us eliminate waste products from our bodies, we don't talk about it, at least not in the casual way we talk about the weather or sports or what we did at work. And even those people who do steal don't casually mention that as their occupation when introduced to strangers. Along with

> *What the neurotic flings away as absolutely worthless contains the true gold we should never have found elsewhere.*
>
> CARL JUNG

many other culturally defined taboos, human waste and stealing are in nearly every westerner's shadow in one form or another, and there's probably no great tragedy in that.

Sometimes, however, adults overreact and cause more to end up in a child's shadow than needs to be there. Often children misinterpret the actions of others, and even more ends up in the shadow. Still, the task of childhood and adolescence is to form a sense of self—ego-self—and that necessitates creating a shadow-self to hold all the discarded possibilities.

The Gold We Have No Wish to Own

While forming a shadow is a necessary part of defining who we are in the world, problems arise because we don't know what to do with this shadow-self we've created. Perhaps we remember, however faintly, how threatening it felt to have our beloved, care-giving parents disapprove of whatever aspects they disapproved of in us. Perhaps we simply fear what isn't. Whatever the reason, most of us fear our shadow.

"If this is gold," the ego wants to tell Jung, "it's fool's gold. It's gold I certainly don't want to own." Your ego has spent a lot of time and energy making sure people see you the way you (ego-you) want to be seen. Your ego has been taught to be "good" to survive.

And here is your shadow, the collection of traits and behaviors you don't want others to associate with you. If your ego is good, then your shadow is bad, and if your ego is good to survive, then surely your shadow threatens your very existence. Of course, you (ego-you) disown, fear, and revile your shadow.

Your shadow is all the potential human behavior and beliefs that you cannot tolerate in yourself. Like George Bernard Shaw, nothing human is alien to you. Anything that a human being could say or do or think is something you could say or do or think. But your ego won't admit that.

There is an old saying that the sins that offend us most in others are the sins we fear of ourselves, but won't admit. For example, Ben hates it when his friend Susan is late. Ben insists he is always on time, so he's not just seeing his own bad habit in Susan; this really is Susan's fault. What really offends Ben is what he perceives as lack of courtesy; he believes Susan is saying he doesn't matter enough to be on time for. Yet Ben's own lack of courtesy is reflected in his curtness when Susan

Everyone carries a shadow, and the less it is embodied in the individual's conscious life, the blacker and denser it is. . . . But if it is repressed and isolated from consciousness, it never gets corrected, and is liable to burst forth suddenly in a moment of unawareness. At all events, it forms an unconscious snag thwarting our most well-meant intentions.
CARL JUNG

arrives late at his door again; Ben is saying Susan doesn't matter enough for him to be patient with. If pressed, Ben might say it seems that Susan thinks her time is more important than his, when in fact, Susan just doesn't think that much about time, and it is Ben who really feels his time is more important.

"Murderers should get the chair!" Beth proclaims on Monday. By Wednesday, she seethes about her boss, "I could just kill him for that!" never admitting to herself that she has committed murder in her heart. Patty declares, "I hate racist skinheads!" without acknowledging that she is expressing the same intolerance as the people she's condemning. Al suggests parents who abuse their children should be thrown in prison for the rest of their lives but never thinks twice about rubbing his puppy's nose in its own offal as part of "housebreaking." Nickie deplores the genocide attempted by the Serbs and complains about the United Nation's reluctance to "bomb them until they see the value of peace."

"Well, what am I supposed to do?" our ego-ideal protests. "Admit I have this shadow and then run around murdering people, beating my kids, and harassing people of different races and religions? Maybe I do have a shadow, but at least I have the good taste to hide it."

It is more disturbing to find that you have a profound nobility of character than to find out you are a bum. Of course you are both. . . .

ROBERT A. JOHNSON
Owning Your Own Shadow

The Tarnished Gold We Can't Hide

The problem, as you've no doubt discovered, is that shadow won't stay hidden. It is, as Jacquelyn Small described in *Awakening in Time*, like a beach ball you try to hold underwater. The longer you try to hide this beach ball, the slipperier it gets. And the deeper you push it under, the higher it's going to fly when you lose your grip. You know what it feels like to lose your grip—suddenly you're saying and doing things you would normally never say and do. You protest, "I don't know what got into me. I just wasn't myself." What got into you, or actually what got out of you, was your shadow-self. You truly weren't your usual ego-self.

We all know people who absolutely refuse to even acknowledge they have a shadow-self. These are the people whose shadows have explosive appearances. As Jung observed, the brighter the persona, the darker the shadow.

Like everyone else, I'd just as soon forget about my shadow. Even though I've done a great deal of personal shadow work and spend much of my professional time studying, teaching, and writing about the shadow, when my own shadow pops up, forcing me to acknowledge it, my first reaction is a heavy sigh. Not again. I feel mortified, which interestingly enough means not only humiliated, but also decayed or dead. It does feel like death, like wanting to crawl in a hole and pull it in after me. I wonder why I embarrassed myself so. It happens because I am not only my ego-self; I am also the shadow-self that wants to be seen and acknowledged and accepted.

Much of the emotional pain I feel is the result of my ego's critical analysis, "I shouldn't have said that! Why did I tell that stupid story? Everyone must think I'm an idiot!" My less articulate shadow-self lacks social grace because my ego-self treats that part of me like Cinderella. Of course my shadow doesn't know how to behave at the ball. If my ego weren't so critical and so insistent on being socially acceptable, that shadow part of me could have the acknowledgment and acceptance I need. When my shadow pops out, my ego wants to kill off that part of me. I wish that part of me didn't exist. But as much as my ego hates to admit it sometimes, I am more than my ego.

I am also that larger Self, and the True Center of my psyche wants wholeness more than goodness or rightness. Carl Jung said, "I'd rather be whole than good." I was scandalized when I first heard that attributed to him. Here was Jung, whose insights I deeply admired, saying that wholeness was to be desired above goodness. Worse, it seemed that if one took precedence over the other, then the two must be mutually incompatible. I remember thinking that I wanted to be both good and whole, but if I had to pick, I'd certainly choose to be good. After all, I'd spent my whole life striving to be good, right, perfect. Giving that up would be like giving up my self, like dying. And it is.

It is my ego that has decided I must be good, right, and perfect to survive. But the ego is not the True Center of the psyche. I am more than my ego. We all are more than our egos. The larger Self in all of us follows a higher truth and a deeper wisdom. The psyche strives for the wholeness that comes from the True Center and will sacrifice the ego's definition of goodness to achieve it. The Self knows that wholeness requires acknowledging what the ego wishes to ignore, and so occasionally, we must die the ego-death of social mortification. At those times, every one of us will feel the embarrassment of saying and doing something that

We're made of more than we realize.
CHRISTOPHER REEVE

later we deeply, deeply regret. We can't believe we really did that. It was our shadow-self acting out.

No wonder we're afraid of our shadows!

As mortified as I've been by my shadow from time to time, it's never killed me. It's always made me a bigger person because it leads me away from the ego center to my True Center. As I've increased my capacity to be wholly, fully myself, I've increased my capacity for goodness and my capacity for evil. As I become more fully myself, I become more fully creative.

The ego is not particularly interested in expanding your True Self. For most of us, the ego is downright hostile to the shadow-self and the idea of embracing it. We may say we want to become enlightened, but when it comes down to survival, the ego-self wants nothing to do with anything that threatens its (our) existence no matter how enlightened that thing may make us. This is exactly as it should be. The ego's job is to preserve and protect itself. Your task is not to rid yourself of ego; you'd never survive without that practical part of you that pulls you out of the path of speeding cars or an angry authority figure.

Despite the ego's distaste for the prospect, Jung said that the task of adults who have formed their ego is to acknowledge their shadow. Of course, acknowledging our shadow is a tremendous blow to our ego. Who wants to admit he or she could be as evil as Hitler or as petty as the neighbor who worries about crabgrass creeping from your yard into hers? But Jung reminds us that just as forming a shadow is a necessity in the first part of our lives, accepting it is a necessity in the second part of our lives.

Remember, Jung insisted that we acknowledge our shadow, not that we act it out. He introduced the concept of moral action, which is acknowledging our own hidden potential and consciously choosing what action to take. Instead of denying we're like Hitler, we must acknowledge that we have the same potential for cruelty and then choose our actions accordingly. Instead of denying we could be as saintly as Mother Teresa, we must acknowledge that we have the same potential for compassionate service and choose our actions accordingly. Moral action acknowledges our ego desires and our shadow impulses without acting out either. When we take moral action, we know what our ego wants to do to preserve itself and how our shadow might want to act out, and

Our deepest fear is that we are powerful beyond measure. It is our light, not our darkness that most frightens us. . . . Your playing small doesn't serve the world. . . . We were born to make manifest the glory of God that is within us. It's not just in some of us; it's in everyone.

MARIANNE WILLIAMSON
Return to Love

then we choose what to do based on the moral principles we hold in our True Center.

In keeping with the kind of synchronicity—meaningful coincidence— I've come to expect and respect in doing this work, I had an opportunity to observe my own ego and shadow in action shortly after I introduced the concepts of ego, shadow, and moral action to a class. The first session of the class ran a little late. When the instructor for the next class, which was scheduled to start ten minutes after mine finished, came in, I introduced myself and apologized for being late. Then I flippantly added that I might often finish late. The other instructor said she hoped not, since she believed in beginning on time so she could end on time. My ego was stung. My first thoughts were to wonder who this woman thought she was. Did she think her students were more important than mine? Did she think I should cut my class short just so she could start on time? My ego desire to be considered important was clearly thwarted. My shadowy impulse was to show her! What could she do if I just refused to leave the room when her class was supposed to start? What if I just "forgot" the time and needed ten minutes or so to gather my materials and leave?

I said none of this to her. Sometimes censoring yourself is a good thing. As I drove home, I had a moment of grace when I saw clearly what my ego and my shadow were up to. I started to laugh. I had asked the participants in the class to be on the lookout for appearances from their shadows that week, and I had already had one to talk about. Of course, the one who thought her class was so important that the other teacher should be cut short was me. Here I was blaming the other woman for my own faults. She had only asked me to be considerate of her time. Determining moral action in the situation was easy. Of course I didn't want to act in a way that caused unnecessary conflict with my fellow teachers, and of course I embraced the principle of respecting others. I made sure my class always ended on time.

In the past, I've acted out my ego desires (for importance or whatever else I think I must have to survive), and I've acted out my shadowy impulses (for revenge or something else I don't like to think I'm capable of). I've acted these out outrageously and received great insight from the experiences. No doubt I'll act out my ego and shadow again, but it was a relief, in that particular situation, to have realized what was going on before I got too involved with the drama.

As we act more and more from our True Center, we expand our Creative Center, our creative abilities, and our creative expression. The goal is not to rid ourselves of ego or shadow; ego is absolutely necessary for our existence as human beings, and shadow is always present when ego is. No human lives only from the True Center and never from the ego or shadow, not even saints, who are saintly because they cultivate their awareness of their shadow. Moral action doesn't require living from the True Center; it only requires acting in accordance with the principles we hold there. People who have explored their larger Self and their Creative Center are better prepared to take moral action. And people who act on principles are better equipped to know and express their creativity.

The Gold We Can't Give Away

Still, becoming aware of our shadow can be so painfully embarrassing that we are tempted to argue with Jung. "This person I've spent all my life insisting I'm not holds gold for me? Please say it isn't so." It *is* so, and if we try to refuse the gift of gold the psyche offers by refusing to acknowledge our shadow, we cause great harm.

The alternative to acknowledging our shadow and taking moral action is projecting our shadow onto others. What you cannot admit in yourself, you see in others—just as Ben sees discourtesy in Susan's lateness and Patty sees intolerance in anyone who isn't an antiracism activist.

Usually, the person you see the shadow element in displays some of the quality you've focused on; Jungians call this a hook for the projection. Many people would agree with Ben that Susan's lateness seems to be disrespectful. Many of the people Patty talks to, or more accurately, preaches at, actually are racist. You probably won't see selfishness in Mother Teresa, but you will project it onto your sister-in-law, for example, rather than see it in yourself.

Projection is one way your psyche moves you toward wholeness. When you project a shadow quality onto someone else, it is easier to see. With a little self-reflection you begin to recognize when you're projecting, and, having seen the quality in someone else, you're better able

---

For the wonderful thing about saints is that they were human. They lost their tempers, got hungry, scolded God, were egotistical, or testy or impatient in their turns, made mistakes and regretted them. Still they went on doggedly blundering toward heaven.

PHYLLIS McGINLEY
Saint-Watching

to recognize it in yourself. Once you've recognized a new aspect of your shadow, you can acknowledge it, accept yourself for having this potential, and then choose how to respond with moral action. The aspects you deny most vigorously have great energy surrounding them because your psyche recognizes that these are the keys to wholeness. So the aspects of your own shadow that you most revile are the ones you'll notice reflected by other people.

Patty sees racism as the most significant social problem of our age and has defined her (ego) self as someone who conscientiously works to end racism. She watches constantly for slips that will reveal people's racism and then points out their error. Because she can't or won't acknowledge that judgmentalism is a personality trait she holds herself, Patty becomes rabid about rooting it out in others.

When Patty can acknowledge her tendency to judge others harshly as part of her own shadow and choose a course of moral action to address it instead of denying it, her psyche's desire for wholeness will be satisfied. The urgency she feels to point out others' failings in this regard will fade. And to her ego's surprise, when she stops pointing out people's failings so vigorously, they will be more willing and able to look to her as a model of change. No one really wants to learn from someone who has condemned us.

Projection is a valuable process, a tool our psyche uses to move us toward wholeness. But when projection goes unchecked, it causes everyone a great deal of harm. Perhaps history's clearest example of the dangers of projection is Adolf Hitler's obsession with destroying everyone who wasn't a full-blooded Aryan. Short, dark-haired Hitler never fit the Aryan ideal. Alice Miller, in *For Your Own Good*, suggests Hitler's insistence that citizens prove they weren't "tainted" by Jewish blood for at least three generations back was a response to his fears about his own uncertain parentage and his loathing of the possibility that his grandfather was a Jew. What Hitler couldn't admit about himself, he projected onto others. Jews became his scapegoats, and anything that didn't fit his ideal was projected onto them.

Miller also points out that nearly every German of the time had been exposed to what she calls poisonous pedagogy—child-rearing practices that would be defined as abuse by today's standards. These

When the soul wishes to experience something, she throws an image of the experience out before her and enters into her own image.
MEISTER ECKHART

practices created people who denied their own feelings of vulnerability and hence lacked compassion for others' suffering.

Clearly, projection has dark and dangerous potential. The antidote is acknowledging our own shadow. Like Germany, communities and entire nations have a shared collective shadow. No one individual can take on responsibility for the totality of the collective shadow. All we can do is address our own shadow, and fortunately, that's all we need to do. And let's remember, too, that communities and entire nations also have shared, collective creativity.

What I see in other people is more-or-less correct if it only informs me, but it is definitely a projection if it strongly affects me emotionally.

KEN WILBER
The Spectrum of Consciousness

Exercise: Look into the Mirror

List five people you who really bug you. Not necessarily all the time, but at least some of the time these people really set your teeth on edge. List individuals or types of people and the reason they bother you so much. For example, "Ann really bugs me when she whines and plays the victim," or "I get really upset with people who get waited on at the deli when it's not their turn and then act like they're entitled because they're in such a hurry."

List five people you despise and explain why. List individuals or types of people. For example, "I despise my ex-husband because he was such a coward when he left. I despise people who chicken out."

List five of your pet peeves. For example, "I hate it when people run their fingernails down a chalkboard to get attention."

Consider what you are projecting onto these people. Are these elements in your own shadow? For example, "Do I want to whine about my life? Do I think I'm not getting something I'm entitled to?" "Maybe I take unnecessary risks to prove to myself how brave I am, when in fact I'm really scared." "Do I do annoying things to get attention?"

Now list five people you deeply admire and explain why. For example, "I admire John because he takes action with confidence."

Consider what you are projecting onto these people as well. Are these elements in your own white shadow? For example, are you repressing your own ability to take confident action?

Giving Away the White Gold

Why would we want to project positive qualities onto another person instead of recognizing them in ourselves? Because we fear those qualities. Jeremiah Abrams, a renowned Jungian therapist, editor of *The Shadow in America,* and co-editor of *Meeting the Shadow,* observes: "We often allow other people, who we admire and respect, to carry our white shadow, the unlived parts of ourselves. We let someone like Mother Teresa carry these noble traits because to embody them ourselves would feel too grandiose. Many people fear that if they truly embodied the nobility they experience in others, then, as Robert Johnson says, 'Heaven will come too soon.' We'll finish our purpose here and we'll be out of here."

Abrams emphasizes that the positive qualities we project are at least as important as the negative qualities. I've observed this again and again in my own and others' journeys toward full creative expression. Hero worship is a major activity of artist wanna-bes. Our projections allow us to fantasize "if only" and "someday" instead of focusing on what we can do today. We trade the difficult work and commitment required to make our dreams reality for the ease of fantasizing how wonderful our creative efforts could be if only . . .

Instead of reading a book or taking a class from someone we admire to learn how we can do what that person has done, we reaffirm that that person is truly one of the greats and thus what he or she does is beyond our reach. We push our white shadow onto this other person to get ourselves off the hook. We refuse to see how that person is human just like us so we can ignore the very real possibility that we can learn the techniques he or she used.

Besides the disservice we do ourselves and our community by discounting our own strengths and gifts, we can harm those we push our white gold onto. When we put our white shadow of creativity or spirituality onto a teacher or guru, we give that person the energy and power locked into our shadow. At first, this can feed the teacher's ego, which feels great and gives him or her more energy to do his or her work. But when enough people project their shadow energy onto one person, that person burns out like a fuse overloaded by an energy spike.

This may be why so many renowned artists and gurus act out so

Beyond "infantile grandiosity," which we make fun of in psychology, there is true grandness, the fragrance of greatness in us, the true gold of grandiosity.
ROBERT BLY
Story Food for Men and Women

outrageously with sexual or financial improprieties or become over-bearing or overcontrolling. Unconsciously, they create enormous problems so that their fans will withdraw the energy of their white shadow projections. Unfortunately, the artist or teacher often misses the drama and the old ego-high of adoration and redoubles his or her efforts to gain new followers. This can create a cycle that is dangerous for everyone involved.

Moving through the cycle once or twice can be a marvelous lesson, however. Sometimes we need to project our white shadow onto another person so we can see it more clearly. When we notice we feel uninspired to do our own creative work or when we feel angry because the other person isn't acting as nobly as we'd like, we can see the projection for what it is and reclaim our own power and potential.

It is possible to have mentors and guides without revering them so much that we see only someone to carry our white shadow. Mentors show their human failings and help us see what they've done and how we can apply those lessons in our own journey. There are others, how-ever, who are happy to take the energy of our white shadow as long as we are willing to give it to them.

There is good reason for the old saying "If you meet the Buddha on the road, kill him." It isn't really the Buddha, of course, it's only an illu-sion that creative potential or spirituality or some other positive trait is "out there." This is your road and your journey, after all. Meeting what looks like the Buddha will only distract you from your primary teacher—you and the divine within you.

We do have to be careful how we go about "killing" the Buddha, though. The illusion is created by a mask, and behind every Buddha mask is another human being who deserves our compassion and per-haps our companionship.

Whether they're humble human mentors or gurus wearing Buddha masks, we learn from our guides and then we must symbolically kill them by calling an end to their role as guides. Often from the corpse of a Buddha rises a new friend, peer, and colleague, if he or she is willing to take off the mask and if we are willing to forgive him or her for being human.

Consider the traits you project onto the people you admire. Remem-ber that those traits are yours.

Part of the blame lies with the student, because too much obedience, devotion and blind acceptance spoils a teacher. Part also lies with the spiritual master because he lacks the integrity to be immune to that kind of vulnerability.

THE DALAI LAMA

※ *Guided Imagery*

Because projecting our white shadow on another so often requires fantasies of "someday"—"Someday I'll win an Academy Award" or "Someday I'll have my own gallery showing"—we need to learn the distinction between fantasy and constructive imagination. The crucial difference is believability. When you imagine an outcome that you believe can happen, you're able to act as if, which produces the result you want, even as you also recognize and respond to real doubts and obstacles. Fantasy, on the other hand, can't allow you to act as if, because a part of you always recognizes that the fantasy is just fantasy.

For guided imagery to be useful, then, it must be something you imagine, not fantasize. Used this way, guided imagery provides tremendous power to transform your beliefs and behaviors, which determine your experiences.

Remember to either read these instructions onto a tape and play them back when you're able to relax fully into the guided imagery or have a friend read the instructions to you.

Find a place and time when you can be relaxed and uninterrupted. Lie or sit comfortably and begin to relax. Close your eyes. Take several deep breaths, noticing and following the breath in and out of your body.

Consciously tighten the muscles in your feet and ankles. Notice the tension. . . . Feel the tension in all the muscles in your feet. . . . Hold the tension as long as you like . . . holding it until you're ready to let it go with a sigh. . . . Take a deep breath and notice how it feels to let go, to feel the warm relaxation in your feet. . . .

Now, consciously tighten the muscles in your calves and knees. Notice the tension. . . . Feel the tension in your calves and knees. . . . Hold the tension . . . until you're ready to let it go with a sigh. . . . Take a deep breath and notice how good it feels to let your calves and your knees relax and go slack. . . .

Consciously tighten the muscles in your thighs, buttocks, and pelvis. Notice the tension. . . . Feel the tension in your thighs and buttocks and pelvis. . . . Hold the tension . . . until you're ready to let it go with a sigh. . . . Take a deep breath and notice how good it feels to let the lower half of your body relax more and more with each breath you take. . . .

Take another deep breath and consciously tighten the muscles in your stomach, chest, and back. Feel the tension in your torso. . . . Notice what it feels like to hold tension in this part of your body. . . . Hold that tension . . . until you're ready to let it go with a sigh. . . . Take a deep, slow breath and notice how good it feels to breathe all the way down to your belly . . . how good it feels to let your belly go soft and round with each breath. . . .

Now, consciously tighten your hands into fists. Feel the tension move from your hands to your wrists, your forearms, elbows, upper arms, into your shoulders and the base of your neck. . . . Notice that tension, what it feels like . . . holding it until you're ready to let it go with a sigh. . . . Take a deep breath and notice how good it feels to let any remaining tension ooze out of your fingertips. . . . Notice how good it feels to let your shoulders drop and let your arms relax more and more. . . .

Now, consciously tighten the muscles in your jaw and neck, scrunch up the muscles around your eyes and forehead. . . . Notice the tension in your face and neck . . . holding it until you're ready to let it go with a sigh. . . . Notice how good it feels to let your whole body become more and more relaxed . . . more and more relaxed with every breath. . . .

Continue to breathe deeply. If worries or thoughts about other things come to you, simply remind yourself, "Not this, not now," set the thought aside, and return your attention to your breathing. Allow your breath to assume a slow, natural rhythm.

Experience your whole body now as relaxed . . . your mind as quiet and still . . . your emotions as calm and clear . . . your spirit as peaceful and serene. . . .

From this place of inner serenity, harmony, and relaxation, begin to allow images to occur in your mind. . . . Think of a creative person you admire. . . . Don't worry about having the perfect person in mind; just use the first or second person you think of. . . . Think about all the qualities you respect in this person, especially those qualities you wish you possessed. . . .

Imagine this person sitting or standing next to you and talking with you in a calm, quiet voice. . . . As you two talk, ask this person how he or she got to be such an outstanding creative person. . . . Ask about how this person felt when just starting. . . .

As you continue to talk, you notice that this person had many of the emotions you have now. . . . You begin to see how you can take on some of the qualities you admire so in this other person. . . .

(pause for at least two to three minutes)

You have just met a part of your white shadow. . . . Ask this guide for a symbol or sign of what you can do now to begin to live with the qualities you admire. . . . Don't worry if the symbol isn't clear or doesn't make sense now; your understanding of it will grow over time. . . .

(pause for at least two to three minutes)

When you're ready, gently touch your fingers to your chair or the floor and begin to return your attention to this room. . . . Slowly open your eyes. When you're ready, draw the symbol you received or the colors or images that stand out in your mind. If the symbol wasn't clear to you before, allow it to emerge in the drawing. After drawing, write a few notes if there is anything else you want to be sure to remember.

The truth is, we're all chosen; most of us just forget to rsvp.

SARAH BAN BREATHNACH
Simple Abundance

❋ Creative Shadow Play

One of the times I tried the guided imagery described above, I imagined talking with Anne McCaffrey, author of *Dragonriders of Pern* and all the other delightful Pern books. I heard myself telling Anne that I half-expected to see a fire lizard (a miniature dragon) on her shoulder, and then, with the magic of imagination, I saw a shimmering blue dragon peer through Anne's graying hair. The imagined Anne told me that the dragonet gave her inspiration and support when she was writing, especially if she got stuck wondering what would happen next in a Pern novel. We talked about the mythic and mystical qualities of dragons and about writing. When I finished the visualization, I knew that that blue dragon was an important symbol for me. So I spent time searching for a blue dragon to place near my computer to remind me what Anne told me about writing in general and my writing in particular.

I don't know whether the real Anne McCaffrey would have said the things I imagined, but that's not really important. The key is that I've projected some of my white shadow—qualities I strive to have when I'm feeling bravely expansive or deny I have when I'm feeling fearful and constricted—onto Anne McCaffrey. What Anne told me in the visualization is actually what my larger Self wanted to tell me. The blue dragon on my computer is a daily reminder of that higher truth about myself.

For your creative shadow playtime this week, spend time looking for a concrete representation of the symbol or sign you received in the guided imagery. If Georgia O'Keefe is the artist you admire, perhaps you want to spend time noticing the intense sensuality of fresh flowers at a conservatory or on your dining room table. If you imagined yourself talking with Ansel Adams, maybe it's time to load your camera with black-and-white film and spend the day outdoors. Give yourself the luxury of taking an hour or more to compose one fantastic shot. And remember what it was Ansel told you about patience and learning from mistakes.

Watch for small ways to move yourself closer to that white shadow aspect of you. You don't have to invest thousands of dollars in photographic equipment this week, but do find one tangible reminder of the white shadow you're beginning to claim. Maybe it's framing your own best shot and hanging it next to one of Ansel's. Maybe it's buying a red poppy and using it as the focus of your meditation. Maybe it's reading one of your favorite writer's early books and keeping it on your writing desk to remind yourself that she, too, faltered at her beginning.

Don't worry if you aren't sure what tangible object could represent your guided imagery experience or can't imagine where you'd find it. You may not know what you're looking for until you see it. Enjoy the search as much as the owning. Many of us tend to put ourselves on tight schedules where every moment has a purpose. Taking time to wander about without a clear goal may be exactly the experience you need right now.

⊙ EXERCISE CHOICES

1. Ask a Friend. Ask your partner or a close and trusted friend how he or she sees your shadow side. In *Your Golden Shadow*, William A. Miller, a Jungian analyst, suggests, "If I can see clearly your shadow to which you are blind, then it must follow that you likewise can see clearly my shadow to which I am blind. If I would be more than happy to tell you what I see (in a nice way, of course), then you would probably be more than happy to tell me what you see (in a nice way, of course)." Miller states that asking a friend what he or she sees is one of the most effective ways to gain insight to the nature of your shadow, but it can be threatening to hear, especially from someone close. "Paradoxically," he writes, "the people who are most likely to be helpful are those whom we are least likely to heed. We may accuse them of overt subjectivity, projection, or just plain fabrication. It would be less threatening to hear feedback from a stranger, but strangers are not in the position to give us the kind of authentic perceptions as are those who know us well."

Ask for this information when you're both calm, never when you're in the middle of a conflict. The person you ask may or may not want you to reciprocate. Accept your friend's insight with grace, if not full belief yet. Miller cautions that if you have a strong reaction and think that your friend has lost his or her mind, you've got a substantial clue that this really is a characteristic of your shadow. He suggests you may want to tell another trusted friend what you're doing and ask if he or she agrees with your other friend's assessment.

I've heard it this way: "If one person tells you you have a tail, he or she could very well be wrong. But if five or six people tell you you have a tail, you've probably got a tail."

2. Ask the Mirror, "Mirror on the Wall, Who's the Fairest One of All?" List the qualities you deeply admire in other people. Think about the people you regard as heroes, role models, or mentors. What is it about these people that attracts you so? What qualities do they exhibit that you admire?

After you've made your list, put a check mark next to the qualities that you feel you already possess, at least partially. Put a star next to the qualities that you would like to possess or exhibit more often. These starred qualities are aspects of your shadow—your white shadow—and they are qualities you will begin to show more and more as you continue exploring your creativity and your shadow.

Practice one of the starred qualities this week. Post a reminder in your date book or on your bathroom mirror: "Be courageous today!" or "Practice being compassionate today." Watch for opportunities to practice this quality in *small* ways every day. If you wish, keep a record of your small successes.

3. Ask the Mirror, "Mirror on the Wall, Who's the Ugliest One of All?" List the qualities you dislike in other people. In addition to your usual pet peeves, like people who are late to meet with you or who cut you off on the highway, think about the qualities you not only dislike, but actively and energetically hate. Think about the people you regard as villains, the people you would never want to be like. What is it about these people that angers or disgusts you so? What qualities do they exhibit that you abhor?

After you've made your list, put a check mark next to the qualities that you feel you possess, at least some of the time. Put a star next to the qualities that you want to exhibit less often or never. These starred qualities are aspects of your shadow—your dark shadow—and they are qualities you will begin to see in others and yourself more and more as you continue exploring your creativity and your shadow.

Be aware of your tendency to project your shadow onto others, particularly the starred qualities. When someone does something that offends you, be aware that you may be more sensitive and less objective because of the work you've begun here. Ask yourself how this other person's behavior reflects your own shadow. A normal response will be to insist you would never do *that*, whatever *that* is. Look again. Maybe you wouldn't do what this person did, but you may often behave in a way that reflects a similar "failing." Because you may be more sensitive and less objective, you may want to ask someone you can trust for feedback.

4. Ask Yourself, "Who Is That Person in the Mirror?"
Rapidly list:

- five things you dislike doing in general
- five things you dislike doing when engaged in a creative effort
- five mistakes you tend to make in general
- five mistakes you tend to make when engaged in a creative effort
- five things you have difficulty coping with in general
- five things you have difficulty coping with when engaged in a creative effort
- When I'm tired, I _____.
- When I'm sick, I _____.

- When I'm under stress, I _____.
- When I'm under the influence of drugs (alcohol, nicotine, caffeine, etc.), I _____.
- When I'm creative, I feel _____.

These lists will give you additional information about your shadow and how it interacts with your creative expression.

5. Remember When . . . Remember the last time you felt embarrassed. Warning: if you claim you can't remember an embarrassing scene, your shadow, who is delighted that you're finally going to listen, will be tempted to give you a fresh embarrassing moment to work with. Shadows are like that.

List as much as you can remember about why you felt embarrassed. You may feel embarrassed all over again just thinking about it, but go ahead and write it out anyway. Give yourself ten or fifteen minutes to remember as much as you can. Include the details of what you said, what others said, how you looked, how others looked, what the environment was, and so on. Don't worry about getting the information down in any particular order, just write it all down.

Then, switch your pen to your other hand, the one you don't usually write with, and write about what you intended to say or do, how you were misunderstood, how you were hurt, what you wish you could just forgive yourself for and accept about yourself. Give yourself about twice as much time as you took for the first writing.

Switch hands again and write about how your larger Self or even your Higher Power (the God of your understanding) might perceive your actions and feelings in the situation. If you are ready to forgive yourself, write that intention. If you're ready to accept a part of your shadow, write that intention. If not, perhaps you're willing to become ready.

6. Go Public — An Advanced Exercise. Select one of your most trusted friends or a stranger you can trust to keep your confidence (such as a clergy member or therapist). Tell this person about the embarrassing experience you wrote about in exercise 5. Contemplating this usually feels scary or overwhelming, but as the millions of people who have done Fifth Steps as part of their Twelve Step recovery have discovered, it is a relief to acknowledge these dark truths about ourselves. When you reveal something you feel shameful about to a trustworthy person who witnesses your admission not with disgust but with loving acceptance, you grow in your own capacity to accept yourself and others. It is a truly healing gift you give yourself.

If you want more information on how and why this works and how to select someone to hear your "personal inventory," refer to AA's Big Book, officially titled *Alcoholics Anonymous,* or AA's *Twelve Steps and Twelve Traditions,* or any of the other good books available on Twelve Step recovery.

7. Go Public—Just for Fun. Get a beach ball or volleyball and go to a public pool. Play around with the ball for a while, remembering Jacquelyn Small's metaphor of the shadow as a ball we try to hide underwater. Notice how high the ball flies in relation to how deep you hold it under. Notice how much attention and energy it takes to keep the ball submerged all the time. Notice how difficult it is to hold on to the ball when it's just below the surface, compared to how easy it is to maneuver if you let it float.

Invite friends to bring their own balls (shadows) and play with you. Invent some games or races that require keeping the balls (shadows) hidden underwater at all times. Try games that allow the balls to surface or be shared. You may want to explain Small's metaphor and talk about your experiences.

If you're part of a committed group where everyone feels safe and accepted, you may want to try a game where the tosser calls out someone's name and tosses the ball to that person. The catcher calls out one of his or her own shadow traits when catching the ball. Because announcing your shadow traits can leave you feeling vulnerable, follow this game with a variation where the tosser calls out another player's name and what the tosser admires or loves about that other player before tossing the ball to him or her. For example, a tosser might call, "Bill, I respect your courage." Reserve time after the game to give everyone a chance to talk about their emotional responses.

CHAPTER 4

Tossing Psyche's Coin

SUPPOSE I GAVE YOU A COIN with a golden sun on one side and a jet-black night sky embossed with pinpricks of silver stars on the other. Suppose I promised that if you tossed the coin and it landed sun-side up, you'd have a peak creative experience. You know the feeling: when you're creating something and everything flows; when you feel fully alive and focused; when you're joyful even though you're not quite sure what to do next; when your ego takes a backseat to the something larger that you're creating, and you feel more fully yourself, detached from petty concerns.

But, suppose I also promised that if the coin landed night-side up, you'd have an entirely different experience—a shadow experience. You'd feel emotions you didn't like: anger, fear, jealousy, or confusion; certainly pain and shame. You'd say and do things you wouldn't ordinarily say or do. You'd realize you weren't yourself, but it would seem as if you couldn't quite catch up to stop yourself, or you wouldn't realize until later how out of control you really were. You'd feel terribly frustrated.

Would you toss this coin? What if I told you that the coin defied the laws of probability, that the chances of the coin landing sun-side up were greater the first twenty times you tossed it, but after that the chances were greater the night side would come up? What if I added that when the night side first appeared, the experience would have greater intensity but that the intensity would gradually diminished after, say, fifty times?

There is such a coin—the coin of our life force. The faces represent the bliss of flowing in our creativity and the pain of encountering our shadow. It has been my experience that fate favors those who are first exploring their creativity with more sun-side experiences. It has also been my experience that the first fifty or so times we encounter our shadow, it is painfully intense.

I've seen people enthralled with exploring new creative outlets, happily tossing the coin again and again—until the shadow face lands in their laps. For example, Alan is bravely, joyfully writing short stories and getting wonderful praise from his friends and teachers. Then he savagely reviews another student's work in an advanced class, realizing only much later it may have been his jealousy speaking. Whatever it was, he doesn't feel safe in the class and stops writing altogether.

Alice, who has been delighted with how easily she's been writing poetry after reading just one wonderfully empowering book, decides to write about her family and realizes her sister or her father may be offended by her public perceptions. She backs away from writing that poem and finds she can't write anything else with the ease she's come to expect.

Rachel starts a dance class with great enthusiasm but quits when the combination of the movement and a careless comment from another participant brings up painful issues about her body image.

Nick has been having great fun trying new techniques with his camera and playing with wood sculptures. He remarks, "I never thought I could have so much fun." A week later, his primary relationship is in trouble and he's struggling with painful emotions, both past and present.

I know how painful and embarrassing it can feel to see the shadow side of yourself. I know it is even more painful and embarrassing if you're expecting the creative side and find yourself sideswiped by your shadow.

As mentioned in chapter 1, I put the coin aside for years. Every once in a while, if I had a flash of inspiration that gave me a complete story without struggling too much, I'd write. Otherwise I'd just talk about writing or read another book about writing. Not tossing the coin left me feeling half-dead—clinically depressed, the professionals called it. Tossing the coin was unpredictable and therefore scary; not tossing it was predictably awful.

That's the crucial piece of information you need before you can decide whether to toss the coin. Avoiding the coin keeps you safe from

A dim premonition tells us that we cannot be whole without this negative side, that we have a body which, like all bodies, casts a shadow, and that if we deny this body, we cease to be three-dimensional and become flat and without substance.

CARL JUNG

those shadow experiences, but at a cost. People who avoid the coin lose the opportunity not only to have peak creative experiences but also to have most other experiences. Sustained abstinence will leave you feeling empty, vague, half-dead, diminished.

If you've read this far, you've probably decided that you don't want to go through the rest of your life as a zombie. You're willing to risk the shadow side, if only because you can't stand the thought of nothingness.

Once you've learned that the shadow side can appear with any toss and you've decided to risk it, there is a bonus: you discover the shadow-side experience is at least as valuable as the creative-side experience. Alan stops taking classes, but he continues to write in his journal, where he comes face-to-face with his own jealousy and recognizes that this jealousy shows him what he truly wants. Alice keeps writing poetry even though it's not always easy, and she finds she's able to do other difficult things as well, like asking for a raise. Rachel finds a therapist to help her address the issues she has about her body and reclaims not only her right to be in a dance class but also her right to be in her body. Nick talks with his wife and commits to working through their relationship difficulties. All the while, Nick is fully aware of his shadow popping out, saying outrageous things. As he learns to acknowledge his part in the difficulties, he finds he has a new level of intimacy with his wife and with himself.

When you surrender to the possibility of your shadow appearing, you learn to accept, even embrace, its appearance. You begin to see the gifts each experience has to offer, and you begin to agree with Jung's observation that the shadow—your shadow—is 90 percent gold.

Once you have made that observation, it doesn't matter so much which side of the coin is revealed. In fact, you notice that the distinguishing marks start to fade and both sides of the coin look remarkably alike. But that happens only when you've handled the coin so much that you start to rub away those distinguishing marks, and only when you stop looking so closely and with so much trepidation to see which side you've gotten on this toss.

You have to leave the city of your comfort and go into the wilderness of your intuition. What you'll discover will be wonderful. What you'll discover will be yourself.
ALAN ALDA

Outside the Comfort Zone

Knowing what you now know about this coin, will you toss it? How often? The reason you may be hesitating is that the shadow side is outside your comfort zone; in fact, the creativity side may also be outside your comfort zone.

Your comfort zone is the collection of things you feel comfortable having, doing, being, feeling. It is what you're familiar with. It probably includes things like reading, writing, and speaking English. It probably doesn't include reading, writing, or speaking ancient Greek. For some people, feeling anger is inside the comfort zone; for others, it is outside. For still others, feeling anger is inside the comfort zone, but expressing it honestly and directly is outside the zone. Some people are comfortable having a lot of money; others are not. Some people are familiar with being alone; others find solitude difficult. No two people have the same comfort zone.

Comfort zones not only vary between individuals, they also change over time. All of the activities now inside your comfort zone were once outside—activities like driving a car, getting dressed in the morning, swimming, walking, having a job, and paying your bills. Even breathing was once outside your comfort zone. Growing up and gaining life experience expands your comfort zone. Seen this way, growing up is more like growing out.

On the other hand, there may be some things that you were comfortable doing, being, having, and feeling when you were younger that are no longer familiar or comfortable. Maybe you no longer want to be seen holding hands with your best friend. Maybe you don't do somersaults on your front lawn anymore. Maybe you're no longer comfortable coloring with crayons. Pablo Picasso said, "Every child is an artist. The problem is how to remain an artist once he grows up."

Still, your comfort zone as an adult is larger than it was when you were a child. And if it seems that your comfort zone has moved sideways so that some of the creative joys of childhood are outside your current area, you can reclaim the old territory without giving up the larger adult zone.

Anytime you venture outside your comfort zone to try something new, you grow. Comfort zones tend to expand symmetrically, maintain-

Some things do make you bigger, and taking risks is one of them. Not taking risks is the way we insist on staying small.

JULIA CAMERON
The Vein of Gold

ing a circular shape. One benefit of this is that when you venture outside your comfort zone to try a new creative activity, such as exploring new media in your painting, your entire comfort zone grows. You not only become familiar with the new style of painting, you're also comfortable trying other things that were once beyond your scope. It's amazing, but true, that trying a new creative outlet could also give you the courage to ask for a raise or challenge the status quo in an unsatisfying relationship.

Comfort zones also contract symmetrically. When you avoid a new challenge just outside or right on the edge of your comfort zone, you don't pull away from just that challenge, you pull your entire comfort zone in. We all pull back from time to time, because what lies outside the comfort zone is always frightening.

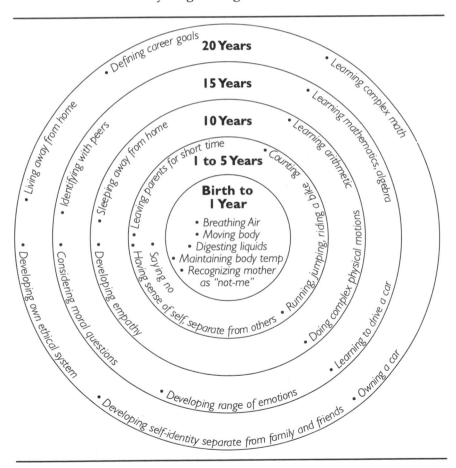

For example, when Alice shied away from writing poetry about her family because she was afraid they wouldn't like what she wrote, she was unable to write any poetry. Her comfort zone had recently expanded to include writing poetry and then quickly constricted. By continuing to write poems for herself, despite her discomfort and the difficulty, Alice pushed the bounds of her comfort zone outward again. And something unrelated to writing poetry, asking for a raise, also became possible for Alice because her comfort zone had expanded symmetrically.

Of course Alice was frightened when she continued to write poetry. Fear always lies outside our comfort zones. Some people call the emotion that accompanies moving just a little outside their comfort zone "excitement" or a "thrill." People who continue to push the bounds of their comfort zones, who are willing to try new things, seem to have a greater tolerance, even enjoyment, for this level of fear. They trust themselves and their ability to handle whatever happens when they venture into unfamiliar territory.

Getting something you want almost always requires you to grow past your comfort zone, which defines what you already have. The very essence of desire is that you desire what is outside familiar territory. Once we recognize that we must move outside the comfort zone to grow and that doing so always entails some degree of fear, it's easy to see fear as a necessary part of growth. Fear is an excellent indicator that you are pursuing your dreams. The reverse is also true—a lack of this kind of fear indicates that you've given up on your dreams.

The circle that represents the comfort zone is static only in the imagination; in real life, our comfort zone is constantly fluctuating. Progress is never a straight line; it's always two steps forward, half a step back, three steps forward, two steps back. Our comfort zone moves out, we feel afraid, and we pull back a little. We push out, pull back. If we aren't constantly pushing a little, we begin to constrict. People who consistently pull back into the familiar and comfortable when they feel threatened find that they are increasingly fearful until they eventually view everything as a threat. The underlying fear of not trusting themselves to handle what might happen becomes overwhelming.

Fear is inescapable. We either fear the new territory we're moving into or we avoid moving into new territory because we're afraid. Of the two, the fear of being afraid, the fear of not trusting ourselves, is more

> *To live a creative life, we must lose our fear of being wrong.*
> JOSEPH CHILTON PEARCE

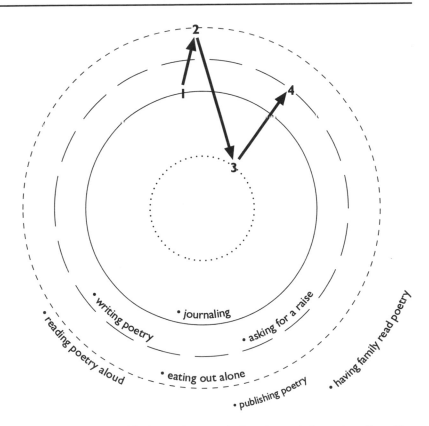

- **writing poetry**
- **journaling**
- **asking for a raise**
- **reading poetry aloud**
- **eating out alone**
- **publishing poetry**
- **having family read poetry**

1. The solid circle represents Alice's comfort zone before she started experimenting with writing poetry. Journaling was inside this comfort zone; writing poetry was just outside.

2. The largest circle represents Alice's comfort zone when she felt the first thrill of success with her poetry. By writing some poetry, she had pushed the boundaries of herself. She had a greatly expanded sense of self and was willing to take new, unrelated risks, like dining out alone. But reading poetry aloud was outside her comfort zone, publishing her poetry was even farther out, and having her family read her poetry was very far outside her comfort zone.

3. The smallest circle, drawn with dots, shows how Alice constricted inward when she realized how frightened she was of her family's possible reactions to her poetry. She pulled in on herself so much that even journaling felt uncomfortable.

4. The circle drawn with long dashes shows how Alice expanded herself again when she pushed through her fear. She's willing to ask for a raise, but not ready to go to a restaurant by herself again. Continuing to journal and experiment with poetry will expand her sense of herself even further.

painful and limiting. People who constrict their comfort zones are usually filled with pain. In a misguided attempt to avoid fear, they fill their lives with low-level fear of just about everyone and everything.

If Alice had given up writing poetry when she encountered her first block, not only would she have lost that method of expressing and exploring her creativity, but she also would have constricted even more. With the taste of fear in her mouth, she may have found the journaling that brought her to poetry was a little too threatening and backed away from that. Without her journaling to give her a safe place to explore and express her emotions, she may have found many of those emotions too frightening and begun to shut down her awareness of how she truly felt.

Backing away from fear can become a pattern that closes our eyes and our hearts. We begin to constrict, collapsing our comfort zones smaller and smaller. We all know how this feels: we have an off day, feeling a bit less competent and more vulnerable than usual, and someone makes a comment that touches a nerve. If we are feeling expansive, in the habit of pushing our comfort zones outward, we might share the incident with a friend and laugh it off. We would trust ourselves to handle the situation.

But when we are in a constricting pattern, we retreat home to lick our wounds and nurse the grievance. We spend the night in front of the TV, channel surfing and eating Ben and Jerry's ice cream right out of the carton. We pull in the comfort zone and feel even less like encountering the person at work the next day. Maybe we call in sick just to get a break; sleep late, don't take a shower, and now we really feel like losers. We might pull in even more, canceling meetings, or skipping classes that usually excite us, avoiding anything that feels a little risky because we have less and less confidence in our ability to handle what might happen.

This fear that we can't handle "it," whatever "it" is, is what collapses the comfort zone. Our sense of self gets smaller and smaller as we spiral in on ourselves, until we become like the mythic Greek bird that flew in smaller and smaller circles until it finally flew up its own tail feathers and disappeared.

On the other hand, when we take the risk of venturing outside the realm of what is familiar and comfortable, we find that there is more of us. Our sense of self expands with our comfort zone. One way to view the comfort zone is to recognize it as our ego-self. As you recall, most of

It is not because things are difficult that we do not dare; it is because we do not dare that they are difficult.

SENECA

our creativity lies outside our ego. As we expand our comfort zone, we expand our ego-self to include more and more creativity. Of course, we also encounter more of our shadow as we do this.

As our ego encounters creativity and shadow, it grows and moves closer to the True Center or Creative Center. Expanding our comfort zone not only gives us a larger sense of self, it also gives us a larger sense of Self. As you take risks and grow, you become more fully your Self.

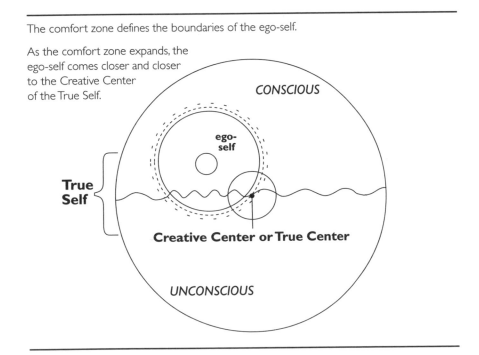

The comfort zone defines the boundaries of the ego-self.

As the comfort zone expands, the ego-self comes closer and closer to the Creative Center of the True Self.

Creativity Just Is

Although we all know what it feels like to be in the creative flow, it is difficult to fully describe the experience. Creativity, like freedom or justice, is an ineffable quality that defies precise definition. One of the best formal definitions I've found is that creativity is combining previously disparate elements into an innovative, cohesive whole. While that covers the bases, it doesn't quite describe the thrill of the game.

To paraphrase William Blake, creativity is the Divine in every person.

Creative expression is evidence of the spiritual force that drives us, body and soul. It is the undeniable urge to express what we see and feel and think.

Creativity is the life force. And the life force will not be denied. Our creativity may be blocked by harmful experiences in our past; it may be repressed by our fear; but it will not be denied. If it cannot flow in the most natural manner, it will nonetheless find a way out, leaking out sideways if it must. The block may be expressed in an addiction or dysfunction, but the creativity always comes out.

The coin will lure you to pick it up again. You'll go to pay for a magazine at a newsstand, and that coin will be handed back with your change when you notice that the cover story is about creativity. Or your boss assigns you to work on a proposal for a social service agency and, since many of their clients are families with young children, suggests you make this one a little lighter, a little more fun. The coin shows up in your paycheck. Suddenly you're pulling in clip art of balloons and kites, and you even think of flying a kite yourself. Or one of your silliest friends, whom you treasure for exactly that reason, buys two water pistols, one for each of you. And there's no telling where that could lead!

So where's the problem? Creativity is a good thing; when people feel the urge, they can just go create something, right?

Wrong. It's important that we don't polarize creativity as good and shadow as bad. Shadow is what your ego has decided is threatening, not necessarily what your True Self recognizes as bad. Likewise, creativity is neither good nor bad; it just is. Being able to flow with it feels great. Not being able to find the flow—being creatively blocked—is painful and unhealthy. Many of us, perhaps all of us, have periods when we feel blocked. We remember the other side of the coin and refuse it, even when offered by our best friend with a water pistol.

I get cranky when I'm not writing. After cranky comes bitchy and then downright mean, usually—but not exclusively—to myself. Then, if I still don't get the message, I feel guilty about being so mean and nasty to everyone and become depressed and feel hopeless about everything. I don't need to castigate myself; I need to acknowledge what harm I've done, mend the situation, and get back to writing.

We cannot escape fear. We can only transform it into a companion that accompanies us on all our exciting adventures.

SUSAN JEFFERS
Feel the Fear and Do It Anyway

When Creativity Just Isn't

If not writing feels so awful and writing feels so good, why don't I just write? Because I am afraid, afraid of what I'll find if I try to write and can't, afraid of what I'll find if I try to write and do. I'm afraid of what I'll find out about myself. I'm afraid of the coin landing night-side up. I'm afraid of my own shadow.

I'm not alone. From talking with other creative people, from reading what others have experienced, and from working with the courageous people willing to participate in the creativity classes I teach, I've learned that we're all afraid of our shadows. I am convinced that the most common cause, perhaps the only cause, of creative constipation is unresolved shadow issues.

Part of my fear about being creative is that I won't do it perfectly, and then I'll feel inadequate and foolish. Another big fear I have is that I can't have the creative life I want and make any real money, that I have to choose between almost having the life I want (*almost* is the operative word here because I won't have enough money to have the life I really want) and earning the money I need by doing work I can barely tolerate, hence living a life I hate.

Both of these are shadow issues for me. Fortunately, my shadow has a way of proving I'm imperfect and leaving me feeling like a fool from time to time in areas other than my writing. I can see that I'm going to play the fool from time to time anyway, so I may as well play it while doing something I love. And as far as never having any "real money" goes, I remind myself that when I wasn't a writer struggling with money, I was a computer programmer struggling with money or a graduate student struggling with money. Money issues are shadow issues for me that I'm learning to deal with regardless of what I'm doing for a living.

Regardless of what your shadow fears are—playing the fool, never making "real money," proving that you really don't have talent, discovering something unexpected about your sex life—regardless of how you dive into the flow of creativity—through writing or sculpting or baking bread—the coin will insist you pick it up again. Your creativity will show itself in surprising ways. And your shadow will present itself

Life shrinks or expands in proportion to one's courage.

ANAÏS NIN

when you least expect it. As the U.S. Calvary learned to say about the Apache warriors, "When you don't see anything, watch out! That's when you're about to be in trouble."

We can't have one side of the coin without the other. To heal the pain we caused ourselves by refusing to pick up the coin of our own life force, we have to risk seeing either side. And it's not enough to just talk about shadow; we must be willing to explore it. We need to notice how creativity and shadow are intertwined in our lives.

Creativity and Shadow Intertwined

For many of us, creativity itself is in the shadow. Creativity is unsafe. It's messy, and we've all heard that old saying about cleanliness being next to godliness. We've been told to stay inside the lines, and being creative is definitely an outside-the-lines kind of behavior and attitude. Creativity requires a willingness to make mistakes, lots and lots of mistakes. Some of us have a bigger problem with this than others, but nearly all of us feel the ego's natural desire to be right. To the ego, entrusted with making sure you survive, mistakes can be fatal. Expressing our creativity is asserting who we really are, and for some people that's a dangerously rebellious and defiant thing to do.

Creativity is often associated with sexuality, and rightly so. If you're familiar with the Eastern philosophy of chakras, which identifies certain centers of energy in different places in the body, you know that the second chakra, located in the lowest part of the abdomen, is linked with both sexuality and creativity. Much of sexuality, if not all of it, is about creating—creating new life, creating pleasure, creating new relationships and connections. Creativity and sexuality share language—to conceive is to both have an idea and have a baby. We talk about a treasured idea as our brainchild; we labor to give birth to our ideas. In the Middle Ages, when the artistry of European women was downplayed because the Muses, being goddesses, would only appear to men, the common perception was that women didn't need any creative outlet other than having children.

So creativity and sexuality, while not identical, are associated with each other. And for the vast majority of us, at least some aspect of our

It is time to throw off the shackles, to reclaim that which every child knows and is taught to forget: the essential right to create without interference or shame.

MICHELL CASSOU
and
STEWART CUBLEY
Life, Paint and Passion

sexuality is in our shadow. Creativity, therefore, becomes shadow-tainted by association.

Finally, "real" creativity is somehow reserved for a class of "special people" we aren't and don't want to be part of. Why wouldn't we want to be "really" creative? Because that would mean we're artists and we all know that artists are, well, you know. Think of a famous artist—writer, painter, photographer, dancer, musician, performance artist—any famous artist who was, or is, insane, crazy, addicted, or mentally ill. Or a famous artist who is weird or wacko or cruel or abusive. Or sexually inappropriate or financially impoverished.

It wasn't difficult to think of several famous artists who are not "normal" in one way or another, was it? We all know the famous examples—Van Gogh, who cut off his ear because he heard voices; Virginia Woolf, Sylvia Plath, Ernest Hemingway, and other gifted writers who killed themselves; Alfred Hitchcock, the ultimate in egomaniacal film directors; the actors and actresses who can't seem to hold a relationship together longer than the time it takes for them to make five tabloid headlines; the multitude of pop musicians whose sexual behaviors are outrageous, some bordering on dysfunctional.

More prevalent than the image of the mad scientist, the crazy artist image keeps many of us from pursuing any hopes of being creative in a big way. After all, the choice constantly paraded before us is either to be a great artist and a rotten human being or to be a decent and normal person.

One cure is to raise our expectations of normal to include expressing creativity in healthy and productive ways. The other cure is to recognize that the either/or choice is a lie. We don't have to be a rotten human being to be a great artist. It may seem that way because the people who have the chutzpah to express their creativity in astonishing new ways often don't have the awareness and courage to confront their shadows and choose their behaviors based on moral action.

If we take another look at the map of the psyche, we can see how the dynamic works. People who are expressing their creativity are going to explore more shadow territory than people who keep themselves locked into their narrow definition of ego-self.

People exploring their Creative Center often find their comfort

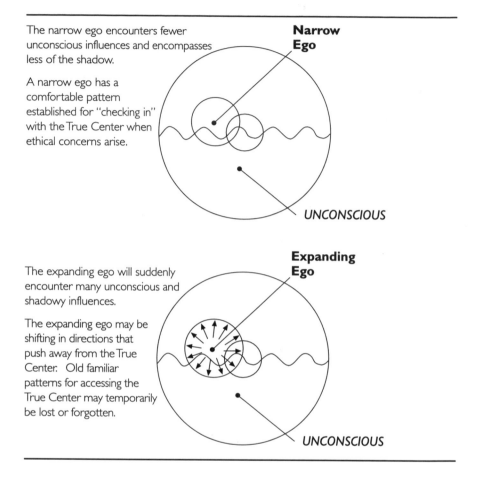

The narrow ego encounters fewer unconscious influences and encompasses less of the shadow.

A narrow ego has a comfortable pattern established for "checking in" with the True Center when ethical concerns arise.

Narrow Ego

UNCONSCIOUS

The expanding ego will suddenly encounter many unconscious and shadowy influences.

The expanding ego may be shifting in directions that push away from the True Center. Old familiar patterns for accessing the True Center may temporarily be lost or forgotten.

Expanding Ego

UNCONSCIOUS

zone—that is, their ego—expands dramatically. Fame has a way of inflating a person's ego. Sometimes these ego expansions happen so fast that the person's ability to move from the ego-center to the True Center, where principled choices are made, can't keep up.

Most of us reading this book have chosen the safer route of limiting our creative expression rather than risk losing our minds, our friends, or our family relationships. But we've based this choice on the lie that we have to choose between being a great artist and a decent human being. We don't have to choose; we can be both. We do, however, have to choose between being creative and always feeling safe.

✍ Exercise: List Your Fears

We have many fears about our creativity based on both erroneous information and accurate intuition. We fear that if we are fully and clearly creative, we'll lose our

- family's respect and acceptance
- spouse or partner
- children, since we'll be declared unfit parents
- job
- house, car, and other material objects
- friends
- safe way of life
- sanity

List your fears about becoming more creative. Start by writing, "What if I _____ and then _____" at least ten different ways. For example, "What if I wrote that screenplay, and then my family felt betrayed and they all hated me for it?"

The only difference between a rut and a grave is their dimensions.
ELLEN GLASGOW

Struggle and Transition Required

It is tempting to assure you that none of these fears will come true. But the truth is that some of them just might. As we become fully and clearly creative, as we become our authentic Self, some of these things or people may fall away from us. It is tempting to suggest that by then, we won't be bothered by the loss of an old friend who hindered us in some way or a luxury car we didn't really need and that didn't truly satisfy us. But the truth is that we will grieve each loss regardless of the necessity of it and the hidden blessing it holds.

To become fully and creatively yourself requires not just changes, but transformation. Does the butterfly mourn the loss of the chrysalis? I don't know. I have been told that if a butterfly doesn't struggle to emerge from its cocoon, if some kindhearted, well-intentioned person comes along and, seeing the butterfly's struggle and pain, cuts it free of the cocoon, that butterfly will die. It's an awareness we may wish we could ignore, but our pain is a vital part of our journey toward wholeness.

M. Scott Peck wrote it so simply in *A Road Less Traveled*:

> Life is difficult. This is a great truth, one of the greatest truths.
> It is a great truth because once we truly see this truth, we tran-
> scend it. Once we truly know that life is difficult—once we
> truly understand and accept it—then life is no longer difficult.
> Because once it is accepted, the fact that life is difficult no
> longer matters.

Pain is inevitable.
Suffering is optional.

KATHLEEN C.
THEISEN

A therapist I know has a sign in her office that says, "Pain is necessary.
Suffering is optional." We cause our own suffering when we resist the
necessary pain of transformation.

But let's not forget the pure joy and thrill of being in the flow of creative expression. I've been told that after the incredible pain of giving
birth, one of the most significant creative experiences of all time, there
is undescribably sweet joy that washes away the memory of the pain.
You can see it in the face of a woman when she holds her newborn. You
may not suffer so to give birth to a poem, but I suspect the joy of the experience isn't as great either. The degree of pain and joy change with
various creative experiences, but the ratio remains.

Creativity has been explained as a process of opening ourselves to
our own unconscious. We learn to drop into the stream of the unconscious. When we dive into that stream, like Gollum finding the golden
ring of power in *The Lord of the Rings*, we're likely to find a treasure glit-
tering on the bottom. It's not so much that sometimes we find creativity
and other times shadow; it's that we always find both. We want to know
the fullness of our creativity, and so we must be willing to explore the
depths of our shadow.

Your Life Is Your Art

Anton Chekhov said, "If you want to work on your art, work on your
life." It's another way of observing how creativity and shadow are intertwined and how exploring your shadow makes way for greater creative
expression. In fact, your creative expression is limited by the maturity
you've gained through your life experiences.

For example, when I was in my twenties, I wrote the first two-thirds of a novel about a young woman who has to face a monster. The wowa-kata, a beast from my imagination inhabiting a science fiction universe I created, was semisentient and had legitimate interests of his own, but these interests were incompatible with the heroine's. The friends who read the incomplete draft sympathized with both characters and asked, "So what happens next? How do they get out of this?" I didn't have an answer. I didn't want the wowakata to kill the heroine, and I didn't want the heroine to kill the wowakata, but it sure seemed as if one was going to have to kill the other. Like most writers, I wrote about characters who were aspects of myself—I was the heroine and my depression was the monster. I couldn't figure out how to solve my heroine's problem because I hadn't figured out how to deal with the depression-monsters in my own life. I couldn't write my way out of a situation I hadn't lived my way through yet.

All the arts we practice are apprenticeship. The big art is our life.
M. C. RICHARDS

This dilemma isn't true only for writers. Your creativity is an expression of you, and you can't create something you haven't lived through. Of course, art is more than autobiography, but we always draw on and expand from our own experiences. When Bill was studying to be an actor in college, he once stayed awake for thirty-six hours to finish a paper. At the end of his physical limits, he had the presence of mind to tell himself, "I want to remember what this feels like in case I ever get the part of an old man."

The reverse of Chekhov's observations holds true as well—if you want to work on your life, work on your art. Creative expression is often used to facilitate personal growth. This is demonstrated by the effective work of professional art therapists and dance and movement therapists. I haven't finished the novel about the woman and the wowakata, and I may never see it published, but it highlighted a struggle in my life and helped me identify the conflict I needed to focus on. Once I worked through those personal issues, I lost interest in the novel.

Nor is it vital that I finish that novel. Not all creative effort needs to be made public. An important distinction needs to be made between process and product. Some of the creative work we do is valuable because it results in art, that is, a product that connects us to others and that earns the acknowledgment and financial rewards we want and deserve. Other creative work is valuable in and of itself: the process of doing the work is more important than the product that results from doing the work. Some creativity leads to art, some creativity leads to life. The work we do to support our creative process eventually supports the production of art, and the production of art invariably supports our own and others' creative processes.

Because working on your life supports working on your art, it doesn't surprise me that my spiritual community—a group of friends committed to giving each other unconditional love and support as we continue exploring our shadow through a technique called integrative breathwork—scheduled a fun, creative activity at many of our get-togethers. We started by drawing mandalas, then created magic wands, sculpted beeswax candles, and made masks. We've led each other through guided imagery, played silly games together, served each other special dinners. Because we are safe to cry or scream or grieve with each other, we are also free to create and play together.

Nor is it surprising that people I trust to guide me in my shadow exploration understand the importance of creativity. We don't just sit around and talk about our fears; we draw them and sculpt them in clay. We don't just confess the aspects of ourselves we'd rather forget; we dress as our own shadow and dance at the best costume parties of all time.

Exploring shadow brings clarity to creativity. Creative expression brings clarity to shadow exploration. This is so because they are faces of the same coin.

✳ Guided Imagery

As you've done in earlier guided imageries, find a place and time when you can be relaxed and uninterrupted. Lie or sit comfortably and begin to relax. Close your eyes. Take several deep breaths, noticing and following the breath in and out of your body.

Consciously tighten the muscles in your feet and ankles. Notice the tension. . . . Feel the tension in all the muscles in your feet. . . . Hold the tension as long as you like . . . holding it until you're ready to let it go with a sigh. . . . Take a deep breath and notice how it feels to let go, to feel the warm relaxation in your feet. . . .

Now, consciously tighten the muscles in your calves and knees. Notice the tension. . . . Feel the tension in your calves and knees. . . . Hold the ten-

sion . . . until you're ready to let it go with a sigh. . . . Take a deep breath and notice how good it feels to let your calves and your knees relax and go slack. . . .

Consciously tighten the muscles in your thighs, buttocks, and pelvis. Notice the tension. . . . Feel the tension in your thighs and buttocks and pelvis. . . . Hold the tension . . . until you're ready to let it go with a sigh. . . . Take a deep breath and notice how good it feels to let the lower half of your body relax more and more with each breath you take. . . .

Take another deep breath and consciously tighten the muscles in your stomach, chest, and back. Feel the tension in your torso. . . . Notice what it feels like to hold tension in this part of your body. . . . Hold that tension . . . until you're ready to let it go with a sigh. . . . Take a deep, slow breath and notice how good it feels to breathe all the way down to your belly . . . how good it feels to let your belly go soft and round with each breath. . . .

Now, consciously tighten your hands into fists. Feel the tension move from your hands to your wrists, your forearms, elbows, upper arms, into your shoulders and the base of your neck. . . . Notice that tension, what it feels like . . . holding it until you're ready to let it go with a sigh. . . . Take a deep breath and notice how good it feels to let any remaining tension ooze out of your fingertips. . . . Notice how good it feels to let your shoulders drop and let your arms relax more and more. . . .

Now, consciously tighten the muscles in your jaw and neck, scrunch up the muscles around your eyes and forehead. . . . Notice the tension in your face and neck . . . holding it until you're ready to let it go with a sigh. . . . Notice how good it feels to let your whole body become more and more relaxed . . . more and more relaxed with every breath. . . .

Continue to breathe deeply. If worries or thoughts about other things come to you, simply remind yourself, "Not this, not now," set the thought aside, and return your attention to your breathing. Allow your breath to assume a slow, natural rhythm.

Experience your whole body now as relaxed . . . your mind as quiet and still . . . your emotions as calm and clear . . . your spirit as peaceful and serene. . . .

From this place of inner serenity, harmony, and relaxation, begin to allow images to occur in your mind. . . . Imagine yourself sitting in a very comfortable chair in a very familiar and comfortable room. . . . Notice the colors and shapes all around you. . . . In your mind's eye, see yourself in this room. . . . *Notice the textures . . . the sounds . . . the smells. . . . Use as many of your senses as you can to see and feel and know you are in this comfortable, familiar room. . . .*

In this familiar room, you have all your comfortable things around you . . . the things you treasure. . . . And you have all your comfortable beliefs around you . . . the ideas and perceptions you treasure. . . . You're surrounded by familiar and comfortable beliefs. . . . Notice how those ideas and beliefs feel. . . . Begin to imagine what those old familiar ideas and comfortable beliefs look like, what they sound like. . . . Give these old familiar and comfortable ideas form, let them take shape and color. . . . Notice how much space they take in your comfortable room. . . .

You notice that this comfortable room has a door. . . . You know that outside the door are all the beliefs and ideas that are not familiar or comfortable for you. . . . At the door, watching carefully, is your skepticism. . . . Your skepticism has served you well in the past. It has kept you safe, kept the uncomfortable ideas outside. . . . But in a moment, you're going to tell your skepticism doorkeeper to take a break. . . . In a moment, you're going to go to the door and open it. . . . Will you be willing to step out into the unknown to experience new ideas and beliefs? . . . Know that you will always be able to find your way back to the familiar and comfortable room. . . .

When you're ready, you get up from the comfy chair or couch and walk to the door. . . . You slowly open it and look outside. . . . Notice what it looks like outside the familiar and comfortable room. . . . Notice the light, the colors, the shapes. . . . Notice the sounds outside the familiar room. . . . If you are willing, step outside the door. . . . If you're not willing to leave the familiar room yet, stand in the doorway and watch. . . .

Notice how the ideas and beliefs outside have shape and color. . . . But they have no weight, no density, so they just float past you. . . . Without judging, without denying or accepting, just notice the ideas and beliefs that float by. . . .

Consider each new idea that presents itself. . . . Ask yourself: What merit does this idea have? . . . How will this belief serve me and my creativity? . . . How will it help me serve others by being creative? . . .

For a few moments, just observe these new beliefs, ideas, adventures, and dreams. . . . Trust that at least one of these is sent to you for your greater good. . . . Decide which ones you want to invite to return with you to the comfortable room. . . .

(pause for two or three minutes)

When you're ready, step back inside the comfortable room. . . . Notice how it has gotten larger to accommodate the new ideas you returned with. . . . Ask your skepticism to return to its duty of watching the door and keeping you safe. . . . Notice that there are now windows in the room so you can see what's outside. . . .

When you're ready to return from the comfortable room to the physical room you're in, gently touch your fingers to the floor or the sides of your chair and slowly open your eyes. . . . Move slowly to find a marker or crayon. Sketch the new ideas or beliefs that you invited in or that were sent to you. After drawing your impressions, write for five or ten minutes to record anything else you want to be sure to remember.

There is such a thing as sacred idleness, the cultivation of which is now fearfully neglected.
GEORGE MacDONALD

❋ Creative Shadow Play

In *If You Want to Write*, Brenda Ueland observed, "The imagination needs moodling—long, inefficient, happy idling, dawdling and puttering."

She writes,

> If your idleness is a complete slump, that is, indecision, fretting, worry or due to over-feeding and physical mugginess, that is bad, terrible and utterly sterile. Or if it is that idleness which so many people substitute for creative idleness, such as gently feeding into their minds all sorts of printed bilge like detective stories and newspapers, that is too bad and utterly uncreative.
>
> But if it is the dreamy idleness that children have, an idleness when you walk alone for a long, long time, or take a long, dreamy time at dressing, or lie in bed at night and thoughts come and go, or dig in a garden, or drive a car for many hours alone, or play the piano, or sew or paint ALONE; or an idleness—and this is what I want you to do—where you sit with pencil and paper or before a typewriter quietly putting down what you happen to be thinking, that is creative idleness. With all my heart I tell you and reassure you: at such times you are being slowly filled and re-charged with warm imagination, with wonderful, living thoughts.

For your creative shadow play this week, schedule at least two hours of moodling. You can spend your moodling time all at once or spread out over several days. Notice your reactions. Do you feel decadent or deserving? Many of us have put "laziness" in the shadow, and anytime we aren't doing "something worthwhile," we feel anxious. Yet this idle time is crucial to the creative process.

You have been warned against letting golden hours slip by. Yes, but some of them are golden only because we let them slip.

J. M. BARRIE

⊙ EXERCISE CHOICES

1. Continue to List Your Reasons for Not Being Creative. Respond to "I don't want to be creative because _____ " as many ways as you can. If there is a particular project or activity you feel blocked in, include that in the statement, "I don't want to _____ because _____."

Record every possible answer, even the ones that don't make sense. Often our biggest blocks disguise themselves, so we won't pay attention to them and they get to stay in place. You don't have to do anything about these now. For the time being, it is important only to notice what ideas and beliefs have gotten in your way. What you're noticing is how creativity and shadow have gotten tangled up together in ways that don't help you.

2. List the Times You've Risked Exploring Your Creativity. Include as many creative experiences as you can think of. Indicate whether the experience was a sunny-side or a night-side flip of the coin.

3. Draw Your Creative Comfort Zone. Get a large sheet of paper and draw a circle in the middle of it. Inside the circle, list all the creative activities you are comfortable and familiar with. If you've been writing poetry for a while, put "poetry writing" inside the circle. If you've just started writing poetry and don't feel completely comfortable with it yet, place "poetry writing" at the edge of the circle, perhaps half in and half out, if that represents your comfort level.

Outside the circle, list all the forms of creativity you don't feel familiar or comfortable with. Put the ones that feel the strangest to you at the far edges of the page. Closer to the circle, place the activities you would consider trying because they seem possible and not too scary.

List as many forms of creativity as you can think of, both inside and outside the circle. You can add to this drawing over the next few days.

The forms of creativity outside your comfort zone are in your shadow for now. For me, that means oil painting and sculpting and calligraphy and gourmet cooking and puppet making and a lot of other fun stuff is in my shadow. So moving toward my True Center and being more fully my Self will mean I get to try all these fun things. Thinking about it that way makes my shadow seem far less frightening.

In this exercise, you're only identifying what is inside and outside your creative comfort zone. In the next exercise, you can play with a creative activity outside your comfort zone. When we get to chapter 10 and have our support systems in place, we'll discuss the principles we can use to expand our creative comfort zone throughout our life.

4. Make a Mess. Pick one form of creativity that is outside the creative comfort zone you drew in exercise 3 (if you didn't do exercise 3, pick any form of creativity that you don't have experience in and aren't comfortable with) and explore that new-to-you creativity this week.

For example, if drumming is in your creative shadow, get a CD or cassette that has lots of percussion and tap and bang your hands on a table along with the music. Don't give up just because you can't always follow the beat; playing around with making mistakes is exactly what this assignment is about. You may discover you want to buy a pair of inexpensive drumsticks and become a dashboard drummer, tapping on your steering wheel with one hand as you drive. (Note: This is shadow play, but reckless driving is something you probably should avoid acting out, so please keep one hand on the steering wheel.)

Your task is to gather the necessary supplies and make a mess. If you also produce something, that's okay, but focus on the process. The process you're looking for is to be messy and inaccurate. So if writing is something you feel uncomfortable with, grab a pad of paper and a pen and write. You'll know you're doing this exercise right when you have a collection of crumbled up wads of paper scattered all around the room and pieces of paper covered with lots of messy scribbles.

Or if oil painting is your creative shadow, go to an art supply store and buy a few oil paints, brushes, a small canvas, and cleaner; then take it all home and make a shadowy mess out of it all.

Creativity is almost always messy, which is why at least some kinds of creativity are relegated to the shadow—most parents and teachers tell children to not make such a mess. Remember that this week you're supposed to make a mess and lots of mistakes trying a kind of creativity you aren't sure about.

5. Surrender Perfection, Make Mistakes. To make good art, you have to be willing to make bad art. To live a good life, you have to be willing to make mistakes. Mistakes are part of the process. If you had given up trying just because you made a few mistakes, you never would have learned to walk or speak or ride a bicycle or . . .

This week celebrate your mistakes. Notice them. Congratulate yourself for your willingness to be fully human. Making mistakes is almost always in our shadow; embrace this part of yourself this week. Keep a journal—just for yourself or to share with others if you wish—of the mistakes, large and small, you make this week.

6. Try Bubble-Brainstorming. Select one form of creativity that you put outside the creative comfort zone in exercise 3 (if you didn't do exercise 3, select a form of creativity that you aren't comfortable with). Write that form of creativity in the middle of a blank sheet of paper and draw a bubble or oval around it. Then let associations bubble up from your unconscious. Write related ideas as they occur to you; draw a bubble around them and then a line connecting the new bubbles to the first. Continue to write down one or two words for ideas that are connected to any of the other ideas, draw ovals around each word or short phrase, and then draw a line to connect it to the idea it's related to. If a word is related to more than one idea, draw a line for each connection.

The drawing on the next page is an example of one of my bubble-brainstorms. The numbers next to the ovals are there only to show you what order the ideas occurred to me. As you can see, your ideas may jump around in this free-association process. The order of the

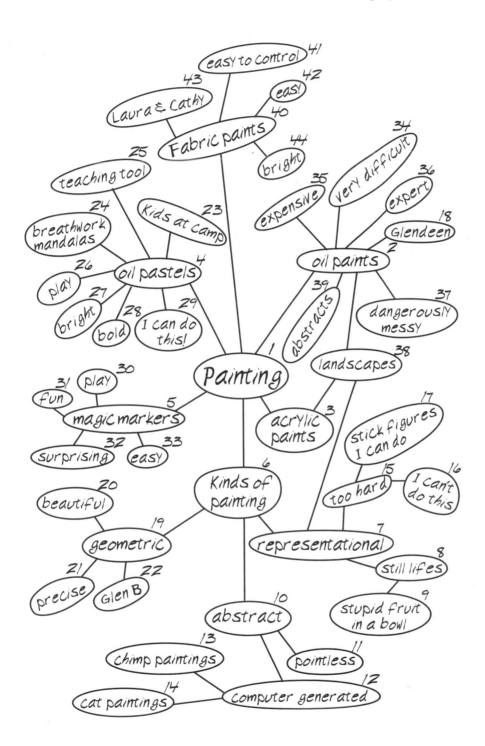

ideas is not important, and there's no need for you to number your ideas.

As you free-associate about the form of creativity you put at the center of your bubble-brainstorm, you may come up with people who are associated too. Write their names down, put a bubble around them, draw a line, and keep going.

You may find that there are some aspects of this form of creativity that you feel good about and that actually are in your creative comfort zone. I found that some aspects of painting weren't completely in my creative shadow. For example, I've had great experiences playing with oil pastels with kids at a camp where I was a counselor, I've used them as a teaching tool, and I've had fun playing with them myself. I'm also learning that I can experiment with magic markers and feel good about the results, which reminded me that I've learned from my friends Laura and Cathy that fabric paints are easy for me to control and are fun to play with.

Don't worry about figuring out what the ideas mean as you're bubble-brainstorming. Although a good deal of understanding will come naturally as you brainstorm, save pondering for later. For example, my sister Glendeen is who I think of when I think of oil paints, so I wrote her name down. Later I thought about the insights I've gained in the past few years about my relationship with Glendeen and how that has affected the ways I've allowed myself to be creative. When we were kids, I didn't like the way my dad treated my sister, so I decided I wouldn't be like Glendeen, and then my dad would treat me differently. Glendeen had long hair, I cut mine short. Glendeen was always thin, I was always chubby. When Glendeen was a teenager, she was seen as being rebellious, so I was always a goody two-shoes. And significantly, Glendeen was the one in our family who could draw and paint and play a musical instrument well. So I'm not surprised to find drawing, painting, and playing music in my creative shadow.

You may or may not find such associations as you bubble-brainstorm. If you do, wonderful. If you don't see such associations immediately, have patience. Insights will occur to you at unexpected moments in the next few days or weeks.

CHAPTER **5**

Telling Psyche's Truth

IN THE FIRST FOUR CHAPTERS, we talked about shadow and creativity as general concepts. No doubt you caught glimpses of your personal shadow and your creative self as you worked through the exercises so far; now we're going to take a good long look at these aspects of ourselves. We'll use two different identification systems to do this.

The MBTI Identification Kit

The Myers-Briggs Type Indicator (MBTI) is a self-measure of your preferences. Katherine Briggs, a contemporary of Jung, was very interested in the concept of personality types. She and her daughter, Isabell Briggs Myers, spent over thirty years gathering data and conducting tests to make Jung's theory of typology accessible to more people and to expand his theory.

The MBTI can be helpful in identifying what form your shadow will usually take. For example, some people are usually cool, calm, and collected, and their shadow often appears as unexpected, sometimes explosive, emotion. A person like this may have outbursts of anger, perhaps even violent rage, may break into unexpected sobbing, or may be suddenly overwhelmed by a wave of inexplicable jealousy. For other people who usually see the bigger picture, their shadow might appear in nitpicking and focusing on relatively minor details that take on inordinate significance to them, leaving others perplexed, wondering why this little thing is suddenly so important.

Only individuals who have trained with the Association for Psychological Type are truly qualified to administer and interpret the results of the MBTI. You can locate a qualified Myers-Briggs administrator in your area through your Yellow Page directory or by contacting the Association for Psychological Type, 9140 Ward Parkway, Kansas City, MO 64114, (816) 444-3500.

Using the MBTI to Identify Your Shadow

Once you know your Myers-Briggs type, use the following chart to identify which of the four MBTI "functions" you use most and which one you tend to avoid using.

ISTJ or ISFJ or ESTP or ESFP		INFJ or INTJ or ENFP or ENTP	
Dominant (most preferred) function	S	Dominant (most preferred) function	N
Least preferred function	N	Least preferred function	S
ISTP or INTP or ESTJ or ENTJ		ISFP or INFP or ESFJ or ENFJ	
Dominant (most preferred) function	T	Dominant (most preferred) function	F
Least preferred function	F	Least preferred function	T

Your least-preferred function is the one you are least developed in, and it is usually the form your shadow will take. The content of your shadow appearances will change over time, but the way your shadow comes out remains surprisingly consistent.

For people whose type is ISTJ, ISFJ, ESTP, or ESFP, the least-preferred or shadow function is Intuition. When people with these types are under enough stress to bring their shadow out, they often feel the situation is hopeless because their Intuitive shadow cannot see possibilities. For these people, it's as if God Herself couldn't find a way out of the difficulty. There are no alternatives. If a friend suggests considering the possibilities, the Intuitive shadow is at a loss. What possibilities? If the friend makes specific suggestions, the Intuitive shadow may dismiss them out of hand or declare that the friend's ability to see solutions is a bit magical.

People whose type is INFJ, INTJ, ENFP, or ENTP will find that their shadow function is Sensing. Shadows of these people tend to be the nitpicking variety described earlier. The Sensing shadow not only becomes unexpectedly obsessed with a minor detail, it will often get that detail incorrect. A person with this form of shadow may fret and fume, "You took Mother's dragonfly stickpin when she died; I know you did!" The bewildered sister may protest that their mother never had a dragonfly stickpin, that their mother gave a butterfly broach to a grandchild years ago, but the Sensing shadow will hear none of that. Moreover, the loss of the nonexistent jewelry will be seen as the source of a much larger conflict.

People who have ISTP, INTP, ESTJ, or ENTJ types have Feeling as their least-preferred or shadow function. Feeling shadows are the ones that appear as the unexpected, sometimes explosive, emotional outbursts described earlier. The emotions expressed are often much deeper and more powerful than the situation would evoke in someone without a Feeling shadow, partially because these types tend to repress their emotions until these shadow episodes bring the emotions out. It might be five or fifteen years of anger that explodes one day. Or the loss of a contract at work might push the normally cool and collected businessperson into raging tears of impotence that are more about the loss of a love ten years ago.

Finally, those of us with ISFP, INFP, ESFJ, or ENFJ types have Thinking as our shadowy least-preferred function. When we're so stressed our shadow appears, we tend to draw erroneous conclusions from limited information, certain all the while that our obsessive thinking must be correct. We will go over the argument in our heads again and again, always leaping to the same incorrect conclusion. For example, I've had arguments with a roommate that left me certain I would have to put my dog to sleep because, of course, the argument was unresolvable because I was right and she was wrong and wouldn't admit it. So of course I would have to move. And I'd never find another apartment where I could have a dog, so I would have to put my dog to sleep. And furthermore, how could I even consider living with such an inconsiderate so-and-so who would rather see my dog put to sleep than admit when she was wrong? My thinking shadow has led me through whole lines of faulty reasoning like this until I learned to stop thinking and give it a rest before making any final decisions.

To confront a person with his own shadow is to show him his own light. . . Anyone who perceives his shadow and his light simultaneously sees himself from two sides and thus gets in the middle.

CARL JUNG

Using the MBTI to Understand Your Shadow

From a Myers-Briggs perspective, we can see why our shadow often takes the form it does. If you examine the chart on page 78, you'll notice that people who are typed ISTJ, ISFJ, ESTP, or ESFP not only share Intuition as their least-preferred function, they all strongly prefer Sensing (making Sensing their dominant function). On the other hand, the INFJ, INTJ, ENFP, and ENTP types share Sensing as their shadow function and Intuition as their dominant function. What the Sensing-dominant types (ISTJ, ISFJ, ESTP, and ESFP) do exceedingly well on an everyday basis is what the Intuition-dominant types (INFJ, INTJ, ENFP, and ENTP) overfocus on and make mistakes about from a shadow place. And, of course, what Intuition-dominant types excel at, Sensing-dominant types mess about with when they're in a shadow place.

The same holds true between the Thinking-dominant types (ISTP, INTP, ESTJ, and ENTJ) and the Feeling-dominant types (ISFP, INFP, ESFJ, and ENFJ). Thinking-dominant types have the qualities associated with the Feeling function as their shadow form, while Feeling-dominant types have the qualities associated with the Thinking function as their shadow form.

Remember that the words *thinking, feeling, sensing,* and *intuition* are used in specific ways in Myers-Briggs terminology. It does not mean that a person who has Thinking as his or her dominant function doesn't have feelings or is insensitive, or that someone with Feeling as the dominant function is incapable of rational thought. People whose dominant function is Feeling prefer to focus on the subjective elements and the human costs when making decisions, while Thinking types prefer to focus on the objective elements like policy statements when making decisions. It is our *over*-reliance on what we prefer (our dominant, most-preferred function) that leads us down the garden path into our shadow.

Most of us focus on perfecting our dominant function; it's only natural. But it's not productive. The last thing we need to focus on is our most-preferred function. We already know how to do that well. What we need to attend to is our least-preferred function. The more we consciously develop our least-preferred or shadow function, the less likely we are to act it out in unfortunate ways when we find ourselves

One does not become enlightened by imagining figures of light, but by making the darkness conscious. The later procedure, however, is disagreeable and therefore not popular.

CARL JUNG

stressed. Remember, Carl Jung said that creativity comes from the least-preferred function, that is, our creativity comes from our shadow!

We can develop our shadow function in a number of ways. A good first step is to acknowledge the importance of that "opposite" function. Thinking-dominant types begin by acknowledging that subjective data is valuable, that the human costs need to be considered, and that sometimes policies need to be changed or simply set aside. Feeling-dominant types can stop gloating now and begin to acknowledge that objective data is valuable, that there are important factors to be considered in addition to how we feel about a decision, and that we may need to have a policy for standard operating guidelines. Likewise, Sensing-dominant types can begin to appreciate the ability to step back from the details and pay attention to the big picture from time to time, while Intuition-dominant types can appreciate that a step-by-step approach that focuses on the little details is sometimes exactly what is needed.

✍ Exercise: Be All You Can't Be

Review the characteristics of your least-preferred Myers-Briggs function, as listed on the following chart. Highlight those traits which are most contrary to your usual approach in creative endeavors. Then find a role model—someone who prefers those

Sensing Characteristics	Intuitive Characteristics
Notices sensory details	Notices the big picture and patterns
Notices what is actually there	Notices what could be
Highlights relevant facts	Suggests new possibilities
Keeps precise track of essential details	Keeps track of trends and predicts future
Takes a realistic approach	Takes an innovative approach
Focuses on the present situation	Focuses on the future potential

Thinking Characteristics	Feeling Characteristics
Relies on logic and objective thinking	Relies on person-centered values
Seeks an objective standard of truth	Seeks a personal standard of what is right
Analyzes evidence, considers cause and effect	Considers the impact on people involved
Good at analyzing what is wrong	Good at appreciating and persuading
Consistently holds to a policy	Acknowledges the need for flexibility
Stands firm in conflict or contention	Looks for consensus

characteristics—and follow his or her lead. For an hour or two a day, assume the outlook of your role model. Do what he or she does; make choices the way he or she would. Consciously practice the traits you highlighted no matter how foreign they feel, and keep yourself open to surprising changes in your creative energy and output.

Shadowing Your Shadow

Spending time with people who have our shadow function as their dominant function is an excellent way to begin to acknowledge and appreciate the value and significance of our shadow. Ask these people how and why they do the things they do and stretch yourself to see things from that perspective. Intuitive-dominant types might want to actually follow the instructions when putting an "assembly required" toy or piece of furniture together. Sensing-dominant types might want to censor themselves when giving directions. Instead of drowning your listener in the details of "You'll see a SuperAmerica on your right and a McDonald's on your left; that's Third Street, keep going. You'll go past Hardee's, a Taco Bell, six maple trees, and come to Fourth Street, keep going. . . ." simply state, "Go to Sixth Street and turn left."

So often the behaviors that are inconceivable or grating or horrible to contemplate are the ones we'll most benefit from trying. They are from your shadow function, and practicing that way of being will both immunize you from some shadow outbursts and bring you freer access to your creativity. Intuitive musicians, for example, who hear the entire symphony in their heads, may benefit most from practicing scales in preparation for the bigger picture the concert will bring. Sensing graphic artists need to remember to step back to view not only the whole layout, but also the entire campaign the piece in question is a part of. Feeling-dominant writers may need the gift of structure that a strict policy regarding regular work hours can provide. Thinking-focused architects may need to consciously consider the emotional states of the people using the spaces they design. (Of course, these are only examples; not all musicians have strong preferences for Intuition, nor are all graphic artists going to be Sensing. Writers aren't necessarily Feeling types and architects aren't all Thinking types.)

The Enneagram Identification Kit

Another excellent tool for gaining insight to the ways your shadow will present itself is the Enneagram. The Enneagram is an ancient system of grouping people into nine personality types, which are represented by nine points on a star. The Enneagram helps you understand not just your behavior (what you do) but also your motivation (why you do what you do).

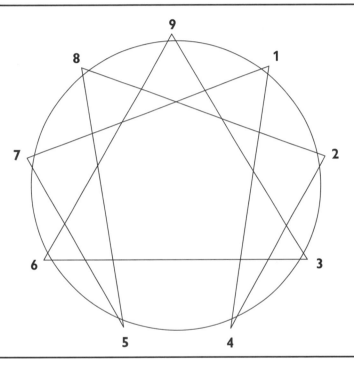

If you don't already know your Enneagram type, use the Primary Enneagram Characteristics chart to make a preliminary selection. Keep in mind, however, that it can be difficult to accurately identify your type from a short description. To fully understand all the subtle nuances of type, read one of the excellent books devoted to the Enneagram listed in the resource directory at the end of this book. Or attend a workshop; I recommend The Enneagram Experience®, facilitated by Kathy Hurley and Ted Dobson or by someone who, like me, has been certified by Hurley and Dobson to lead the workshop.

Type	Primary Characteristics

Ones   Ones value taking action, developing and manifesting ideas into something tangible, and the joy of completion. They focus on reacting spontaneously to overcome a sense of being unimportant. Ones are hardworking people who strive for perfection. They have very high standards and often experience an insistent inner critical voice. Life rarely measures up to Ones' standards, yet directly expressing their anger about that would not be "the right thing," so they seethe with resentments. At their best, Ones are ethical, organized, idealistic people who are willing to make sacrifices to do "the right thing."

Twos   Twos value relationships, intimacy, and emotional awareness. They focus on relationships to overcome a sense of being unlovable. They are caring people who need to be needed. Known for being considerate and empathic, they take great pride in being supportive. They focus on others so they can remain unaware of their own uncertainty and emotional needs. If others don't express appreciation for all the Two does for them, Twos can become resentful, possessive, and manipulative. At their best, Twos have deep understanding and offer unconditional love and support.

Threes   Threes value relationships, intimacy, and emotional awareness. They focus on relationships to overcome a sense of being unlovable. They are charming and put intense pressure on themselves to perform. They are always aware of their image and will work hard, maneuver others, and even massage the truth if necessary to protect their image of success. They tend to be personable, but impersonal, and rarely reveal their deeply passionate nature and their inner emotional life. At their best, Threes are effective leaders, enthusiastic promoters, and authentic friends.

Fours   Fours value relationships, intimacy, and emotional awareness. They focus on relationships to overcome a sense of being unlovable. They are sensitive, self-aware people who strive to feel special. Fours believe their emotional intensity is vital, although they sometimes have difficulty sorting out their feelings. Fours may act superior, but often feel inferior and long for what others have. They tend to focus on the lost ideal or unavailable lover. At their best, Fours are original, insightful, and creative, and can be gifted counselors and loyal friends who offer true compassion.

Fives   Fives value thinking, planning, and abstracting. They focus on thinking to overcome a sense of being incapable. Fives are emotionally detached, objective thinkers who use their accumulation of knowledge to stave off fear and to feel full. Fives protect their time alone to ponder new information and fit it into their own unique system. They appreciate new adventures and eccentric perspectives. Fives fear commitment and are often uneasy in social situations. At their best, Fives offer valuable diversity of ideas and encourage others to make their own decisions.

Sixes   Sixes value thinking, planning, and abstracting. They focus on thinking to overcome a sense of being incapable. They are responsible, energetic people who usually feel low-level anxiety and want to be connected to others and know the rules to help them feel safe. They lack awareness of their own inner authority. They are gracious but can be stubborn if they feel pushed or crossed. At their best, Sixes are keepers of tradition who are loving and are willing to sacrifice for their family or community.

Sevens   Sevens value thinking, planning, and abstracting. They focus on thinking to overcome a sense of being incapable. They are charming, optimistic thinkers who want to have fun. They have active minds and can see multiple possibilities but have difficulty following through, especially if a project stops being interesting. Sevens are very social and know how to use humor to deflect tension and mask the underlying anxiety they usually feel. At their best, Sevens are visionaries whose optimism and playful nature facilitate important change.

Eights   Eights value taking action, developing and manifesting ideas into something tangible, and the joy of completion. They focus on reacting spontaneously to overcome a sense of being unimportant. Eights are forceful people who make things happen. Eights abhor weakness in themselves, but will fight for justice for those they believe can't fight for themselves. They are willing to express their anger openly and are surprised when others tell them they are intimidating. At their best, Eights are selfless champions of the underdog who learn to express their tenderness as well as their strength.

Nines   Nines value taking action, developing and manifesting ideas into something tangible, and the joy of completion. They focus on reacting spontaneously to overcome a sense of being unimportant. Nines are easygoing, even obsessively ambivalent in their effort to feel peaceful. They will avoid conflict at almost any cost. Yet, they usually do only what they want to do. What Nines see as acceptance, others might see as laziness or passive-aggressive anger. They resist change and need a quiet place to withdraw. At their best, Nines are excellent mediators and combine gentleness with stamina to put their compassion into action.

In books about the Enneagram, different authors use different names for the same points. For example, the One point is alternately titled the Perfectionist, the Reformer, or the Achiever. Yet some authors call the Three point the Achiever, while others call it the Succeeder, the Performer, or the Motivator. To avoid confusion, I will simply refer to the points by their numbers.

As you read about the Enneagram, keep in mind that although all nine types have both positive and negative aspects, much of what has been written about the Enneagram focuses on the negative aspects that need improving. Also be aware that although some authors suggest that some points are more creative than others, this is a misunderstanding of creativity. It's true that the Four point fits the stereotypical view of the "artistic" personality more closely than other points, but all human beings are inherently creative and no type is more creative than another.

To use the Enneagram to gain insight to your shadow and your creativity, you need to know that the theory underlying the Enneagram assumes that our type reflects our chosen response to a particular kind of childhood wound. All of us were wounded when we were children, and this is not necessarily because our parents did a bad job. The source of some people's childhood wound is obvious: growing up in a war zone; experiencing sexual abuse, physical abuse, trauma; losing a parent or other family member; enduring natural disasters; and so on. For some of us, the wound is not so obvious. But no one comes through childhood unscathed; learning how to respond to rejection and pain is part of the human experience. Because of our significant childhood wound, we decided the world was a certain kind of place and we needed to respond to it in a certain way. Some of us decided we couldn't trust other people; some of us decided we couldn't trust ourselves. One child may have decided it wasn't safe to love others, while another kid in a similar situation might have given up hope in other people.

Creation is never about changing yourself; it is about meeting yourself, probing deep into your own core. Creation wants only to fulfill your deepest desire: to know and accept yourself as you are.
MICHELL CASSOU and **STEWART CUBLEY**
Life, Paint and Passion

Type	Childhood Wound	Lost the ability to
One	Was betrayed	Trust others
Two	Was betrayed	Trust self
Three	Was emotionally alienated	Love self and others
Four	Was abandoned	Hope in others
Five	Was abandoned	Hope in self
Six	Was betrayed	Trust self and others
Seven	Was emotionally alienated	Love others
Eight	Was emotionally alienated	Love self
Nine	Was abandoned	Hope in self and others

When we were children, our choices were limited and our assumptions tended to be rigid. Even as adults, we tend to see only what we expect to see; we lock ourselves into believing reality is what we've come to expect it to be. Our behavior reinforces our worldview even when it is no longer valid. For example, if you believe no one else can ever live up to your standards, you'll constantly be on the lookout for other people's mistakes. Other people will soon learn that you're impossible to please and will give up trying. Vióla, your expectation that no one is as precise and exacting as you are is reaffirmed.

Each point on the Enneagram represents an assumption about the world and the typical responses for someone who sees the world that way. The perspective of each point is valid at different times and in different circumstances. We cause ourselves problems, though, when we assume our worldview is valid in all circumstances. To be a completely balanced person, we would need to move from response to response as the situation calls for.

Studying the Enneagram helps you identify your typical responses and learn to see beyond those responses. Your typical responses are the negative traits associated with an obsessive reliance on a limited worldview. Identifying those traits gives you your first glimpse of your shadow. Remember the following chart shows the *shadow* traits of each point—by no means a complete description of all the qualities associated with that point.

Do not keep the creative power away by telling yourself that worst of lies—that you haven't any.
BRENDA UELAND
If You Want to Write

SHADOW ENNEAGRAM CHARACTERISTICS	Type	Shadow Characteristics
	Ones	Perfectionistic, critical, have excessively high standards that few people or situations meet. Angry that nothing is as it should be. Seethe with resentment because expressing anger directly isn't "correct" behavior.
	Twos	Proud of ability to understand and help others, unaware of own needs and unbalanced by giving too much. May present different selves to different associates. Manipulative, seek love and approval by anticipating another's needs and being indispensable.
	Threes	Competitive, opportunistic, obsessed with image and the appearance of success. Control how much to reveal and massage the truth as necessary to support the image of success.
	Fours	Self-focused to the point of selfishness. Focused on the lost ideal and the lost lover; the present is never as good as the past. Moody, melancholy, and depressive. Special, exempt from the rules ordinary people follow.
	Fives	Other people's needs drain them; they seek privacy and withdraw emotionally from others. Cynical, aloof, sometimes lacking interpersonal skills. Greedy for knowledge, cerebral, preoccupied with ideas, want to be seen as wise. Stingy with their time, attention, and emotions.
	Sixes	Anxiety and fear dominate existence. Either phobic, procrastinating to avoid the risk of change, or counter-phobic, rushing out to meet fear to get it over with. Defensive, conservative keepers of tradition regardless of the need for change, antiauthoritarian. Seek connection with others to soothe fears of being left out.
	Sevens	The Peter Pan of the Enneagram; just want to have fun. Childish, gluttons for the "high" of life, will ignore or become angry at whatever pulls them from enjoying life. Superficial, overextended, undisciplined. Lack the fortitude to commit fully in loving relationships, especially when difficulties arise.
	Eights	Aggressive, confrontive, direct with anger, can be hard-hearted. Respect only those who are strong enough to stand up to them. Lust for power and control. Blunt, bossy, domineering. Excessively energetic.
	Nines	Passive and passive-aggressive. Obsessivly ambivalent and complacent. Can see every side to an issue, always willing to go along with others, and thus lose own direction. Simplify or ignore problems. Subtly stubborn; quietly and passively resist change. Substitute busyness for real goals, fantasy for realistic planning. Tend to space out with TV, computers, food, drugs.

In addition to providing insight to the characteristics of your type, the Enneagram's system of arrows identify which point you'll move to when you're under stress. Since stress often provokes a shadow appearance, the characteristics of your stress point provide additional insight to your shadow.

When stress causes a shadow outburst, the tendency is for Ones to take on the most negative aspects of the Four point; Fours to take on the most negative aspects of the Two point; Twos to take on the most negative aspects of the Eight point; Eights to take on the most negative aspects of the Five point; Fives to take on the most negative aspects of the Seven point; and Sevens to take on the most negative aspects of the One point. Notice that the Three, Six, and Nine points form a triangle distinct from the six-pointed star. When moving toward shadow, Threes take on the most negative aspects of the Nine point; Nines take on the most negative aspects of the Six point; and Sixes take on the most negative aspects of the Three point.

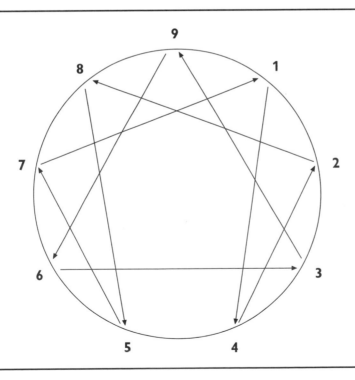

The triangle formed by Three, Six, and Nine are the core points for three centers which, like the points themselves, have different names depending on the author discussing them. I use the names Kathy Hurley and Ted Dobson give the centers, with the exception that what they call the Creative Center, I call the Action Center to avoid any misunderstanding that one center is more creative than the other two. Hurley and Dobson offer significant insight to modern understanding of the Enneagram with their theories of the Preferred and Repressed Centers, which we will discuss shortly.

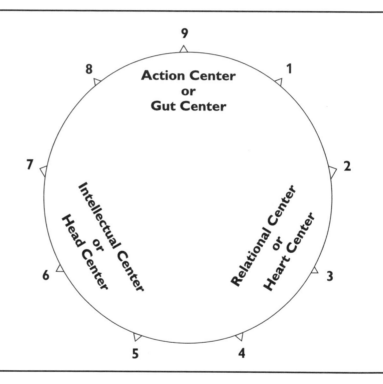

But first, let's take a look at Helen Palmer's explanation of the predominant emotion in the three centers. Eight, Nine, and One form what Palmer calls the Gut Center or Anger Center. This is not to say that Eights, Nines, and Ones don't feel other emotions or that the other points don't feel anger. It does highlight the most prevalent emotion Eights, Nines, and Ones experience is anger. Each point expresses anger differently: Eights tend to be confrontive, even adversarial; Nines tend to repress anger and become passive-aggressive; and Ones seethe with resentments that explode from time to time.

Palmer calls Two, Three, and Four the Heart Center and says that the predominant emotion for people in this center is the question "what am I feeling?" We can also describe the predominant emotion felt by Twos, Threes, and Fours as confusion or uncertainty. Again, this does not imply that Twos, Threes, and Fours don't feel other emotions or that other points aren't occasionally uncertain about their emotions. The points in this center also express their prevalent confusion or uncertainty differently: Twos tend to ignore the question of how they feel by focusing on other people's needs and emotions; Threes tend to substitute a focus on their success for awareness of their feelings; and Fours tend to obsess on their emotions, firmly believing that if only they understood their own feelings and could make others understand them as well, there would be no conflict or problems.

Palmer refers to Five, Six, and Seven as the Head Center, with the predominant emotion of fear or anxiety. Again, this does not imply that Fives, Sixes, and Sevens feel only fear or that other types don't experience fear. And again, the types in this center experience the prevalent fear differently: Fives distance themselves from the fear through an accumulation of knowledge; Sixes either express their fear outright or become counter-phobic (rushing toward what they are afraid of); and Sevens attempt to repress their underlying anxiety by focusing on having and being fun.

According to Hurley and Dobson, although each of us has all three Centers of Intelligence—Action, Relational, and Intellectual—we prefer one center, which we overuse, and repress another, which we underuse. Hurley and Dobson explain: "To prefer a center means that the issues of the center become the issues of the person—you see life through the values of this center. . . . To repress a center means that generally only its lowest expressions are readily available to the person. This is the center you don't like to use and often can't use creatively." Obviously, the Repressed Center is the home of the shadow, which will lead you to the resolution of your creative blocks and unlived dreams.

The fear of confronting monsters can keep even sensitive and willing people from diving into the creative sea. . . . Quite often, these demons guard the doors of our inner world and must be faced before we can enter the heart chamber of our mysterious existence.

MICHELL CASSOU
and
STEWART CUBLEY
Life, Paint and Passion

Center Values and Higher Purpose

Center	Preferred by	Repressed by	Values		Higher Purpose
Action	Eight, Nine, and One	Four, Five, and Nine	Doing, being, survival, spontaneous action, search for value, instinctive love		Awareness of life, enactment, manifestation, development, completion, genuineness
Relational	Two, Three, and Four	Seven, Eight, and Three	Relating on personal level, emotional reactions, search for meaning, emotional passion		Awareness of love, relatedness, transcendence, conscience, synthesis, true understanding
Intellectual	Five, Six, and Seven	One, Two, and Six	Logical thinking, investigating, planning, search for insight, love of learning		Awareness of light, vision, discernment, discovery, pondering, true knowledge

The information in this table is condensed from *What's My Type? Use the Enneagram System of Nine Personality Types to Discover Your Best Self* (San Francisco: HarperSanFrancisco, 1992) and *My Best Self: Using the Enneagram to Free the Soul* (San Francisco: HarperSanFrancisco, 1993) by Kathy Hurley and Ted Dobson and is printed here with their permission.

The combination of Preferred Center and Repressed Center form the unique patterns of the nine personality types. Each type prefers the center it is located within: Eights, Nines, and Ones prefer the Action Center; Twos, Threes, and Fours prefer the Relational Center; Fives, Sixes, and Sevens prefer the Intellectual Center.

What is unique to Hurley and Dobson's theory is the recognition that Threes, Sixes, and Nines, called the Balance Point Numbers, simultaneously repress the center they prefer, while the other numbers—Ones, Twos, Fours, Fives, Sevens, and Eights, called the Wing Numbers—

repress the center opposite their preferred center. Hence, Ones, Twos, and Sixes all repress the Intellectual Center; Fours, Fives, and Nines repress the Action Center; and Sevens, Eights, and Threes repress the Relational Center. (Read *My Best Self* for more information on the Repressed Center.)

Identifying which center you repress clarifies what shadow issues you need to focus on in your life in general and your creativity in particular.

Effects of Repressing the Intellectual Center
If you are a One, Two, or Six, you repress the Intellectual Center.

This doesn't mean that you lack intelligence or don't think. In fact, one of the results of repressing the Intellectual Center is overthinking—obsessively thinking in circles without coming to resolution. Every issue is connected to and affected by every other issue, so it's hard to separate issues and come to a conclusion. You lose touch with your ability to see the big picture and to think and plan for yourself. You become dependent on what other people think and let them set the agenda, which creates tension with your standards and can lead to resentment. You tend to substitute opinions for thinking.

If you are a One, Two, or Six, you need to develop your ability to think objectively and linearly. You can learn to listen to and accommodate the opinions of others and still come to your own decisions. Broaden your focus beyond the immediate situation and plan for the future. When you embrace the highest purposes of the Intellectual Center—vision, discovery, discernment, and true knowledge—you will be able to break through creative blocks and begin to live your creative dreams.

Effects of Repressing the Relational Center
If you are a Three, Seven, or Eight, you repress the Relational Center.

This doesn't mean you don't have feelings and relationships. In fact, one of the results of repressing the Relational Center is that you have many feelings that you don't express directly. You may secretly fear that your emotions would overwhelm you and others, so you repress your awareness of these feelings. You may have many relationships, but you tend

Out beyond ideas of wrong doing and right doing there is a field. I'll meet you there.

RUMI

to be personable on the surface and not deeply personal. You have a great deal of energy and value making changes and getting things done. Because you repress your awareness of your own needs and emotions, you inevitably disregard the needs and emotions of others as you drive yourself and them to make the changes you believe are necessary.

If you are a Three, Seven, or Eight, you need to develop your sensitivity to yourself and others. You can learn to feel and face your own fears while maintaining your optimistic approach to change. You will discover that your willingness to explore and express deep feelings decreases your need to defend yourself and brings meaning to your life. When you embrace the highest purposes of the Relational Center—spiritual love; true intimacy with self, others, and the Divine; and moral awareness to guide your actions—you will be able to break through creative blocks and begin to live your creative dreams.

Effects of Repressing the Action Center
If you are a Four, Five, or Nine you repress the Action Center.

This doesn't mean you don't take action. You may tend to be inactive or you may be busy most of the time; the key distinction is that if you repress the Action Center, you tend to do only what you want to do, not what you need to do. While you appreciate intricacy and ponder life, you tend to substitute thinking, feeling, and/or talking for actual doing. You may also tend to substitute addictive activities or pleasures for the effort required to pursue what would bring you true pleasure. You believe you can't really change the world, so you detach and withdraw, repressing the Action Center, which in turn reinforces your belief.

If you are a Four, Five, or Nine, you need to develop your confidence that you can make a difference. Develop your assertiveness and take action. You have always sought enlightened solutions, now you need to learn to put those solutions into practice. As you take the risk of being fully involved, rather than detached, and begin to spontaneously follow your ideas instead of just thinking about them, you will discover the satisfaction of completing the creative process. When you embrace the highest purposes of the Action Center—manifestation, development, and the joy and delight of completion—you will be able to break through creative blocks and begin to live your creative dreams.

The shadow never lies; it's the ego that lies about its real motives. That's why successful psychotherapy, and any genuine religious conversion, requires absolute honesty about oneself.
JOHN A. SANFORD

No matter what type you are, remember that type is only a part of who you are and how you express yourself.

✍ Exercise: Take My Advice

Your Repressed Center provides valuable information about your shadow and the traits you can consciously bring to your creative efforts, just as the traits of the your least-preferred Myers-Briggs type show the way to maximum growth.

First, identify your Enneagram type and which center you repress if you haven't already done so. Highlight the qualities listed on the Center Values and Higher Purpose table (page 92) that you need to develop.

Finally, follow the advice below. This advice is based on my theoretical understanding of the types combined with years of experience in helping people with different types work through their own unique creative blocks. In addition to reading what is written specifically for your type, you may also benefit from reading the advice written for the other two types that repress the same center you repress.

If a piece of advice written for your type doesn't fit your situation, ignore it. But if it confuses, angers, or scares you, take another good look at it; a strong emotional response usually means there's a bit of shadow being activated, which always brings growth.

If you are a One:
- Beware of your tendency to overwork and to overfocus on the project with the most pressing deadline.
- Plan for your creativity beyond just today or this week.
- Schedule time for yourself to play, relax, and feed your soul with inspiring images.
- Enlist the help of a Seven who can lead you in having fun and developing long-range strategies.
- Loosen up—mistakes are essential in the creative process.
- Surrender your desire to be perfect.
- Learn to ignore the inner critical voice in the early stages of developing a project.

When one first sees the shadow clearly, one is more or less aghast. . . . A genuine insight into the shadow also calls out what Jung called the Self, the creative center. And then a million things begin to move.

JOHN A. SANFORD

If you are a Two:
- Beware of your tendency to take care of everyone else at the expense of your own self-development and expression.
- Get to know your own feelings so you have a self to express.
- Plan time for your creativity and stick to the plan despite other people's "emergencies."
- Schedule time alone so you won't be distracted by the needs of others.
- Give yourself approval and love as you wean yourself from manipulating others to appreciate you.
- Trust yourself—you do have important, original ideas to share.
- Enlist the help of a Five, who can help you focus on facts, rather than exclusively on feelings.

If you are a Three:
- Beware of your tendency to make your image of success more important than achieving what your heart truly yearns for.
- Be willing to be a beginner; take pride in being mediocre.
- Stop working so hard and make time for frivolous, relaxing play.
- Stop censoring your deep passions.
- Experiment with different kinds of creative play to find ways to express your deep feelings.
- You may want to narrow your social connections so you can develop a few solid friendships in which you can express whatever you feel without worrying about how it will look.
- Look to a Six for an example of defying authority and staying connected to the people who really matter.

If you are a Four:
- Beware of your tendency to express your feelings about expressing your feelings instead of expressing your creativity.
- Stop telling the long, involved story that explains why you haven't done what you know in your heart you need to do and *just do it.*
- Be spontaneous.
- Take action, especially action you know you need to take but are reluctant to initiate.

- Trust your ability to use symbols and images to share all the beauty you have inside.
- Let a One be your role model in buckling down.

If you are a Five:
- Beware of your tendency to substitute doing research for completing the creative process.
- Stop gathering facts and do something with the information you already have.
- Don't wait until you have the final, definitive word on something.
- Add passion to your dispassionate approach; consider feelings as well as facts.
- Let others see your creative process; push yourself to find creative allies.
- Follow the Eight's example for taking the risk of putting yourself out there, right or wrong.

If you are a Six:
- Beware of your tendency to let fear rule your life.
- Stop obsessing about the scary possibilities and observe how Sevens focus on future possibilities for fun to dispel anxiety.
- Use your gift for connecting with others to gather creative friends to support you in taking risks.
- Discover your own vision and purpose and make plans to accommodate your discoveries.
- Use your energy to take the leap of expressing your creativity.
- Stop dismissing all change as bad; learn to trust your powers of discernment.
- Enlist the help of a Nine in broadening your perspective, keeping your energy in reserve for creativity, and going with the flow.

If you are a Seven:
- Beware of your tendency to abandon a project when it stops being fun or interesting.
- Overcome your resistance to being vulnerable so you can express the deep passions of your heart and soul.

The journey to happiness involves finding the courage to go down into ourselves and take responsibility for what's there. All of it.
RICHARD ROHR

- Deepen a few relationships so that you can let go of the fear that others will abandon or reject you if you express "negative" emotions or show vulnerability.
- Stop overscheduling yourself (which you do to keep yourself entertained).
- Keep time and energy in reserve for your creativity.
- Take "drama" lessons from a Four to develop sensitivity to the needs and feelings of others and yourself.

If you are an Eight:

- Beware of your tendency to rely only on yourself and to overuse your own strength.
- Use your courage to surrender to the open, out-of-control state that is a vital part of the creative process.
- Stop hiding your vulnerability and tenderness.
- Slow down and experiment with less-intensely active ways to express your feelings.
- Develop tolerance for weakness so you can practice true compassion, which is necessary for meaningful creative expression.
- Follow the Two's example in developing sensitivity to the needs and feelings of others and the Four's example in developing sensitivity to your own needs and emotions.

If you are a Nine:

- Beware of your tendency to keep yourself so busy with trivia that you never have time for the meaningful creative projects you have been called to manifest.
- Take heart—you can create important things and there are people who appreciate your creative efforts.
- Stop stockpiling art supplies and start using them.
- Trust that one small step repeated every day can change your life.
- Stop using your strength to resist change and start using it to maintain your own momentum and direction.
- Watch a Three in action for a role model of how to accomplish tasks.

Why should we all use our creative power? Because there is nothing that makes people so generous, joyful, lively, bold and compassionate, so indifferent to fighting and the accumulation of objects and money. Because the best way to know the Truth and Beauty is to try to express it. And what is the purpose of existence Here or Yonder but to discover truth and beauty and express it, i.e. share it with others?

BRENDA UELAND
If You Want to Write

✍ *Exercise: Find the Hidden Picture*

Look for similarities between the two systems. I was impressed to discover that Hurley and Dobson's insights revealed that my Repressed Center is the Intellectual Center, which overlaps with my least-preferred Myers-Briggs function, Thinking.

Review the traits you highlighted in your least-preferred Myers-Briggs function for the Be All You Can't Be exercise earlier in this chapter (page 81). Compare that list to the higher purpose of your Repressed Center as listed in the Center Values and Higher Purpose table on page 92.

What qualities do both the Myers-Briggs Type Indicator and the Enneagram suggest you need to develop?

When a woman tells the truth she is creating the possibility for more truth around her.
ADRIENNE RICH

☀ *Guided Imagery*

As you've done in earlier guided imageries, find a place and time when you can be relaxed and uninterrupted. Lie or sit comfortably and begin to relax. Close your eyes. Take several deep breaths, noticing and following the breath in and out of your body.

Consciously tighten the muscles in your feet and ankles. Notice the tension. . . . Feel the tension in all the muscles in your feet. . . . Hold the tension as long as you like . . . holding it until you're ready to let it go with a sigh. . . . Take a deep breath and notice how it feels to let go, to feel the warm relaxation in your feet. . . .

Now, consciously tighten the muscles in your calves and knees. Notice the tension. . . . Feel the tension in your calves and knees. . . . Hold the tension . . . until you're ready to let it go with a sigh. . . . Take a deep breath and notice how good it feels to let your calves and your knees relax and go slack. . . .

Consciously tighten the muscles in your thighs, buttocks, and pelvis. Notice the tension. . . . Feel the tension in your thighs and buttocks and pelvis. . . . Hold the tension . . . until you're ready to let it go with a sigh. . . . Take a deep breath and notice how good it feels to let the lower half of your body relax more and more with each breath you take. . . .

Take another deep breath and consciously tighten the muscles in your stomach, chest, and back. Feel the tension in your torso. . . . Notice what it feels like to hold tension in this part of your body. . . . Hold that tension . . . until you're ready to let it go with a sigh. . . . Take a deep, slow breath and notice how good it feels to breathe all the way down to your belly . . . how good it feels to let your belly go soft and round with each breath. . . .

Now, consciously tighten your hands into fists. Feel the tension move from your hands to your wrists, your forearms, elbows, upper arms, into your shoulders and the base of your neck. . . . Notice that tension, what it feels like . . . holding it until you're ready to let it go with a sigh. . . . Take a deep breath and notice how good it feels to let any remaining tension ooze out of your fingertips. . . . Notice how good it feels to let your shoulders drop and let your arms relax more and more. . . .

Now, consciously tighten the muscles in your jaw and neck; scrunch up the muscles around your eyes and forehead. . . . Notice the tension in your face and neck . . . holding it until you're ready to let it go with a sigh. . . . Notice how good it feels to let your whole body become more and more relaxed . . . more and more relaxed with every breath. . . .

Continue to breathe deeply. If worries or thoughts about other things come to you, simply remind yourself, "Not this, not now," set the thought aside, and return your attention to your breathing. Allow your breath to assume a slow, natural rhythm.

Experience your whole body now as relaxed . . . your mind as quiet and still . . . your emotions as calm and clear . . . your spirit as peaceful and serene. . . .

From this place of inner serenity, harmony, and relaxation, begin to allow images to occur in your mind. . . . Imagine yourself sitting in a very comfortable chair in a very familiar and comfortable room. . . . Notice the colors and shapes all around you. . . . In your mind's eye, see yourself in this room. . . . Notice the textures . . . the sounds . . . the smells. . . . Use as many of your senses as you can to see and feel and know you are in this comfortable, familiar room. . . .

In this familiar room, you have all your comfortable things around you . . . the things you treasure. . . . And you have all your comfortable beliefs around you . . . the ideas and perceptions you treasure. . . . You're surrounded by the familiar and the comfortable. . . .

Now you notice there is a mirror next to the chair you're sitting in. . . . You look in the mirror and you see your reflection . . . you see your

> *Nothing is more dangerous than an idea when it's the only one you have.*
> EMILÉ CHARTIER

face the way it looks today . . . very familiar . . . reassuring. . . . Watch your-self as your reflection changes to show you doing the kinds of things you usually do. . . . See yourself in the mirror saying the things you usually say . . . thinking and feeling the way you usually think and feel. . . . Watch your familiar reflection show the comfortable and familiar way you have of being in the world. . . .

Watch as the mirror goes blank and then shows a very different face . . . a very different person . . . who does things you would never do . . . who says things you wouldn't say . . . who thinks and feels things so differently from you. . . . As you take some time now to watch this person in the mirror, you realize he or she is showing many of the traits and per-ceptions of your Repressed Center or least-preferred function. . . . As you watch this person in the mirror, you begin to understand why he or she acts, thinks, and feels so differently. . . . And you begin to see the value in his or her actions, thoughts, and feelings. . . .

Watch as the face in the mirror changes again . . . blending the face of the person who is so different with your own familiar face . . . until you begin to see yourself acting, thinking, and feeling in those strange, unfamiliar ways. . . . Notice how you feel watching yourself change in these ways . . . watching yourself transform . . . watching yourself grow in new ways. . . .

(pause for two or three minutes)

Expand your awareness now beyond the mirror . . . notice the familiar and comfortable room. . . . Look around now and see how the room has changed . . . how much bigger and more open it feels. . . . Look around and see if there is a symbol or image in the room that draws your attention . . . a symbol or image that will remind you of this experience of seeing yourself in the mirror. . . . Don't worry if the symbol isn't clear or doesn't make sense now; your understanding of it will grow over time. . . .

(pause for two or three minutes)

Slowly return your attention to body, to your breathing. . . . When you're ready, keeping your symbol with you, touch your fingers to your chair or the floor. Slowly open your eyes and draw the symbol or image you found in the guided imagery. After drawing, write a few notes if there is anything else you want to record.

There is nothing in this world more dangerous than sincere ignorance and conscientious stupidity.

MARTIN LUTHER KING JR.

❋ *Creative Shadow Play*

Make a collage of the qualities in your Repressed Center and your least-preferred MBTI function. Display your collage where you will notice it each day. You may want to add a statement of your willingness to embrace and embody these qualities to your daily prayers or meditation.

◎ **EXERCISE CHOICES**

1. List Your Role Models. Make a list of the people you know who excel at the qualities in your Repressed Center and your least-preferred function. Explain that you need to develop some of their strengths and ask them for advice. Make an agreement to call them when you're in a crunch and really need their insight.

2. Stretch Daily. Each day for a week (or longer if you like), select one quality or attribute from your Repressed Center or least-preferred function to focus on that day. Consider what this quality means to you as you stretch your arms over your head, from side to side and down to the ground. Move your body slowly, steadily stretching your muscles to a comfortable reach. Take mini breaks throughout the day to stretch your body, and, as you do so, consider how you could stretch your mind and emotions to practice that quality on whatever activity is in front of you.

3. Cross Over Daily. Each day for a week (or longer if you like), select one quality or attribute from your Repressed Center or least-preferred function to focus on that day. (You can do daily stretches and daily crossovers with the same quality.) Consider what this quality means to you as you stand and do crossover stretches, touching your right hand to your left shoulder, then your left hand to your right shoulder; your left hand to right hip, then right hand to your left hip; your right knee to your left elbow, then left knee to right elbow, and so on, mixing body parts to touch right to left. Take mini breaks throughout the day to get your body and brain crossing hemispheres, and as you do so, consider how you can cross over from your usual perceptions to seeing the world from the viewpoint of your Repressed Center or least-preferred function.

4. Draw Your Shadow and Your Creativity. Ask your shadow-self to do a self-portrait, to draw your ego-self, or to draw how your shadow sees your creativity. You may want to do some of these drawings with your nondominant hand (if you're right-handed, use your left hand; if you're left-handed, use your right hand). Sometimes it's easier for a hidden aspect of ourselves to emerge when we use the nondominant hand. Ask your creative self to do a self-portrait or to draw your shadow-self. (Use either hand.)

5. Describe Your Shadow- and Creative-Self. Describe your shadow-self. What characteristics have you identified so far that you (ego-you) have pushed away? What does your shadow look like, act like, sound like, think about, plan? How does it feel? What does your shadow want most?

Describe your creative-self. What do you think your creativity looks like, acts like, sounds like? How do you express your creativity? What does your creative-self want most?

Then, switch to your nondominant hand and let your shadow-self and creative-self both describe your ego-self. Stay with this nondominant hand and ask your True Self to describe this larger you.

6. Correspond with Your Shadow. Write your shadow a letter, telling this part of you what you're afraid of, what you want and need from it, and anything else you might want to say (for example, you may need to offer an apology). Then, switch to your nondominant hand and let your shadow write back, telling you what your shadow-self is afraid of, what it wants and needs from the other aspects of your Self, and anything else this part of you wants to say.

7. Correspond with Your Creative-Self. Write a letter to your creative-self, telling this part of you what your fears and hopes are about exploring your creativity further. Then switch to your nondominant hand and let your creativity respond.

8. Begin a Slip Journal. Keep a journal of your shadow's appearances. Describe what happened and how you felt just before, during, and after your shadow's appearance. Watch for little "slips" as well as major shadow outbursts. Slips can be a slip of the tongue where you say something you didn't intend, but if you take a close look, you see you said what you really meant. They are usually very embarrassing; in fact, your embarrassment is a sign that this is a significant mistake. Or you may have a slip of behavior, where you do things you would never usually do. Again, your embarrassment about your mistaken behavior is a sign that it was significant. Be sure to notice when these slips are connected to a creative activity or to a feeling of being blocked from fulfilling a creative dream.

CHAPTER **6**

Honoring Psyche's Swings

DO YOU REMEMBER THE JOY OF SWINGING ON A SWING? How you lean back and pump your legs and then tuck them under your body so you can swing higher and faster? How you put your whole body into the motion, going higher and higher with each sweep forward and backward, until you almost fly free?

Now imagine how high and free you would fly if you decided that the backswing was bad. How much momentum would you generate if every time you pushed yourself forward, you dug your heels into the ground at the midpoint to keep yourself from swinging backward? You would use a great deal of energy pushing yourself forward, then use even more energy to prevent the backswing, and you would never experience the exhilaration of breaking free of gravity even for a moment.

This, unfortunately, is what many of us do with our creativity. Creation is the forward motion of the pendulum swing of the life force. Destruction is the backswing of that pendulum. We have decided that only the forward (creative) swing in the cycle is valuable. We resist the other half of the cycle with all our might, and because of that, we break our momentum and squander our creative energy.

✍ *Exercise: Experiment with Practical Physics*

Try a practical demonstration of how energy moves in a swinging cycle. Get a hammer, a couple of nails, and a board. Begin with the assumption many of us have about our creativity—that only forward motion is desirable. You want to drive the nail into the wood, so why would you pull the hammer away from the nail? Put the nail on the board; place the hammer on the head of the nail and push! No, don't pull the hammer back to strike the nail, just push, push, push. Come on, put your whole body into it. You're supposed to be putting this nail into the board! If you can't get the nail into the board like this, tell yourself that you're just not cut out to drive nails, that you lack nail-driving talent, and that you may as well just give up now and leave it to the real experts.

Oh, all right, try it your way. Instead of putting all your energy into pushing the nail into the board (the way you've been told to do it), go ahead and squander your energy by raising that heavy hammer away from the board, away from the direction you really want the nail to go, and then let the hammer fall. Go ahead and just try pounding a nail like this (like I'm sure *that* will work).

Remember, this is a metaphor for creative energy. Practice with another nail, keeping in mind that you are illustrating the full spectrum of the creation-destruction cycle.

Think about the way skilled carpenters use a hammer. They tap the nail once or twice to set it in place; then they swing the hammer all the way back and *wham, wham*, it's in. Think about the way people who aren't experienced with a hammer use one; we choke the hammer and tentatively *tap, tap, tap, tap* until we either bend the nail or coax it all the way in. Skilled carpenters trust themselves enough to get a good backswing behind their efforts. Those of us who haven't used a hammer a lot don't trust ourselves.

Just as the serpent stands for the power that heals as well as corrupts, so one of the thieves [crucified next to Jesus] is destined upwards, the other downwards, so likewise the shadow is one side regrettable and reprehensible weakness, on the other side healthy instinctivity and the prerequisite for higher consciousness.

CARL JUNG

🖎 *Exercise: Notice Your Backswing*

Write for five or ten minutes about the parts of your creative cycle that you avoid. Do you hate to make a mess? Are you constantly straightening and organizing when you need to crumble the paper, spill the paints, and let the drops fall where they may? Or do you waste time trying to find supplies in the cupboard you never make time to organize? Do you fear making a mistake? Are you so focused on getting the beginning just right that you never move on to the middle and end of the project? Do you pull out so many imperfect stitches you never finish the quilt? Or do you throw things together willy-nilly and promise that someday you'll do it right? What are you afraid of ruining, wrecking, destroying? Where do you stop your momentum? Where do you drag your feet and dig your heels in?

After you write, let these questions percolate in the back of your mind. In a day or two, sit down and write again to see what other insights bubble to the surface. Or go to a park and put your body in motion on a swing and see what occurs to you.

If Creativity Is Good, Then Destructivity Is . . .

We have a prejudice against destruction in our culture. Destruction is not always bad or evil. And creation is not always good. For example, cancer is a result of cells being overcreative. Cancer cells grow and reproduce too fast, making more and more of themselves until they crowd out the cells that should be present. Cancer is creation gone wrong. And our cures for cancer—surgery, chemotherapy, radiation—are all attempts to destroy the cancer without harming the noncancer cells too badly.

We have accepted the belief that creation is always good and destruction is always bad without thinking it through. And this belief gets in our way. It keeps us from surrendering ourselves to the full swing, the full cycle of the life force.

It's ironic, but the biggest obstacle to expressing our creativity freely and fully is often our deep desire to do so. We become so attached to the ideal of creation that we begin to fear and loathe its counterpart, destruction. We begin to believe that destruction is always evil and ignore the fact that destruction is part of the cycle.

I see a similar phenomenon with people who want to live only in "the light." They spend a lot of time visualizing themselves in white light and asking for guardians to keep them in the light. If a friend is in crisis, they pray that the friend be returned to the light, unaware that the crisis may be exactly what the friend needs to propel him or her into the next stage of life. These light-only seekers are unwilling to do shadow work. Perhaps they fear that exploring the shadow inside themselves would invoke the powers of darkness. But true evil lurks not in the shadow itself, but in the act of disowning our shadow, which sends that shadow unmonitored out in the world to do whatever mischief is necessary to get our attention again. That's what Hans Christian Andersen's story *The*

The more you give, the more you will receive because you will keep the abundance of the universe circulating in your life.
DEEPAK CHOPRA
The Seven Spiritual Laws of Success

Shadow (see appendix A) says to me. And that's why Jung advised, "One does not become enlightened by imagining figures of light, but by making the darkness conscious."

I don't think we can live only in the light or that we're meant to live only in the light. We are humans, not angels. We live in the physical plane and we are meant to be physical. We live in a world of duality and we are meant to experience both ends of all continuums. It's not a matter of living either in the light or in darkness. It's both-and.

Exploring Both-And

Likewise, we cannot choose to be only creative. Creation and destruction are ends of the same continuum, stages of the same cycle. To embrace one is to embrace both.

Whenever we create something, we destroy something else: Create music, and you destroy silence. Create a painting, and you destroy the blank canvas and all its possibilities. Create wisdom, and you destroy ignorance and innocence. For every yin, there is a yang. If you are willing to go only this far with the yang of destruction, you can go only that far with the yin of creation. The degree to which you deny your capacity for destruction is the degree to which you limit your capacity for creation.

Creation and destruction are part of the life-and-death cycle that all living (and dying) things participate in. Each plant survives by taking up the space, sunlight, water, and nutrients another plant could have used. The spider survives by eating the fly. The wolf thrives on the lifeblood of the deer. It's not quite as the narrator dramatically proclaims in a TV nature documentary, "Eat or be eaten!" It is actually, "Eat *and* be eaten." Eventually the wolf feeds the flies, the crows, and the worms. Of all living things, only we humans try to remove ourselves from the cycle.

We resist physical death, which is only natural, but we also resist the cycles of spiritual life and death. From time to time, our ego needs to die so our psyche can be reborn. Ego-death can come with the loss of a job, a divorce, the onset of menopause, or a balding head. It comes whenever we are forced to die to who we were, so we have room to become who we will be. It comes when we need to destroy the old self to create the new self.

The psychic totality, the self, is a combination of opposites. Without a shadow, even the self is not real. It always has two opposites, a bright and a dark. . . .

CARL JUNG

The Pendulum Swings

If you suspend a pendulum above sand and let it swing, it creates diminishing, circular patterns in the sand as it gradually loses momentum and comes to a stop. But if you pull the pendulum to the right and then block it from moving to the left, the pendulum simply stops. You cannot draw gradually diminishing half-circles. You cannot swing a pendulum in only one direction.

Resisting our own capacity for destruction prevents us from fully and freely expressing our creative capacity. In practical terms, it isn't enough for a writer to be willing to delete paragraphs that don't work or abandon a story that isn't going anywhere. If a writer wants to keep growing enough to avoid falling into a formula of his or her own making, he or she has to endure the painful times of transition. Like a boy soprano on the verge of puberty, the writer doesn't know how, or even if, the once-powerful, now-disintegrating "voice" will reemerge.

The same kind of experience awaits all of us who want to keep our creativity growing. Painters, sculptors, healers, leaders, actors, fabric artists, designers, musicians—however we express the creative force that swings through our being, we all face the choice to either stagnate or risk transforming our style to keep pace with our development as human beings. And there are no guarantees that the style changes will be welcome. Bob Dylan alienated his folk audience when he went electric. Nor are there guarantees that the changes will all be recognized as "progress." The only guarantee is that there will be times when we will be lost betwixt and between, neither here nor there. At these times we must trust that these passages through the valley of the shadow are necessary and will revitalize our creativity eventually. At these times, we need to remember that the more we resist, the more we slow the entire cycle and prolong the periods of being lost and adrift.

Like the daily cycle of night and day, the monthly cycles of the moon, the yearly cycles of the seasons, and the lifelong cycles of birth, death, and rebirth, our creativity-destructivity comes and goes in cycles. At times, it seems we can't take a wrong step; every project we attempt develops and bears fruit beyond our hopes and dreams. Other times, it seems we can't find our momentum. Everything we try turns to dust between our fingers and ashes in our mouths. The cycles of lush

No matter what our art form, we work along on a certain level and then the creative syntax breaks down and falls in a heap (*&%#!), and it's really hard working for a while. We paint, act or write "badly." Then something shifts and the work comes back together at a different level.

JULIA CAMERON
The Vein of Gold

productivity and destructive droughts are less predictable than the cycles of the moon, but it helps tremendously to remember that the cycle keeps turning. Knowing this helps us stay humble in the midst of lush creativity and hopeful in the middle of the drought.

Every swing to the left brings a complementary swing to the right. Shadow compensates for our ego, especially our ego excesses. The more we are invested in our ego-selves being one way, the more our shadow will take on the opposite attribute. For example, if our ego denounces the pleasures of the flesh as sinful, then our shadow will be fascinated with sex and the shadow energy behind that will eventually cause us to act out sexually.

In our culture, and especially for those of us who are actively interested in being more creative, creativity is seen as the good. We have invested our ego-selves in being creative. Since our ego-selves deny and denounce destruction as bad, we shouldn't be surprised if our shadows are filled with and energized by a fascination with destruction.

Honoring the Destroyer Within

In other cultures around the world, people have ways to honor the archetype of the Destroyer. Hindus honor Shiva, the Destroyer, who destroys the universe so it can be reborn. Most indigenous people have rituals to honor animals that are killed for food and to purify hunters or butchers after the killing. Many cultures have rites of passage for young males that recognize and sanction their roles as hunters and/or warriors. These cultures often have rites that prepare warriors to leave the destruction of war and return to the creation of living within the group again.

But Western tradition has no rituals to honor the Destroyer, no rituals to provide a safe container for us to express destructive energy. When we try to block destruction, we cause unconscious, random violence. Violence isn't limited to physical abuse; it is often present in the way we speak to each other and the way we treat each other. Every time we curse another driver in rush hour traffic, every time we gossip or complain about a family member or friend, all the while we hold grudges and act superior we are perpetuating verbal, emotional, and spiritual violence. We commit murder in our hearts.

Because we have relegated it to the shadows, destruction fascinates

Existence is sustained by the on-off pulse, the alternating current of the two forces in perfect balance. Unchecked, the life force is cancer, unbridled, the death force is war and genocide.

STARHAWK

us, often in ways that are vaguely unsettling even to ourselves as we engage in them, sometimes in downright disturbing ways. Some people are fascinated with serial killers and the latest movie of the week about them. Some people are fascinated with the violence of professional sports. After all, gathering with friends to watch your (football, hockey, basketball) team and scream, "Kill 'em!" is a kind of ritual. So is getting together with friends to watch a horror movie. This fascination with destruction obsesses some of us with horrific news reports and disasters, like the sinking of the *Titanic* or the latest tornado to hit Somewhere Else, Kansas.

We do need to release destructive energy, and we need the safe containers and parameters that rituals provide. Because they aren't provided with a rite of passage that is led and supervised by elders, adolescents and young adults in the West end up hazing each other, often with disastrous results. We denounce this kind of behavior as primitive and uncivilized, but young people need rituals to help them through the transition to adulthood. If adults don't provide meaningful ritual, young people will provide it themselves.

I was horrified by the news reports of Marine pilots using their fists to hammer metal wings into the chests of the junior pilots who had just earned them. I could see that these warriors needed a ritual that included enduring physical pain with honor. My opinion is that, because the ritual was unsanctioned and unsupervised, it was excessively violent and dangerous. Yet I've heard reports of the men who were beaten saying it was one of the best moments of their lives.

I do know that westerners need to find ways to honor the purpose and beauty of destruction. We need to find ways to honor the Destroyer within without harming ourselves or others. Our current course of denying the Destroyer has brought the entire world to the brink of destruction.

Without ways to honor and express our destructivity, we stop the entire cycle. If we want to be creative, we have to trust ourselves to be appropriately destructive. That's the key, of course: discerning what is appropriate destruction. Because we have attempted to banish the destructive aspects of our nature to the shadow, we don't trust our ability to discern what form of destruction might be appropriate, necessary, and valuable for our growth.

If the soul could have known God without the world, The world would never have been created.
MEISTER ECKHART

This lack of trust explains why so many people we applaud as being tremendously creative so often exhibit self-destructive (or other-destructive) habits, like smoking, drinking, sexual promiscuity in the age of AIDS, temper tantrums, infidelity—the list goes on. When we swing to the far end of the creativity continuum, we must swing to the far end of the destruction side of that same continuum. If we aren't conscious of this fact, we will be unconsciously destructive. Only by becoming conscious can we hope to find ways to make the complementary swing to the destruction end in ways that do not violate our values and principles.

Only when you drink from the river of silence shall you indeed sing.

KAHLIL GIBRAN
The Prophet

Welcome to Your Dragon's Den

It's one thing to come to a philosophical understanding of the way creation and destruction are ends of the same continuum and so accept the necessity of the Destroyer as an archetype. It's quite another challenge to acknowledge your own personification of the Destroyer. It takes a great deal of courage and commitment to say, "This is when and how and why I am destructive. This is when and how and why I am violent." It is so hard to admit this aspect of ourselves. We all want to pretend we're only half, the so-called good half. Sometimes we pretend so well that we begin to believe it, and then our troubles really start.

To be whole, we have to be willing to be both-and. Both creative and destructive. Both good and bad. Both living and dying. We have to be willing to enter the Dragon's Den.

To me, the dragon is an excellent symbol of the combination of creation and destruction. I've explored some of the myths and stories different cultures tell about dragons. For some, the dragon is totally evil and should be destroyed by a courageous saint. For others, the dragon is the symbol of the Divine, of emperors (sons of God), or at least of nobility. The dragon is seen as friend, as foe, as ally, as enemy. The ancient Welsh (a strand in the twists of my ethnic heritage) saw the dragon as a symbol of the life force. The dragon is both-and, just as creation-destruction is both-and.

When you become aware of your own tremendous potential for both creation and destruction, you enter the den of your own inner dragon. And in the dragon's den, the only thing you can do is dance. I have danced there in the presence of my dragon-self in terror and in ecstasy. I've danced to keep my feet from burning, I've danced to express my joy, I've danced to avoid the dragon's ire, I've danced to invite and invoke the dragon's power. Dancing is another both-and. Dancing can be an expression of creative energy, and like Kali, a goddess in the Hindu pantheon who dances people to death, an expression of destructive energy. Dancing is a way to become conscious.

✍ Exercise: Identify the Best of the Worst

We need to find ways and rituals to appropriately honor our own inner Destroyer. Because we have historically associated the Destroyer with villains, we'll start looking there. Using only fictional characters, not real people, quickly list

- five memorable fairy-tale villains
- five memorable villains from TV, movies, or fiction
- five bad guys or bad girls
- five scoundrels or scamps
- five fools or simpletons

You may want to give yourself a day or two to add to these lists. It's fun to brainstorm these lists with a couple of friends or co-workers. You'll be surprised how many villains you can remember with a little help. When you've got a good long list of baddies, select your top ten, the ten most memorable bad guys, the best of the worst.

Stop reading until you've selected your top ten. Once you've selected your top ten, go on with the next paragraph.

Your choices are not random. They reflect an underlying consistency of your personality. If you think they're meaningless because you just thought them up, ask yourself where you think your creativity comes from, if not from making it up. Find the common themes reflected in your choices for the best of the worst. If you have trouble seeing the commonalities yourself, read the list to a couple of friends and ask them to help you find the common threads.

For example, many of the characters might be powerful, "witchy or bitchy" women (this is equally possible for men and women). Many might be nonhuman monsters. Or they might be judgmental and vindictive. Or sneaky. Or dumb. Begin with the obvious connections (perhaps most are human men) and then leap to the more far-fetched ideas (hmm, Darth Vader, Dr. Frankenstein, and Jack in *The Shining* are all bad fathers).

Look for the ways the characters express your inner Destroyer or fit patterns in your life. For example, most of the characters on my list tend to be loud, shouting, and roaring their displeasure. As a kid, I was told I was "too loud," and my choices reflect both my lingering shame and rebellious pleasure about being loud.

❋ Guided Imagery

As you've done in earlier guided imageries, find a place and time when you can be relaxed and uninterrupted. Lie or sit comfortably and begin to relax. Close your eyes. Take several deep breaths, noticing and following the breath in and out of your body.

Consciously tighten the muscles in your feet and ankles. Notice the tension. . . . Feel the tension in all the muscles in your feet. . . . Hold the tension as long as you like . . . holding it until you're ready to let it go with a sigh. . . . Take a deep breath and notice how it feels to let go, to feel the warm relaxation in your feet. . . .

Now, consciously tighten the muscles in your calves and knees. Notice the tension. . . . Feel the tension in your calves and knees. . . . Hold the tension . . . until you're ready to let it go with a sigh. . . . Take a deep breath and notice how good it feels to let your calves and your knees relax and go slack. . . .

Consciously tighten the muscles in your thighs, buttocks, and pelvis. Notice the tension. . . . Feel the tension in your thighs and buttocks and pelvis. . . . Hold the tension . . . until you're ready to let it go with a sigh. . . . Take a deep breath and notice how good it feels to let the lower half of your body relax more and more with each breath you take. . . .

Take another deep breath and consciously tighten the muscles in your stomach, chest, and back. Feel the tension in your torso. . . . Notice what it feels like to hold tension in this part of your body. . . . Hold that tension . . . until you're ready to let it go with a sigh. . . . Take a deep, slow breath and notice how good it feels to breathe all the way down to your belly . . . how good it feels to let your belly go soft and round with each breath. . . .

Now, consciously tighten your hands into fists. Feel the tension move from your hands to your wrists, your forearms, elbows, upper arms, into your shoulders and the base of your neck. . . . Notice that tension, what it feels like . . . holding it until you're ready to let it go with a sigh. . . . Take a deep breath and notice how good it feels to let any remaining tension ooze out of your fingertips. . . . Notice how good it feels to let your shoulders drop and let your arms relax more and more. . . .

Now, consciously tighten the muscles in your jaw and neck; scrunch up the muscles around your eyes and forehead. . . . Notice the tension in your face and neck . . . holding it until you're ready to let it go with a sigh. . . . Notice how good it feels to let your whole body become more and more relaxed . . . more and more relaxed with every breath. . . .

Continue to breathe deeply. If worries or thoughts about other things come to you, simply remind yourself, "Not this, not now," set the thought aside, and return your attention to your breathing. Allow your breath to assume a slow, natural rhythm.

Experience your whole body now as relaxed . . . your mind as quiet and still . . . your emotions as calm and clear . . . your spirit as peaceful and serene. . . .

From this place of inner serenity, harmony, and relaxation, begin to allow images to occur in your mind. . . . Imagine a beautiful and peaceful place outdoors. . . . Notice the colors, shapes, and textures. . . . Notice the feel of the ground beneath you. . . . Notice the sounds around you. . . . Notice the freshness of the air. . . . Begin to see yourself relaxing in this beautiful place. . . . Feel yourself there. . . . Experience being completely comfortable and relaxed in this beautiful, peaceful place. . . .

And now you notice the trickling sound of water flowing over rocks. You look around and find the stream you hear. . . . Follow the stream up and around, following it upstream until you come to its source . . . where you find a cave. . . . Although you might ordinarily be wary of entering a cave

It is important to learn to use destructive energy in a creative way: if you do not, it will turn against you. . . . Handling a destructive urge properly brings a sense of power, for then you feel that anything can be used and expressed, no matter how dark, and then nothing can stop you from creating.

MICHELL CASSOU
and
STEWART CUBLEY
Life, Paint and Passion

by yourself, you know this cave is a sacred place . . . and it is completely safe. . . . The walls and ceiling are solid. . . . There is plenty of fresh air moving in and out of the cave. . . . So you follow the stream into the cave. . . .

You walk slowly in the fading daylight, down into the cave, following the stream. . . . You walk down a tunnel, down into the cave. . . . It gets darker and darker as you go deeper and deeper into the cave. . . . The sound of the water increases, and you find a small waterfall. . . . Behind the waterfall, you find stone steps. . . . You walk down the stone steps as they spiral down and around, deeper into the cave . . . down and around . . . down and around. . . .

Finally you come to an open area deep inside the cave, deep inside your own True Self. . . . You notice that the walls glow slightly . . . just enough for you to find your way. . . . Explore this room. . . . Notice the rocks, the crystals. . . . Notice the sound of water dripping. . . . And here, deep in the cave, deep in your Self, you sit and wait. . . .

You hear footsteps of someone or something coming toward you from the depths of the cave. . . . You turn to see who is coming . . . and as this someone gets closer, you recognize it is one of the bad guys from the best of the worst list you just made. . . . Notice how you feel about meeting this villain, this shadow character here in the cave . . . deep inside your Self. . . .

Notice what this character looks like . . . what clothes he or she is wearing. . . . Notice the mood he or she is in. . . . Notice how you feel about this character appearing here in the cave with you . . . do you feel anger, or fear, or hatred, or awe, or respect, or disgust? . . . Notice the sound of this character's voice. . . . What does this character want to tell you?

You notice that this character holds something . . . something that is absolutely vital for you to live the creative life you yearn for. . . . What is it this character holds? . . . Will he or she give it to you? . . . Will you ask for it? . . . How do you feel? . . . Angry? Grateful? Hopeful? Desperate? . . .

In a few moments, you're going to leave this cave, so finish talking with this shadow character. . . . If you want to, you can invite this shadow character to return with you. . . .

So finish talking with your shadow and begin walking back up and around the stone steps . . . up and around . . . until you emerge from behind the waterfall. . . . Walk back up the tunnel toward the light of day . . . following the stream back, back up the tunnel toward the light . . . back to the sacred and beautiful place where you began. . . . Find a place to sit down and reflect on the gift the shadow character held. . . .

In a few moments, you're going to leave this beautiful and sacred place. . . . Slowly return your attention to this room . . . to your body lying on the floor or sitting in the chair. . . . When you're ready, open your eyes. Move slowly and gently to find a marker or crayon. Draw the shadow character from the cave and the gift he or she held. After drawing, write any other impressions you want to remember.

✸ Creative Shadow Play

Choose the one memorable villain or scoundrel from your best of the worst list that would be the most fun to play the part of in a community play or a movie. It might be the character who visited you in the guided imagery. Give this character a voice or practice the voice you just know this character has. Remember or invent this character's walk, attitude, face. Find this character a prop of some kind.

From time to time this week, rehearse this character as if you were playing the role. Use the voice, walk, attitude, and prop. You can practice when you're in the shower, in your car, alone in the kitchen doing dishes, in an elevator alone. If someone cuts you off on the freeway, definitely use the voice and say what this character would say. Remember, this is *play*. Have fun with it. If you start to scare yourself, back off a little bit. Remember, you're acting, not acting out. In fact, the acting may alleviate the desire to act out.

You don't need to act this character to extremes. I certainly don't suggest you start kidnapping Dalmatian puppies if the villain you choose is Cruella De Vil. But you may want to give yourself permission to wear outrageous clothes, make grand entrances, wave a long cigarette holder in expansive arm gestures, and yell from time to time, "Get those puppies!" Let your body feel and play the part as much as your mind.

As the week goes on, you'll gain a deeper understanding of what this character has that you want or what aspects of your own shadow this character expresses. As your awareness grows, you may want to repeat the guided imagery and see what bubbles up from

Dr. Marie-Louise von Franz and Barbara Hannah, who shared a household in Küsnacht, Switzerland, had the custom of requiring whoever had some especially good fortune to carry out the garbage for the week.

ROBERT A. JOHNSON
Owning Your Own Shadow

your unconscious the second time around. This is a very powerful exercise. While doing it, you may want to give yourself extra time for journaling or schedule an appointment with your therapist or lunch with your best-listening friend.

⊙ **EXERCISE CHOICES**

1. Research Your Shadow Character. If the character you're playing for the Creative Shadow Play is a character from fairy tales, for example, read as many different fairy tales as you can find with that type of character. Or read as many variations on a specific fairy tale as you can find. If your shadow character is from a movie, rent and watch the movie and others with similar characters.

2. Dress Your Shadow. As part of your shadow play this week or as a different exercise, create a costume for your shadow-self and let your shadow-self play dress-up. This is what many people do unconsciously at costume parties. Because a shadow belief I once had was that having lots of money gave people power over others, and part of my shadow was having that kind of power, one of my shadow costumes was to wear a pinstripe suit with money falling out of my pockets. I threw this (fake) money around, using it to boss people around at a shadow party.

If you're feeling adventurous, host a shadow costume party. Invite your guests to come dressed as some aspect of their shadow.

3. Dress Your Creative-Self. Create a costume and find props for your creative-self. Maybe your creative-self wants to wear a beret and dress like a beatnik. Maybe your creative-self wants to have a magic wand and a fairy costume. Maybe your creative-self needs a white smock or a wrist pincushion. Maybe your creative-self needs a carpenter's apron and cap.

You can have a creativity costume party, where everyone comes dressed as their most creative-self.

4. Wreck Something Big. If you have plans to remodel your home, or know of someone else who does, this is an excellent opportunity to get in touch with your destructive-self. One of the great satisfac-

> *Judging your work is one of the hardest challenges in the painting process. It is the immediate reaction of a consciousness long bent on protecting itself, and is felt with such conviction that there seems to be no arguing with it. A disheartening judgment is the last resort of a threatened self-image, and it can attack with the desperation of a cornered animal, endangering your openness and enthusiasm.*
>
> MICHELL CASSOU
> and
> STEWART CUBLEY
> *Life, Paint and Passion*

tions of remodeling is the preliminary deconstruction. Sledge hammers can be fun! (Caution: Don't take down any load-bearing walls.) Be prepared for a huge mess. And you should have a plan for how and when you'll do the creative part of remodeling, which can also be satisfying. If you don't have walls, ceilings, or floors that need replacing in your house, check with friends and neighbors and volunteer to help if they do. You have the fun of taking out the old, and then, best of all, you get to walk away from the sometimes tedious work of putting in the new.

5. Wreck Something Smaller. Find ways to wantonly destroy something. (This is difficult for me, as a rabid recycler, to even suggest. But senseless—yet safe—destruction does have its place and provides a big payoff.) None of that sissy hitting-pillows-with-tennis-rackets stuff. Wreck real stuff. Smash glass. To be safe, you can put a glass in a bag and smash it with a hammer, or put it in a pillow case and smash it on concrete. Shred paper with your bare hands. Rip cloth into useless strips. Put a perfectly good pencil in a pencil sharpener and grind it down to a worthless nub. Get a scissors or a knife to cut up a stuffed animal, then rip the stuffings out and throw it around the room. Break old albums on the edge of a table. Burn something. (Perhaps the reason so many New Age rituals involve burning something is to honor this need for conscious destruction.) Be very conscious and intentional about destroying some tangible thing. This exercise works best if you can find or pay someone to clean up the mess for you—knowing you'll have to clean it up can inhibit you.

6. Revisit What Good Girls and Big Boys Don't. Look at your responses to exercise 2 in chapter 2, where you made a list of what good girls or big boys (depending on your gender) don't do. If you didn't do this exercise before, take a few minutes to respond to it now. Go over the list and pick one or two things you could do without harming yourself or anyone else. Do those things this week to honor your contrary side. You might buy and wear a leather jacket with chains, get a tattoo (temporary or permanent), refuse to share your toys, mope in your bedroom, whatever. Explore the one thing

I have put duality away and seen the two worlds as one.

RUMI

that would give you the most guilty pleasure without really harming anyone.

7. Drive a Bumper Car (at a Fair or Amusement Park) with a Vengeance. Feed the blood lust you repress every time you're in rush hour traffic. Keep score. Yell triumphantly every time you hit someone. Vow, seek, and get revenge every time someone hits you. Don't worry about what the other drivers think—you'll never see them again, and besides, it's what you're supposed to do with bumper cars. So what if you get into it a little more than usual?

8. Honor the Cycles. Every day for a week, notice that each time you make anything, you are also destroying something. Make a sandwich—destroy the individual slices of bread and meat. Cultivate your garden—destroy the weeds. Feed the cat—destroy the fish. Drive your car—destroy the gasoline, weaken the atmosphere, and wear the engine. Draw a picture—dry out the marker and ruin the plain paper. The purpose of this exercise is *not* to riddle you with guilt or produce a maudlin fascination with destruction. The purpose is to become conscious of the cycles of give-and-take in creation and destruction.

9. Dance with Your Dragon. Get a copy of Gabrielle Roth's videocassette *The Wave* and follow her instructions for a moving meditation. As you dance and move, contemplate the image of a dragon living inside you. As you move with the music, imagine yourself dancing with your dragon. Explore what moves your dragon wants to make, what it has to say, and what it has to give you.

10. Slay the Old You. Gather pictures of yourself from childhood until the present. Notice how you have changed physically over time. Remember that every cell in your body is replaced within seven years. Select a photo and either write or talk to a friend about how you have changed since that photo was taken. What parts of you had to die for you to become the person you are today? Then describe the person you want to be in five years and talk about what parts of your current self you need to "kill" to become that future you.

For example, to write this book I had to kill certain parts of the old me. The part of me that wanted to write only when struck by inspiration had to die so a new me who writes on a schedule could grow. The part of me that wanted to remain unnoticed so my flaws wouldn't be criticized had to die so that my willingness to share my ideas in meaningful ways could develop.

What parts of you need pruning so that more of your True Self can emerge? How can your inner Destroyer assist your inner Creator?

11. Host Your Own Wake. Invite some of your closest friends to a party to celebrate the life and death of the old you that you identified in exercise 10. Encourage your friends to bring photos of their old selves that have recently "passed away" as well. Raise a toast, tell stories, sing "Amazing Grace" or other songs that seem appropriate to honor the passing of the old and the coming of the new.

12. Honor Your Values. List two or three of your most important values. What are the principles you want your choices to uphold? Then watch for small ways you can honor those values and principles in both creative and destructive acts. For example, I want my choices to be life affirming, beauty enhancing, and generous. I can weed the garden (destroying some plants) because it is life enhancing for the other plants and for my family and neighbors. I can throw out a ratty, ugly shirt and wear a hand-painted shirt instead. I can send checks to the organizations I believe will do the most to protect and enhance the environment for all living things. What can you destroy to honor your values? What can you create to honor your principles?

Help us to be the always hopeful
Gardeners of the spirit
Who know that without darkness
Nothing comes to birth
As without light
Nothing flowers.
MAY SARTON

TWO

EMBRACING YOUR SHADOW, EXPRESSING YOUR CREATIVITY

✳ ✳ ✳ ✳ ✳ ✳ ✳ ✳ ✳ ✳

CHAPTER 7

Enlist Your Allies

Everyone Needs Allies

PART 1 OF THIS BOOK gave you information about your creativity and your shadow and the connections between the two. Part 2 challenges you to use this information to begin the long journey to being fully creative and fully yourself, your True Self. No one else can make this journey for you, but you don't have to travel alone. In fact, you're not supposed to travel alone.

One of my mentors, Luis Cordoba, once said, "If you were meant to do it alone, you'd have your own planet. There are plenty of them in the universe." Luis challenges our assumption that we are supposed to be independent, that somehow we're supposed to figure everything out all by ourselves and do it all by ourselves. We do need to make the journey *for* ourselves, but we can't complete it *by* ourselves. We simply are not independent; all life on Earth is interdependent.

Intellectually, I know this. I write and talk about how we all need other people to support us. But in the very human tendency of failing to practice what I teach, I occasionally struggle with this concept myself. In fact, I was good and stuck in writing this chapter until I recognized I wasn't reaching out for the support I needed. Once I availed myself of the support all around me, the writing started flowing again.

It is silly, but when I'm in a shadow place, feeling fearful and resistant, I'm likely to say something along the lines of, "I don't *need* you! I don't *need* anybody!" Sometimes I say this under my breath, sometimes I shout it out loud. It's not attractive. Not wise. Not true. It's my awkward way of trying to disentangle myself from being overly dependent on one person. Wiser people have taught me that we all need to depend on something or someone greater than ourselves or other people, *and* we need to be part of communities where all the members cherish, support, and challenge each other.

Dependence on other people is necessary when we are children, but it doesn't work when we're adults. We struggle to be independent in our early adulthood, and sooner or later we discover that that doesn't work either. As wisdom comes (and goes and comes back again), we recognize we are interdependent with all other living beings. We come to rely on something greater, whether we call that by one of the many names for the Divine (God, Christ, Goddess, Allah, Mohammed, and so on) or simply recognize it as the Life Force. However we come to understand it, the truth is we cannot become who we are meant to be without help.

Where to Find Traveling Companions

Trust me, you need traveling companions. As valuable as I hope this book will be for you, no book can ever provide enough support in facing this challenge. Where do you find traveling companions? As a general rule, you find them on the road, traveling the way you are, seeking a similar destination—a creative and meaningful life.

You need a variety of people who can and will support you. It is too much to expect one or two people to be your sole emotional support or to give you feedback on all your creative endeavors. To get the variety of viewpoints you need, find some kind of support in each of these major categories: creative support, spiritual support, therapeutic support, and interpersonal support. (See appendix B for details on locating people who provide each of these kinds of support.)

You may find that a person or group that supports you in one category provides other kinds of support as well, but ask yourself whether you are trying to avoid acknowledging your need for support in that other area. For example, if you're willing to do therapy but are resisting spiritual support, you might be tempted to point out that you and your therapist often talk about spirituality. Ask yourself whether talking with your therapist fills you the way regular spiritual practices and rituals can. Likewise, your friends say they like your painting, poetry, or plum pudding, but do they know enough about painting, poetry, or

We read books to find out who we are. What other people, real or imaginary, do and think and feel is an essential guide to our understanding of what we ourselves are and may become.

URSULA LE GUIN

pudding to give you creative support that will challenge you to grow artistically?

Creative Support

I teach and write about the creative process, so I tend to look for process-related solutions when people tell me they feel frustrated or daunted about expressing their creativity. I ask if they are making time for their creativity, if they have encouragement, if they express themselves just for process every day (with "morning pages," a dream journal, or dancing in the dining room for the sheer joy of moving). I look first for unresolved shadow issues that lead to blocks or stagnation. But sometimes the frustration isn't a creative process issue at all; sometimes it's a question of knowing enough about technique. Sometimes we need to ask for help from someone who knows how to do what we're struggling with. In short, we need support, encouragement, and guidance for both creative process and production.

Support for creative production is often found in classes, specifically in classes with skilled and talented instructors who can show you how to improve your technique and polish your craft. If you want to write better poetry, take a poetry class from a good poet. If you want to plant a better garden, take a gardening workshop from someone who knows the intricacies of things like soil pH, crop rotation, and which good bugs eat bad bugs.

On the other hand, sometimes you don't need a class that focuses on the product of your creativity as much as on the creative process itself. Often we can trust our innate talent to shine forth in our own unique style without the structure of learning a particular school of thought or technique. Sometimes, creative process classes are what you need. At those times, classes that focus on books like *The Artist's Way* or *The Vein of Gold* or this book can be good sources of support.

Other classes that may indirectly support your creative and shadow work are classes in Jungian psychology, psychic development, or dream interpretation. Or take a class in a kind of creativity you aren't "serious" about. How would a class in watercolor painting help a short-story writer? How would a course in architecture help a quilter? How would a semester of studying geology help a sculptor? Think of it as creative

One of the reasons real life is difficult is that we don't ask for assistance — from family, friends, co-workers, strangers. We feel uncomfortable, as if asking for help is confirmation that we're completely inept or spongers.

SARAH BAN BREATHNACH
Simple Abundance

cross-training. Often a class you take just for kicks through a community or continuing education program provides a fresh perspective and brings new vitality to your creative endeavors.

What do you do when a class ends? You can start another class or you can start an ongoing support group. You can form a creativity and shadow support group with as few as three truly committed individuals or as many as ten or so. The guidelines provided later in this chapter will help you determine your group's mission and policies, but the primary purpose is usually to give members a safe place to be honest and open about the struggles and successes of exploring and expressing their creativity as they learn to accept and embrace their shadow. A creativity and shadow support group usually focuses on the creative process and so may benefit from having members with a variety of interests and expressions.

On the other hand, some creativity support groups share a common form of creative expression and focus on the creative product. For example, a group of novelists might meet twice a month to read and respond to each other's work in process. Their common interest makes the feedback meaningful and on target and makes it possible for group members to commiserate about the challenges they all face.

Call it a clan, call it a network, call it a tribe, call it a family. Whatever you call it, whoever you are, you need one.
JANE HOWARD

Spiritual Support

One of the basic premises of Julia Cameron's book *The Artist's Way* is that creativity and spirituality are essentially the same thing. (In fact, *The Artist's Way* is an excellent resource for exploring the spiritual side of creativity and the creative potential of spirituality.) In many ways, receiving support for your creativity is spiritual support. I make a distinction between spiritual support and creative support here only for convenience.

There are several sources of spiritual support. And you don't have to be "religious" to avail yourself of these.

First and probably foremost, you will find spiritual support by approaching the God of your understanding through a practice of prayer and meditation. As you explore the untapped potential of both your shadow and your creativity, it is comforting to know that all you are comes from something greater. Regular prayer and meditation will smooth some of the volatile emotions that shadow work can stir up, giving you a place to rest spiritually and regroup mentally. Practicing quiet will reveal that difficulties are rarely as big as we fear or imagine them to be. And prayer brings grace and offers a place to surrender the difficulties that really are too big for us alone.

A spiritual director or clergy member can guide you as you learn to look for the Divine within and the Divine all around. If it seems strange or pointless to you to rely on the Divine, perhaps because you were taught erroneous and toxic beliefs about God, a spiritual director can help you explore what the truth might be.

You may also find that the members of your spiritual or religious community not only support your spiritual journey, but also encourage your creative expression. Creativity and shadow are so intimately connected with our spiritual and moral awareness that a spiritual community is a natural place to look for traveling companions. You may want to start a creativity and shadow support group among like-minded members of your church or spiritual organization.

Most Twelve Step group members find that the group itself is an excellent source of spiritual support and connection. Since addiction is often a reflection of shadow issues, you may want to explain your understanding of your shadow to your group or sponsor and ask for feedback.

You may also find spiritual support in the autobiographies and biographies of the saints, mystics, and people like Viktor Frankl who detail their journey through "the dark night of the soul." A multitude of inspirational books and meditation guides are available in most bookstores. Some of my favorites are listed in the resource directory at the end of this book.

Some people use oracles like the *I Ching*, tarot cards and other decks, and rune-stones as a source of inspiration. I see much more value in using these oracles as a starting point for introspection and meditation than as questionable predictors of the future. Taken in that light and with awareness of Jung's concept of synchronicity (that is, that the universe is filled with "coincidences" that are not related by cause and effect but are still filled with meaning), oracles can be intriguing sources that provoke you to ask questions and seek answers you might not have recognized otherwise. My personal favorites are *The Medicine Cards*, *The Druid Animal Oracle*, and *Soul Cards*.

We need to feel the cheer and inspiration of meeting each other. We need to gain the courage and fresh life that comes from the mingling of congenial souls, of those working for the same ends.

JOSEPHINE
ST. PIERRE RUFFIN

Therapeutic Support

Exploring your shadow and expressing your creativity will take you to a deep, archetypal layer of meaning and experience. You are likely to experience intense emotional responses from time to time. Your creative and shadow work will bring you immense satisfaction and joy, but often only after it stirs up old, old emotional pain.

If you haven't worked with a therapist in the past (or if you haven't had the opportunity to work with a *good* therapist), you may discover old wounds that you must heal before you can go forward on your creative journey.

If you have done therapy, you may find yourself revisiting issues you thought you had worked through and finished years ago. Think of this as your psyche, your Higher Self, taking a walk down memory lane. You, your ego-self, may not want to take this sentimental journey, but your Higher Self has a purpose in reminding you of your origins.

Either way, you will benefit greatly from having a professional guide to point out the highlights and pitfalls along the way. You need a good therapist. If you haven't worked with a therapist (or recognize your old therapist isn't really helping), ask people you respect who they would recommend. Do brief phone or in-person interviews to see which therapist fits best with your perspective, goals, and style. If you're working with a therapist now, you will naturally talk about where your shadow and creative work is taking you. If you had a therapist you are no longer seeing, be prepared to schedule some follow-up sessions.

I know, I know. Therapy can be hard work. And you may not want to do it, or you may feel like you've already done it and don't want to have to do it all over again. But most people need the support of a talented mental health professional as they take this journey, if only to assure them that the emotions and issues stirring around inside them are the signs that they are finding their True Selves, not losing their minds.

You can get the therapeutic support you need in one-to-one sessions or in a therapy group or both. Personally, I have found integrative breathwork (or holotrophic breathwork or shamanic breathwork) to be an excellent supplement to working with a therapist. Breathwork recognizes the healer within each of us and provides a witness and trained facilitator to support that inner healer. It gives me a place to physically work

---

Science teaches us that we can understand the universe only in terms of relatedness, that things are nothing in themselves, in isolation, that even the atom has significance only in some pattern of organization. Carbon atoms, for example, form charcoal when related in one way and become diamonds when related in another. A lone atom is a meaningless atom. A related atom is the building stone of nature. A lone human being is a destroyer of values; a related human being is the builder of individual and social peace. Our interdependence is the most encompassing fact of human reality.

JOSHUA LIEBMAN
Peace of Mind

through emotional issues. It has also strengthened my ability to intentionally and safely enter different states of consciousness, and ultimately that is what creativity is, an altered state of consciousness. (You'll find names and phone numbers of breathwork practitioners who can more fully explain this work listed in appendix B.)

Keep in mind that mental health practitioners are not the only sources of therapeutic support. All too often we think of therapy as a mental and emotional issue only, forgetting how much our bodies are involved in the whole process. Likewise, some of us think of creativity as primarily a mental and emotional exercise, forgetting how important physical movement is when we're looking for movement in our psyche and our art.

I suspect writers may be especially prone to overlook the physical nature of creativity, which is probably why Brenda Ueland extolled the virtues of walking in *If You Want to Write*. She wrote, "For me, a long five or six mile walk helps. . . . It is at these times I seem to get recharged." But anyone who wants to expand his or her creativity benefits from the movement and new perspective and images walking provides. As Julia Cameron highlights in *The Vein of Gold*, "Treadmills and Stairmasters provide exercise, but they do not provide an image flow. Consider them a last resort."

Walking isn't the only way of moving your body to enlighten your mind. You can swim, run, hike, cross-country ski, bicycle, dance, row, paddle, and climb your way to expanded creative horizons. Any regular, rhythmic movement of your body will facilitate your creativity and help you work through shadow issues. Finding ways to move in fresh air with beautiful surroundings makes the movement both more enjoyable and more effective.

Creativity comes through our bodies—we use our bodies to make our creative urges manifest in the world. So we need to treat our bodies well. This can be difficult to acknowledge. For most westerners, the body is a shadow issue. We are taught that our body has hungers that will interfere with spiritual growth, even spiritual salvation. We are taught to disregard, deny, or denigrate the "sinful pleasures of the flesh." That's why so much of our awareness of our bodies and the physical pleasures we can find in and through our bodies becomes repressed into the shadow. The upside of this is that we can release the energy locked in

Mentally (at least three or four times a day) thumb your nose at all know-it-alls, jeerers, critics and doubters.
BRENDA UELAND
If You Want to Write

the body-shadow as we learn to treat our bodies well. We find an easy access to our shadow and our creative energy through being physical.

People who are trained to work with the human body and its energy can support you in your creative growth. Massage isn't just something that feels good; it will help you release energy into your creative endeavors. A skilled bodyworker can do wonders for your creativity. Explore different modalities—all the different kinds of therapeutic massage, chiropractic, shiatsu, acupressure, acupuncture, reiki, Feldenkrais, aromatherapy, reflexology, among others. See which ones suit your body and your creativity best.

Honest communication among artists is necessary and it won't happen at openings.
SALLY WARNER

Interpersonal Support

The first people many of us turn to for support are our partners, family members, and friends. After all, they know us better than strangers do; sometimes they know us better than we know ourselves. Your spouse or partner or a friend you've known for a long time is probably the person who knows your creative dreams and recognizes your shadow better than anyone else. He or she can be the best ally you have for your creative efforts or your worst detractor; sometimes both on the same day. You need to find the balance in how much of your creativity to share with your partner and in how much his or her opinions and insights will influence you.

From my own experience and the experiences of couples taking my classes together, I can affirm that working through the creative and shadow exploration together can deepen and strengthen relationships. Some people are hesitant to start shadow exploration with their spouse, partner, or close friend. They fear that talking about shadow will cause conflict and dissatisfaction, perhaps even end the relationship. But the truth is, sooner or later, you're going to reveal your shadows to each other anyway. You can't help it. Real intimacy requires that we share all of ourselves, the best and the worst aspects. So why not enter the journey intentionally and with a shared understanding of the creative gifts you'll gather along the way?

Remember, shadow calls shadow. When you're stressed to the point that your shadow puts in an unexpected appearance, your reactions will probably send your partner into a shadow place as well. Be compassionate with each other and with yourselves. And remember that creativity calls creativity too. When you take the risk to share the deepest, most beautiful parts of yourself and express that creatively, the people you share it with will feel the urge to express their creativity as well.

Another important source of interpersonal support can be found with a personal coach. My coach, Valerie Olson, president of Designed Alliance (her coaching business), defines her role this way: "A coach is a partner, catalyst, and sounding board, trained to help you achieve your personal and professional goals. A coach offers a wealth of knowledge and skills to motivate, inspire, and encourage you to move toward your highest potential." Personal coaches are skilled listeners who know when to affirm and encourage, when to challenge, when to clarify, when to make requests, and when to brainstorm possibilities.

Working with a coach usually involves an in-depth interview to establish values and long-term goals, and then a weekly telecoaching session of about a half hour. Many coaches offer voice mail or e-mail services for clients who want to check in between sessions. Coaching is quite affordable and, because it is done over the phone, available to most people no matter where they live.

A coach is skilled and trained to give you useful feedback as you learn to hold yourself accountable, which, I have found, most of my coaching clients need. As creative people, we need to find ways to actually do what we dream of doing, and being coached is one way to help yourself make that happen. You'll find more information about personal coaches in appendix B.

Remember, too, that humans are not the only life-form on the planet. Find a place where you can be a steward of the land, a place where you are reminded how interdependent all life is. It might be a garden or a stretch of riverbank or a grove of trees or a part of a park that you assume responsibility for without the hubris of attempting to control. Awareness of your connections with the plants and animals you share that land with will promote your creativity in unexpected ways.

Finally, don't underestimate the power of a companion animal to be an unconditionally loving, life-sustaining ally. SARK is absolutely correct when she writes in *Inspiration Sandwich,* "Dogs are miracles with paws." One of my greatest spiritual teachers was my dog Bear, who modeled, among other things, what it means to be fully present and to trust your

Our perfect companions never have fewer than four feet.
COLETTE

own instincts. Of course, cats are unparalleled teachers of sensuality. I'll leave it to you to explore what your pet has to share with you.

Mix and Match

Notice that the descriptions above include allies found in groups, such as classes and support groups; allies found in one-to-one relationships, such as with a friend, therapist, bodyworker, or coach; and allies found through introspection, such as meditation and reading.

It is important to ask for many kinds of support. Take a moment to consider which kind of support you gravitate toward. Are you likely to seek support in classes, where you get a variety of viewpoints, but then lose track of people after the class is over? Do you usually call one or two close friends who've known you long enough to give their feedback depth, but because there's only one or two of them, offer more limited perspectives? Are you willing to pay someone to guide your emotional angst, but reluctant to write a check to someone who would pamper your body with massage or energy work? Most of us prefer and tend to rely on the kind of support we're most comfortable with. Of course, the kind of support you tend to avoid or forget to ask for is the kind that will probably provide the greatest rewards.

It is also vital that you seek allies among people who are willing and able to be an ally, as the next exercise will highlight.

I have seen that in any great undertaking it is not enough for a man to depend simply upon himself.
LONE MAN

Exercise: Identify Your Allies

Freewrite for five minutes or so, beginning with: "I recognize I need support in exploring, expanding, and expressing my creativity. The people I would like to support me and the ways I want them to support me are . . ."

Then, in the smallest circle in the drawing on the next page, write the names of people you know who are strongly committed to living a creative life and who are willing to explore the shadow issues necessary to live that life. They aren't perfect, but they make progress. They may get stuck from time to time, and when they do, they endure. Over the long haul, they are committed to living a satisfying, creative life.

In the outside circle, write the names of people you know who are not committed to living a creative life. They're unwilling to face the difficult issues that come with that commitment. They never have the time, the energy, or the inclination. They get blocked and stay blocked. They may talk about being creative but don't put it into action. Or they don't see the value in being creative. They've given up hope of really being creative. This may change for these people, but for now, this how it is for them.

In the middle circle, write the names of people you know who are not fully committed but not fully uncommitted either. Perhaps they don't know they can live a fully creative life or don't know how to do it. Sometimes they find the courage to create, sometimes they don't. They haven't committed to being creative, but they haven't given up either. They're in the middle.

Put your own name in one of the circles. Are you fully committed, kind of committed, or not committed at all? Be honest with yourself.

Somehow animals act as ideal symbols or images of our deepest fears and urges, or of those parts of our psyche which have been denied or repressed or simply neglected.

PHILIP CARR-GOMM
and
STEPHANIE CARR-GOMM
The Druid Animal Oracle

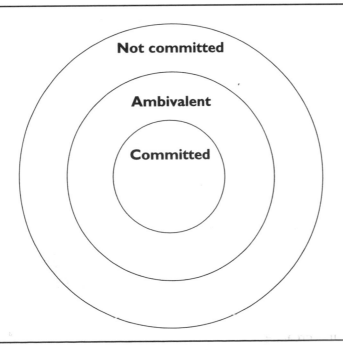

Not committed

Ambivalent

Committed

The people in the smallest circle are your potential allies—the people who can help you in exploring, expanding, and expressing your creativity. They can support you in taking creative risks because they're willing to take the risks themselves.

The people in the middle circle may occasionally be able to support you and may be people you can invite to join you in making a commitment to exploring creativity. But be on the alert; there is always the possibility that from time to time, they may unconsciously try to pull you away from your commitment to justify their own waffling.

Be aware that the people in the outer circle simply cannot give you the support you need. They may say they support you, they may want to support you, but no one can give what they don't have. People who are not living a commitment to their own creativity can't help you live your commitment.

You need to spend time with other people who are doing the work of following their passion, not with people who only talk about doing the work or make excuses for why they aren't doing it. And you need to spend time with other people who are willing to play and to dance, not with people who only give lip service to the value of the play or the beauty of the dance.

This is not to say the people in the outer circle are your enemies. They are simply not your allies. You don't have to eliminate them from your life, but you do need to practice discernment around them. The people in the middle circle may become your allies, but you need to practice discernment around them too.

Practicing discernment means being aware. Pay attention to the other person's words and actions. Are they consistent, or does that person say one thing and do another? Notice how you feel while you're with that person and how you feel afterward. Limit your contact with people in the middle and outer circles when you are feeling uncertain or discouraged. Don't share too much about your creative projects with them, especially in the early stages when the work is fresh and you are vulnerable. Don't cast your pearls before swine, as the saying goes. Don't ask them for feedback. They probably don't know how to give supportive responses, perhaps because they never received any themselves. Be aware of their limitations and don't accept their negativity as truth.

Do you have enough allies in your inner circle? How many of the people included in your freewrite are in the outer circle and thus unable to be your true allies? How many are in the middle circle and thus require discernment in your contact with them? Looking for support from someone who is unable to give it is a common error when we don't know what to look for in an ally. Continuing to look for support from someone unable to give it is a setup for disappointment.

Forming Your Support Network

Stay open to finding new allies; they'll show up in the most unexpected places and bring you the most unexpected gifts. Keep your eyes and ears open for others who are committed to the journey. People who aren't doing the often frightening self-exploration you are may be threatened by your willingness. Others who are growing will be able to support your growth.

If you need or want more allies in your inner circle, invite someone to coffee or tea so you can explore what you may have in common. Don't expect potential allies to reveal everything on the "first date." After all, if they have the kind of wisdom you want in an ally, they're checking you out while you're checking them out.

As you're exploring new potential allies, remember to rely on people you trust. If you're going to share your feelings and experiences about your creativity and shadow with someone, that person needs to be someone you trust to be honest, accepting, and committed to her or his own journey. Everyone is imperfect and fallible, so don't expect your allies to have perfect insight to all your problems or to always be available. But do expect your allies to be trustworthy. Base your commitment to each other on mutual respect and honesty. It is possible, and probably preferable, to know that as trusted friends, you will accept each other's shadows, but you won't allow yourselves to be misused by anyone acting out harmful shadow behavior. It is also important to know that you will be honest and direct with each other. Be conscious of using "I" language

And let your best be for your friend. If he must know the ebb of your tide, let him know its flood also. For what is your friend that you should seek him with hours to kill? Seek him always with hours to live. For it is his to fill your need, but not your emptiness. And in the sweetness of friendship, let there be laughter and sharing of pleasures. For in the dew of little things the heart finds its morning and is refreshed.

KAHLIL GIBRAN
The Prophet

("I feel . . . I've found . . . I believe . . .") that acknowledges the possibility of other perspectives.

Sometimes you will need more support than other times. That's when it's wonderful to have a variety of resources to call on—make an extra appointment with your massage therapist, increase your meditation time, ask your spiritual community to pray for you, call friends, have lunch with your sponsor, or start a new class. And when you're in a more stable place, you can be the one called upon. But to truly benefit from the support available to you, there is nothing like a regular place and time to meet with people you trust.

When one's own problems are unsolvable and all best efforts are frustrated, it is lifesaving to listen to other people's problems.
SUZANNE MASSIE

Forming a Creativity and Shadow Support Group

One of the best things you can do to enhance your journey is to find or form a creativity and shadow support group. Contact some of the people you identified as potential allies and invite them to discuss the possibility of forming a group to support each other as you all explore your creativity and the shadow issues that arise with that exploration. Explain what you've learned so far. Encourage others to talk about what they've found in exploring their creativity. At the end of the discussion, express your own commitment and ask who else is willing to continue meeting as a support group.

I recommend regular meetings—weekly seems to work best because these meetings then become a part of your regular routine. You just get in the habit and don't schedule anything else for the day you've agreed to meet with your group. But if that seems like too much, try every other week or once a month. Make it the same day of the month, for example, the second Sunday of each month.

Discuss what kind of support each of you wants. Write a mission statement for your group. Develop a contract that establishes the ground rules and clarifies what you as a group are able and willing to provide. (Remember that you have multiple allies and don't need to get everything from one source.)

Many groups find it useful to begin with a check-in, which forms the circle and brings everyone's attention to the people present. Over time, the honesty and self-awareness in your check-ins will deepen, and your bond to each other will grow. You will have valuable witnesses as you begin to hold yourself accountable to making the changes you want to make. After check-ins, your group may want to have time for creative play, guided imagery, shadow exercises from this book or others, or for giving each other feedback on recent creative efforts. It is particularly useful when members share their goals for the coming week at the end of one meeting and then check in about those goals at the beginning of the next meeting.

I recommend the leader or facilitator role "float" from person to person each week. If some of the members of your creativity and shadow support group have been in a Twelve Step group, ask them to explain the "trusted servant" concept.

☀ Guided Imagery

As you've done in earlier guided imageries, find a place and time when you can be relaxed and uninterrupted. Lie or sit comfortably and begin to relax. Close your eyes. Take several deep breaths, noticing and following the breath in and out of your body.

Consciously tighten the muscles in your feet and ankles. Notice the tension. . . . Feel the tension in all the muscles in your feet. . . . Hold the tension as long as you like . . . holding it until you're ready to let it go with a sigh. . . . Take a deep breath and notice how it feels to let go, to feel the warm relaxation in your feet. . . .

Now, consciously tighten the muscles in your calves and knees. Notice the tension. . . . Feel the tension in your calves and knees. . . . Hold the tension . . . until you're ready to let it go with a sigh. . . . Take a deep breath and notice how good it feels to let your calves and your knees relax and go slack. . . .

Consciously tighten the muscles in your thighs, buttocks, and pelvis. Notice the tension. . . . Feel the tension in your thighs and buttocks and pelvis. . . . Hold the tension . . . until you're ready to let it go with a sigh. . . . Take a deep breath and notice how good it feels to let the lower half of your body relax more and more with each breath you take. . . .

Take another deep breath and consciously tighten the muscles in your stomach, chest, and back. Feel the tension in your torso. . . . Notice what it feels like to hold tension in this part of your body. . . . Hold that tension . . . until you're ready to let it go with a sigh. . . . Take a deep, slow breath and notice how good it feels to breathe all the way down to your belly . . . how good it feels to let your belly go soft and round with each breath. . . .

Now, consciously tighten your hands into fists. Feel the tension move from your hands to your wrists, your forearms, elbows, upper arms, into your shoulders and the base of your neck. . . . Notice that tension, what it feels like . . . holding it until you're ready to let it go with a sigh. . . . Take a deep breath and notice how good it feels to let any remaining tension ooze out of your fingertips. . . . Notice how good it feels to let your shoulders drop and let your arms relax more and more. . . .

Now, consciously tighten the muscles in your jaw and neck; scrunch up the muscles around your eyes and forehead. . . . Notice the tension in your face and neck . . . holding it until you're ready to let it go with a sigh. . . . Notice how good it feels to let your whole body become more and more relaxed . . . more and more relaxed with every breath. . . .

Continue to breathe deeply. If worries or thoughts about other things come to you, simply remind yourself, "Not this, not now," set the thought aside, and return your attention to your breathing. Allow your breath to assume a slow, natural rhythm.

Experience your whole body now as relaxed . . . your mind as quiet and still . . . your emotions as calm and clear . . . your spirit as peaceful and serene. . . .

From this place of inner serenity, harmony, and relaxation, begin to allow images to occur in your mind. . . . Begin to imagine yourself in a beautiful and peaceful place, a place where you feel a deep connection to the Divine. . . . Notice the colors and the shapes in this beautiful place. . . . Begin to see yourself in this place. . . . Notice the sounds of this place. . . . Begin to feel yourself in this place. . . . Notice the scents . . . even the tastes of this place. . . . Allow this place to become more and more real with each breath you take. . . .

You begin to explore this beautiful, sacred place. . . . You move around in this place until you find a spiral path. . . . You follow the spiral path . . . walking, or swimming, or even flying, you follow the spiral path, around and in . . . around and in . . . following the spiral path around and into the center of this place. . . . And as you follow the spiral path around and in, you notice there is a fog rising. . . . As you follow the spiral path, it gets darker and darker . . . and you feel more and more alone . . . until you are completely alone in utter darkness. . . . Notice how you feel about being alone . . . how you feel about being in the dark. . . .

You ask for light . . . and now you notice a small spark of light. . . . You move toward the light. . . . The light gets larger and larger. . . . You see it is a campfire. . . . You move to the fire. . . . You come close to the fire and sit down . . . and you know you are at the center of the sacred place. . . . Notice how you feel about the fire . . . the light and warmth provided for you here at the center of the sacred place . . . and notice how you feel about being alone in the flickering firelight. . . .

You ask for guidance . . . for an ally . . . and you wait by the fire . . . until you begin to feel someone or something coming. . . . You can't see past the flickering light of the flames . . . you can't hear anything but the crackle and pop of the fire . . . you can't smell anything but wood smoke . . . but you know there is another presence there with you . . . you know there is another being there with you . . . and you know this being is your ally. . . . You turn slowly and look into the dark until you can begin to see your ally. . . . Your ally can present itself in whatever form it chooses . . . an angel or a totem animal or a spirit guide. . . . As your ally comes closer to the light, you see more and more clearly what form it has chosen . . . and you realize how perfectly that form resonates with your own spirit. . . .

Your ally comes closer and closer until it rests next to you. . . . There are some questions you may want to ask your ally. . . . What is your name? . . . How will you help me? . . . What do I need to know or remember? . . .

Spend some time with your ally now . . . hearing the wisdom it has to share with you . . . heeding the advice it has to give you . . . allowing the love and support of this being to fill your mind, to fill your heart, to fill your entire being. . . .

(pause for several minutes)

In a few moments you're going to leave the fire at the center of the sacred place. . . . You can invite your ally to come with you. . . . Know that your ally is with you always . . . and that you can return to the fire at the center of the sacred place anytime you want. . . . So when you're ready, get up and find the spiral path that will take you back out and around . . . away from the fire . . . out and around, back out and around to the place where you began . . . and as you follow the spiral path back out and around, you notice the darkness fades and the light grows . . . back out and around until you recognize the beautiful and peaceful place where you began. . . .

Take a few moments to contemplate the advice your ally gave you by the fire at the center of the sacred place. . . . Remembering the wisdom and the love your ally showed you, prepare yourself to leave this beautiful and

When the cry goes out, there is a response.
THE TIBETAN

peaceful place and return to your ordinary room. . . . Become aware of your breathing again . . . become aware of the feel of the floor or the chair beneath you. When you're ready, gently touch your fingers together and wiggle your toes. Slowly open your eyes. Move slowly and gently to find a marker or crayon and draw your ally. After drawing, write any other impressions you want to be sure to remember.

When you call upon the power of an animal, you are asking to be drawn into complete harmony with the strength of that creature's essence. Gaining understanding from these brothers and sisters of the animal kingdom is a healing process, and must be approached with humility and intuitiveness.

JAMIE SAMS
The Medicine Cards

✸ *Creative Shadow Play*

Make a collage of your allies, tangible and intangible. Include photos of people who are now allies, pictures of people (or types of people) you want to become your allies, and pictures of the ally you met in the guided imagery. Include a photo of yourself.

◉ **EXERCISE CHOICES**

1. Find Out More about the Ally That Came to You in the Guided Imagery. If your ally was an angel and you know his or her name, ask a reference librarian to help you learn more about that angel. Or read some of the many books about angels that are available. Also check with your family to see if your ally's name is the name of a relative. If so, it may just be coincidence, but ask for stories about that relative to see whether those stories add to your understanding of your ally. If your ally was an animal, find out more about that animal, on both the practical, factual level and the symbolic level. *The Medicine Cards* by Jamie Sams and David Carson, *The Druid Animal Oracle* by Philip and Stephanie Carr-Gomm, and *Animal Speak* by Ted Andrews are excellent resources for exploring the qualities associated with different animals.

2. Be on the Alert for Tangible Representations of the Ally That Appeared in Your Meditation. You might find a sweatshirt with a picture of your ally on it or a small statue or a stuffed animal. Give yourself these tangible reminders that you are not alone in the dark. All you have to do is ask for light and guidance and it will come.

3. List Potential Allies. List people and places where you can find additional support. You might want to begin therapy or find other professionals to help you. Remember that this creative shadow exploration often brings up old, old pain that can be the raw material for significant psychological growth. Get experienced, trustworthy guides.

4. Review Your Commitment Circles. Add the names from the list you just made in exercise 3 to the circles. Are there enough names in the inner circle now?

5. Review Your Commitment. Write your name in the commitment circle you *want* to be in. (It may be the same circle you put yourself in earlier.) Be honest with yourself. If you don't want to be in the inner circle or the middle circle, now is not the time for you to be doing this work. Forcing yourself will not work and will only make you miserable.

6. Freewrite. Use this sentence as the starting point for a five- to ten-minute freewrite: I want _____ (name) to support my commitment to living a creative life in the following ways:
_____.

7. Ask for What You Want. Let the people you want support from know how and when you'd like their help. Ask them if they're willing to do that for you. For example, you might ask your partner or best friend to give you insight to your shadow. But remind this person that the best time to give that insight is *not* when you're in the middle of a shadow outburst—you just won't be receptive. Or, you might ask the members of other support groups you belong to, your writer's group, Twelve Step group, or therapy group to give you feedback on your creative projects or insight in interpreting your dream journal.

8. Begin or Reestablish a Practice of Prayer and Meditation. Ask the God of your understanding to give you insight and support your ability to see yourself honestly and objectively.

9. Try New Sources of Images to Meditate On. I've found the animal allies in *The Medicine Cards* by Jamie Sams and David Carson or *The Druid Animal Oracle* by Philip and Stephanie Carr-Gomm provide insight when I need a new perspective. Some people use a tarot deck, the *I Ching,* angel cards, or rune-stones. Jung believed such tools used the principle of synchronicity and were useful, not for divination purposes, but as a source of inspiration.

10. Take a Trip to the Library. Read about others' journeys through the dark night of the soul. Read biographies of the saints, mystics, and heroes. Read Carl Jung's *Memories, Dreams, Reflections.*

11. Form a Creativity and Shadow Support Group. See pages 138–139 for detailed instructions on forming such a group.

12. List Five Classes That Would Be Fun. List five classes you've wanted to take for a long time. List five classes that would further your usual creative mode (fiction writers might list poetry or play-writing classes, oil painters might list watercolor classes). List five classes that would open new creative possibilities.

13. Sign Up for One (or Two) of the Classes You Listed in Exercise 12. Rank the others and tentatively schedule when you'll take them.

CHAPTER 8

Restore Your Energy

Energy Drain

A **COMMON MISCONCEPTION** about creativity is that creative people are frequently and inexplicably struck with all kinds of outstanding ideas and that these ideas fill them with a feverishly intense inspiration while they flawlessly execute each idea. Like many fallacies, this one contains elements of truth (if there were nothing valid about the concept, we would have dismissed it long ago), but the truths get lost among the exaggerations.

First, it isn't just a few "naturally talented" or "creative" people who get ideas. We all get ideas, all the time, but some people have learned to pay attention to their ideas. Second, it is rare that any idea produces the desired result without a lot of trial and error, mistakes, and missteps along the way. It is the so-called mistakes that help us refine ideas. What looks like a perfectly logical trail leading to the solution can be seen only in hindsight; while we're in the middle of the process, we all face uncertainty about which way to go next.

Still, it is true that being creative requires a receptivity to ideas, and these ideas naturally fill us with enthusiasm to act on the ideas. Many of us doubt our creativity because we so rarely feel even modest enthusiasm, let alone the feverish, wild-eyed intensity we erroneously associate with creative genius. But if we all get ideas, why do so many of us feel a lack of creative energy? Because we squander this energy, draining it away with a kind of mental isometrics without even noticing what we're doing.

When was the last time you thought, even briefly, about doing something a little creative, a little playful—like playing a few scales, or journaling, or working on a project you started and haven't finished, or even just coloring—but then decided you had really better finish that proposal for your boss, or clean the kitchen, or take care of someone else; in other words, do something practical? And then, having abandoned the possibility of creative play and pleasure and instead pushed yourself to be virtuous, found yourself slumped in front of the TV, or staring glassy-eyed at the screen as you surfed the Internet, or numbed out with food, shopping, or mindless reading? It happens more often than we realize. One part of us is pushing one way—I want to create, to play—while another part is pushing the other way—I have to work, be practical, be responsible—with the net result being that we lack the energy to work *or* play.

If the repressed tendencies, the shadow as I call them, were obviously evil, there would be no problem whatever. But the shadow is merely somewhat inferior, primitive, unadapted, and awkward; not wholly bad. It even contains childish or primitive qualities which would in a way vitalize and embellish human existence, but— convention forbids!

CARL JUNG

Stopping the Mental Isometrics

The result of these mental isometrics is a serious creative block. You know what it feels like to wear yourself out this way—you vow that this time you're going to stick to the new diet, the new budget, the New Year's resolution. And then the battle begins. Part of you says, "I will not" (eat a donut, buy a new CD, skip exercising this morning), while another part of you says, "Oh why not, just this once?" Ego demands one thing, while shadow slyly suggests the opposite. You're in a mental shoving match that you always end up losing. Whenever there is a contest between willpower (ego) and shadow, shadow will always win. Your psyche, your True Self, will always side with shadow against ego because your True Self knows that shadow will lead you to wholeness.

In the case of your creativity, you're sure that this is the week you will find time to get out the brushes, or the clay, or that piece you've been meaning to finish. But then, things happen and you just somehow don't get around to it. Or you do force yourself to sit down with the project, and then nothing comes. There's no juice, no energy, no inspiration. You cannot will yourself to be creative.

We spend so much of our energy keeping our shadow in check that we don't have any left over for being creative. We fear the pendulum swing (described in chapter 6) that must come with expressing our creativity, so we use almost all our energy trying to limit our options and hold ourselves in a very narrow realm of possibilities. We may tell ourselves that we have to do whatever it is that saps our energy because that's what respectable adults have to do, but the truth is, if we are excused from those activities (while on vacation or switching jobs), we get anxious and quickly find something else to focus our attention and energy on. Anything but actually playing with our creativity, please!

Trying to deny the shadow is a refusal to accept reality. We refuse to accept that what is, is. Of course, refusing to accept reality doesn't change reality; it only wears us out. Deepak Chopra highlights the futility of this refusal in *The Seven Spiritual Laws of Success*, where he writes, "When you struggle against this moment, you're actually struggling against the entire universe. . . . If you just relinquish the need to defend your point of view, you will in that relinquishment, gain access to enormous amounts of energy that have been previously wasted."

Until we stop the mental isometrics, we wear ourselves out without accomplishing anything.

Before Stopping, Intensify

The first step in releasing the energy pent up in mental isometrics is to identify the opposing forces. Fear is often one force. For me, expectation is the other force. One part of me is demanding, "It has to be . . ." while another fearful part of me keeps bringing up, "But what if it isn't . . ." And I'm caught.

A good way to clearly identify the opposing forces is to let these forces have their say. Dialogue it or write it. Speak for each force, first one and then another and possibly another, letting your voice get louder and louder. Or sit down and write out all the demands and accusations bouncing around in your head. Let each force get bigger, louder, more insistent.

Before you can surrender, before you can let go, you may need to hold on even tighter. That's why when I lead guided imagery, I always begin the relaxation by inviting people to consciously tighten their bodies and to hold that tension until they're ready to let go.

If fear is one of the opposing forces that is sapping your energy and accomplishing nothing, go fully into your fear—scream, cry, thrash about, shake, cower. If expectation is one of the opposing forces, exaggerate it—throw a tantrum, shout demands, hold your breath, pound

Fear is the mind-killer. Fear is the little-death that brings total obliteration. I will face my fear. I will permit it to pass over me and through me. And when it has gone past I will turn the inner eye to see its path. Where the fear has gone there will be nothing. Only I will remain.

FRANK HERBERT
Dune

your fist. You can do this with any emotion at the core of an opposing force. When you let this energy wash over you and through you, you discover it does dissipate. It disappears and you remain. You may want a safe, supportive person there (in other words, an ally) to make sure you're okay as you do this. Integrative breathwork is my safe place to do this kind of intentionally intensified work.

Changing the Mix

Once you've identified the opposing forces and intensified them so that you are ready to surrender one or both, it is time to change the mix. Do something different. If you always work indoors, go outside. If you always rehearse with background music, practice in silence. If you work alone, go to a coffeehouse and soak up the background of half-heard conversations; if you work in a crowded office, create quiet space.

Remember, there is a time to push and a time to let go. If you've been pushing and nothing is happening—that is, you're blocked— then it's time to stop pushing. If you've let go and don't feel a release of energy or if that released energy has dissipated, it's time to start doing again.

The Creative Shadow Play in chapter 4 encouraged you to make time to moodle, to leisurely do nothing. When you feel blocked or drained, it may be time to surrender. Stop trying so hard. Of course, your ego will probably squeal resistance to the idea, but it may be time to give in to your shadow.

Give In to Shadow?

In *Do What You Love, the Money Will Follow,* Marsha Sinetar details how we get caught up in a vision of how we are "supposed" to work or express our creativity. Sinetar shares what a fellow writer has to say about her work habits: "I used to hate seeing myself lie there. It went against all my pictures of what I 'should' be doing and how I 'should' look. In my mind's eye, I felt that I was supposed to be a starched and immaculate vision in white all day, a Betty Crocker of the typewriter, constructively producing neat and clean copy twenty-four hours a day, like perfect cookies from the oven."

The problem is not to get rid of any symptom, but rather to deliberately and consciously try to increase that symptom, to deliberately and consciously experience it fully! If you are depressed, try to make yourself more depressed. If you are tense, make yourself even tenser.

KEN WILBER
The Spectrum of Consciousness

This is the ego's idea of what a writer should look and act like. A painter's ego, a dancer's ego, a quilt-maker's ego—whatever your creative expression, your ego has similarly silly ideas about what your creativity is "supposed" to look like. But, Sinetar points out, creativity doesn't really happen that way. The shadow has its own idea of what creativity looks and feels like, and since most of creativity lies outside the realm of the ego and in the realm of the shadow, the shadow knows! Our ego resists this truth, thus intensifying the mental isometrics.

Sinetar advises we accept our shadow's truth. She writes: "No other part of our personality reveals our basic temperament, our fundamental way of working, more than does our dark side—the part of ourselves which illogically unfolds at its own time and which has its own requirements. I'm referring to our uncontrollable impulses, the habits we simply can't break; the unacceptable, contradictory tendencies moving us in opposition to the way we intended to go."

Of course, these are the tendencies that are unacceptable and contradictory to the way *our ego* intended to go. They are not necessarily contradictory or unacceptable to our True Self, and in fact, may be exactly the tendencies that will revive the flow of our creative "juice."

As Sinetar points out, this realization doesn't mean we should indulge in habits that are truly harmful. (Although, even with harmful habits, the ego's will alone is never sufficient; to truly get past a harmful habit or an addiction, we have to first surrender to it. Once ego surrenders, True Self can act from the Moral Center, and change begins. As long as ego alone struggles with shadow, shadow will always win.)

Sinetar offers questions that we can ask ourselves to discover the value of those behaviors which our ego has decided are "bad habits" even though they aren't truly harmful. For instance, Sinetar asks if you have tried to suppress work habits so you could be more like others, if you have personality traits you thought were wrong and tried to hide, if you've abandoned activities or interests because you were told they weren't important, and if there are "time-out" activities you think you shouldn't do (like watching TV, reading, daydreaming, relaxing) that actually restore your energy.

Once you identify some of these habits, traits, interests, and time-out activities, wallow in them. Why would you want to wallow in bad habits? Think about what happens when you're in a tug-of-war with someone

Where so many hours have been spent in convincing myself that I am right, is there not some reason to fear I may be wrong?

JANE AUSTEN

and one of you suddenly lets go. There is a tremendous release of energy. To stop the mental isometrics, let go. Surrender your will. Consider this an experiment. Watch the cause and effect as you indulge yourself in these so-called bad habits for a while. See if they don't actually restore your energy, improve your life, and boost your creative output.

Once you get your ego out of the way, you allow yourself to receive help from your closest ally.

Yet it is in our idleness, in our dreams, that the submerged truth sometimes comes to the top.
VIRGINIA WOOLF

The Closest Ally of All

As you started identifying your allies in the last chapter, you were probably surprised to realize that some of the people you thought were your allies can't be and that some of the people who really can be your allies are people you hadn't thought of in that way before. But of all the allies you have available to you, your shadow is the best one of all. That's right, your shadow-self, the junk drawer of your psyche where your ego tosses everything it doesn't know what to do with, is the best resource you have in reclaiming your creative energy.

"Wait a minute!" your ego is undoubtedly protesting. "How can all those negative traits I pushed away so that I could be a good person and get along in the world be my best resource? This shadow stuff is what I've got to fight so hard against!"

Most of us have an adversarial relationship with our shadow. We fear it; we loathe it; we try to repress it; we hide it whenever we can. And when we can't hide it, we go to battle to keep it at bay and send it back underground as soon as we can "get control of ourselves" again. This is normal and understandable; after all, your ego is in charge of your survival. Your ego decided very early in your life what your best survival strategy was, and anything that didn't fit that strategy was sent into the shadow. A key piece of information is that your ego made these decisions when you were very young. You based your decisions on your best understanding, but of course, your best understanding of the world when you were five was pretty limited. Many of those decisions no longer apply.

This ego stance of battling the shadow is common and understandable; it's just not a stance that will help you become fully creative and fully your True Self. Your ego wants your shadow to remain hidden, and that means a good part of your creativity has to stay hidden too. On the other hand, your shadow wants to be recognized and accepted, your creative-self wants opportunities to express itself, and your psyche wants wholeness. Wholeness requires allowing your creativity and your shadow to come out and share the limelight with your ego. It means putting your ego in the right relationship with the other aspects of your Self.

Your ego wants to do battle, to conquer the shadow. But the conventional wisdom that "if you don't own your shadow, your shadow will own you" reflects the essential truth that battling the shadow only leads to more shadowboxing, more shadow skirmishes, more shadow warfare. Your shadow can't be defeated, so you may as well give up fighting with yourself. Embrace your shadow instead. You may not act out all your shadow's impulses, but you don't act out all your ego's impulses either. The fear that embracing your shadow will make you a horrible person is just a last-ditch defense by your ego-self, who is understandably worried about giving up control.

Remember you are larger than your ego. That larger Self is wise. By following the wisdom of your True Self, you can embrace your shadow without becoming your shadow. Follow the values and principles in your Moral Center, rather than the demands of either your ego or your shadow. When you do that, you'll find your creative blocks fall away. You will have more energy to do your creative work; you will also have a deeper understanding of humanity that will give your work depth and compassion.

Now the ego that is not in an egocentric state is an entirely different matter; it has a healthy creative relationship to both the shadow and the Self. The ego is not really diminished in the process of integration; it simply becomes less rigid in its boundaries.

JOHN A. SANFORD

Claiming the Saving Grace

Rejected, neglected, condemned, your shadow remains ever faithful. This aspect of yourself has waited and waited for you to turn a kind eye and a welcoming heart. Shadow waits for you because you need it so. You see, your shadow is your saving grace. It is what will save you.

As discussed earlier, you don't need to be Christian to recognize the wisdom of Jesus' words: "If you deny what is inside you, what is inside you will destroy you. If you embrace what is inside you, what is inside you will save you." Jesus didn't use the term *shadow*, but he certainly understood the concept and its significance.

When we look at the characters in a movie or a story as aspects of ourselves, we can gain a deeper appreciation for the story and for our own complexity. For example, in the movie *Forrest Gump*, Forrest can be understood as one aspect of our shadow. He is certainly a shadow figure for the character of Lieutenant Dan. Forrest is innocent and simple, even stupid, and willing to follow orders. Lieutenant Dan, on the other hand, is sophisticated, even cynical, and knows his way around. Dan is supposed to be a leader, and he doesn't want to be like Forrest. Yet while Dan wants to be a hero and a martyr, Forrest is the one who is truly heroic and self-sacrificing. After Forrest saves his life, Dan sees Forrest as the source of all his problems, hates Forrest for it, and tries to kill him.

Grace fills empty spaces, but it can only enter where there is a void to receive it, and it is grace itself which makes this void.
SIMONE WEIL

Not only does Forrest save Dan's life twice—once by carrying him to safety out of a forest in Vietnam and again by carrying him out of the forest of his own self-pity and despair—Forrest also embodies the saving grace Dan needs. Dan needs the kind of self-acceptance that Forrest has. And when Dan humbles himself enough to allow Forrest to be the captain of his shrimp boat for a while, Dan faces his fear and makes his peace with his Creator and his life. Dan is healed; he becomes truly whole. And the next time we see Dan in the movie, he is out of his wheelchair and in a relationship, standing on what Forrest calls "magic legs."

But notice that once Dan has accepted Forrest's lead and becomes whole, he is able to share his own gifts with Forrest. It is Dan's wise investments that ensure Forrest's financial future, something Forrest probably could not have done for himself. Like the combination Forrest and Dan make together, we must develop a right relationship between ego and shadow. We embrace our shadow as our captain, our guide, without letting it become our commander. Hans Christian Andersen's fable *The Shadow* (appendix A) highlights the risk of letting our shadow become our master. The fastest way to allow your shadow to master you is to try to send it away. It is only by accepting our shadow that we can allow it to be our guide. If we can learn to do that, our shadow will bring the saving grace we need to become the creative, wise, and loving people we are meant to be.

✍ Exercise: Accept Your Saving Grace

Remember the shadow character you played the part of in the Best of the Worst exercise in chapter 6. Consider what saving grace that shadow character offers you. Journal about it. Ask trusted friends what similarities they see between you and your shadow character and what that shadow character does well that you may need to work on.

The next time you have a "shadow outburst" or "shadow slip," journal afterward about what you may need to bring from your shadow into your everyday consciousness and behavior. For example, maybe you don't need to snap at people, but you do need to respectfully state your own desires more directly.

❄ Guided Imagery

In this guided imagery, you will return to the same beautiful place and talk again with the same shadow character you discovered in the guided imagery for chapter 6. Before you start this guided imagery, take a few moments to remember the guided imagery you did in chapter 6. Look back at what you drew or journaled at the end of that guided imagery.

As you've done in earlier guided imageries, find a place and time when you can be relaxed and uninterrupted. Lie or sit comfortably and begin to relax. Close your eyes. Take several deep breaths, noticing and following the breath in and out of your body.

Consciously tighten the muscles in your feet and ankles. Notice the tension. . . . Feel the tension in all the muscles in your feet. . . . Hold the tension as long as you like . . . holding it until you're ready to let it go with a sigh. . . . Take a deep breath and notice how it feels to let go, to feel the warm relaxation in your feet. . . .

Now, consciously tighten the muscles in your calves and knees. Notice the tension. . . . Feel the tension in your calves and knees. . . . Hold the tension . . . until you're ready to let it go with a sigh. . . . Take a deep breath and notice how good it feels to let your calves and your knees relax and go slack. . . .

Consciously tighten the muscles in your thighs, buttocks, and pelvis.

> *They (repressed emotions and images) are dangerous only when kept prisoner, and it requires lots of energy to keep them locked up and tranquilized. When they appear on the paper, a vibrant energy floods the body and you feel relieved because you don't have to stand guard anymore.*
>
> **MICHELL CASSOU**
> and
> **STEWART CUBLEY**
> *Life, Paint and Passion*

Notice the tension. . . . Feel the tension in your thighs and buttocks and pelvis. . . . Hold the tension . . . until you're ready to let it go with a sigh. . . . Take a deep breath and notice how good it feels to let the lower half of your body relax more and more with each breath you take. . . .

Take another deep breath and consciously tighten the muscles in your stomach, chest, and back. Feel the tension in your torso. . . . Notice what it feels like to hold tension in this part of your body. . . . Hold that tension . . . until you're ready to let it go with a sigh. . . . Take a deep, slow breath and notice how good it feels to breathe all the way down to your belly . . . how good it feels to let your belly go soft and round with each breath. . . .

Now, consciously tighten your hands into fists. Feel the tension move from your hands to your wrists, your forearms, elbows, upper arms, into your shoulders and the base of your neck. . . . Notice that tension, what it feels like . . . holding it until you're ready to let it go with a sigh. . . . Take a deep breath and notice how good it feels to let any remaining tension ooze out of your fingertips. . . . Notice how good it feels to let your shoulders drop and let your arms relax more and more. . . .

Now, consciously tighten the muscles in your jaw and neck; scrunch up the muscles around your eyes and forehead. . . . Notice the tension in your face and neck . . . holding it until you're ready to let it go with a sigh. . . . Notice how good it feels to let your whole body become more and more relaxed . . . more and more relaxed with every breath. . . .

Continue to breathe deeply. If worries or thoughts about other things come to you, simply remind yourself, "Not this, not now," set the thought aside, and return your attention to your breathing. Allow your breath to assume a slow, natural rhythm.

Experience your whole body now as relaxed . . . your mind as quiet and still . . . your emotions as calm and clear . . . your spirit as peaceful and serene. . . .

From this place of inner serenity, harmony, and relaxation, begin to allow images to occur in your mind. . . . Imagine a beautiful and peaceful place, the same beautiful place you visited before. . . . Notice the colors, shapes, and textures. . . . Notice the feel of the ground beneath you. . . . Notice the sounds around you. . . . Notice the freshness of the air. . . . Begin to see yourself relaxing in this beautiful place. . . . Feel yourself there. . . . Experience being completely comfortable and relaxed in this beautiful, peaceful place. . . .

And now, you notice the trickling sound of water flowing over rocks. You look around and find the stream you hear. . . . Follow the stream up and around, following it upstream until you come to its source. . . . Where you find a cave . . . the same cave you visited before . . . you know that this cave is a sacred place . . . and it is completely safe. . . . The walls and ceiling are solid. . . . There is plenty of fresh air moving in and out of the cave. . . . So you follow the stream into the cave. . . .

You walk slowly in the fading daylight, down into the cave, following the stream. . . . You walk down a tunnel, down into the cave . . . it gets darker and darker as you go deeper and deeper into the cave. . . . The sound of the water increases and you find a small waterfall. . . . Behind the waterfall, you find stone steps. . . . You walk down the stone steps as they spiral down and around, deeper into the cave . . . down and around . . . down and around. . . .

Finally you come to an open area deep inside the cave, deep inside your own True Self. . . . You notice that the walls glow slightly . . . just enough for you to find your way. . . . Explore this room . . . notice the rocks, the crystals. . . . Notice the sound of water dripping. . . . And here, deep in the cave, deep in your Self, you sit and wait. . . .

You hear footsteps of someone or something coming toward you from the depths of the cave. . . . You turn to see who is coming. . . . It is the same character who approached you before . . . the same character you described as one of the best of the worst. . . .

As this character comes closer and closer, notice how you feel about meeting this character again. . . . Notice how you feel as you realize this character carries what you need to live the creative life you yearn for. . . . This shadow figure carries your saving grace. . . . Your shadow is willing to give you this saving grace if you will only ask for it. . . . If you will only open your hands and your heart to receive it. . . .

Here, in the depths of the sacred, in the depths of your True Self, spend some time with your shadow. . . . Spend some time opening your heart to your saving grace. . . . Notice whether there are any other characters who want to talk to you . . . who want to give you gifts of grace. . . .

In a few moments, you're going to leave this cave, so finish talking with this shadow character . . . and begin walking back up and around the stone steps . . . up and around . . . until you emerge from behind the waterfall. . . . Walk back up the tunnel toward the light of day . . . following the stream

I think that when I get blocked, it's that I have something to say but I don't want to say it. So my mind says "I have nothing to say." Closer to the truth is that I have a thought I really would prefer not to have.

PAUL SIMON

back, back up the tunnel toward the light . . . back to the sacred and beautiful place you where you began. . . . Find a place to sit down and reflect on the saving grace your shadow carries for you. . . .

In a few moments, you're going to leave this beautiful and sacred place. . . . Slowly return your attention to this room . . . to your body lying on the floor or sitting in the chair. . . . When you're ready, open your eyes. Move slowly and gently to find a marker or crayon and draw the saving grace and the gifts you received. After drawing, write any other impressions you want to remember.

Creative Shadow Play

Go back to the Creative Shadow Play in chapter 6 and once again play the role of a shadow character, this time the role of the character who appeared in your guided imagery. Notice what saving grace you can find in this character, what gifts this character has that you need to incorporate into your life. Notice, too, what happens to your energy level as you play this role.

⊙ EXERCISE CHOICES

1. Re-examine Your Projections. Take another look at exercise 3 in chapter 3. Can you see what saving grace there may be in things that have always bugged you? Instead of projecting these qualities onto others and wasting energy shadowboxing, consider how you can consciously bring these "negative" qualities into your life. If you're irritated by people who are late, for example, maybe you need to lighten up your perceptions about time. Maybe you need to find ways to "waste" time or not schedule every minute of your day.

2. Add a Drawing or Picture of Your Shadow to the Ally Collage You Made in the Creative Shadow Play for Chapter 7. Or, make a new collage of your shadow and the saving graces it holds for you.

3. Watch for Falling Projections. Remember, we all tend to project our shadow onto others. As you've worked with the material in this book, you've probably noticed that you are both more aware of your shadow and more likely to project it at times. This increased tendency to project your shadow can be disconcerting unless you keep in mind that this is part of your growth process. Just be sure to keep asking yourself how other people's "bad" behavior reflects your shadow. If you're sure you would never do whatever it is you're upset about, you've probably spent a good deal of energy keeping not only the behavior, but also the desire to behave in that way, in your shadow. Keep looking until the projection falls away and you recognize your own shadow.

Just for a kick, not to show anyone, and especially not to beat yourself up with, keep a record of your projections this week. Remember, everyone projects. It's not a sin; it's human nature and your psyche's way of bringing you to wholeness. Just notice the ways you project this week as a source of valuable information.

4. Take Back Your Projected Artist. Make a list of the people you have projected creativity onto or given your creative power to. This may include teachers, authors, "real artists," people who do what you want to do for money, and other experts or authorities. Anytime you've said or thought that another person is a better artist or more creative or talented than you, you have projected your creativity. Call these people or write them a letter to say, "Give me back my artist." They probably won't know what you're talking about, but that's okay, because you do. You are reclaiming your own creativity, seeing it as yours. (You don't have to actually mail the letters, if you don't want to.) If you'd rather, you can visualize or draw yourself taking back your artist, or write about it, or dance it.

5. Make a Gift List. List all the gifts your shadow just might hold for you.

6. Check It Twice. Make a list of the qualities you wish you possessed. How many of these are on the list of gifts your shadow offers you?

7. Remember, Practice Makes Perfect. Practice one of the qualities from exercise 6 daily. Make a reminder in your date book or on your bathroom mirror: "Be outrageous today!" or "Stay open to crazy ideas!" Watch for opportunities to practice this quality in *small* ways every day.

8. Ask Yourself, "What If No One Would Object?" Freewrite for five minutes or so, completing the phrase, "If no one would object, I would _____." Include all the things you censor yourself from doing or trying because you're afraid of what other people would say or think or do if you did these things. Include all the so-called bad habits you think you shouldn't indulge in.

Freewrite for another five minutes completing the phrase, "If no one would object, I would stop _____." Include all the things you make yourself do or try to do because you're afraid of what other people will say or think or do if you didn't.

Do this exercise a couple of times this week. Once you've included as many things as you can think of on both lists, read the following paragraph:

You are not limited by these other people. You are only limited by your chosen responses to their *anticipated* responses. If you believe your happiness is dependent on another person's mood or behavior, *you* have limited yourself severely. You might not decide to do all the things you said you'd try if no one would object, or give up all the things you do because of what others might expect. But do reconsider your reasons. Do you do what you do because of what others will do in response, or do you do what you do because of who you are? Are you reacting or are you self-determining? One perspective is that even being reactionary is a choice—a choice to accept the illusion of limitation.

9. Identify Your Exercises. Make a list of the projects or activities you feel blocked in. These are the projects where you are practicing mental isometrics. I had long periods of struggling with writing a book proposal and then with writing the book itself—my ambition to get the book published on the one hand pushing against my fear and distrust of giving my "baby" to strangers (editors, publishers' sales reps, and so on) on the other. Identifying the sources of the block, where and why you're doing mental isometrics, is an important step.

10. Take a Break. Let go of the struggle you identified in exercise 9. Easier said than done, I know, but it's possible. Consider ways you can work with yourself, not against yourself. I kept asking, "How can I use my fear to get the book published? How can I reassure myself? How can I let go of my mistrust?" The most important recognition is that fighting with yourself is taking you nowhere anyway, so why not just give up, at least for a while. Strange, but it works. Set a time limit on the break, and when time is up, go back to the project. You may be quite surprised to find you aren't struggling to do it, but are simply doing it.

11. Practice Patience. Patience is another name for the card game solitaire. In "With Solitaire, She Lays Her Cards on the Table," an article published in the *Minneapolis Star Tribune*, Trudi Hahn describes how learning a new version of solitaire called *le parterre*, the flowerbed, distracted her long enough to let the solutions to her problems fall into place. She writes, "The crisp flourishes of the shuffles between games became an anchor for my unconscious mind while it sorted questions. . . . The first time I won *le parterre* without violating the rules, the celebration culminated with me at the computer massaging an essay I'd been avoiding. After digging the weeds out of all those flowerbeds (clearing the solitaire layout), writing was easy."

So get a deck of cards and begin shuffling to anchor your own unconscious. Practice patience, with a solitaire deck or another diversion of your choosing. I recommend you start with the real cards rather than the computer version. After you get a feel for what practicing patience feels like with the soothing practice of shuffling the cards with your hands, you can try it with the computer to see if it gives you the same relaxing effect.

The trick is to find something that will distract you, but not completely numb you out. And, of course, try not to spend too much time distracting yourself. How much is too much? Only you can decide, but as in exercise 10, setting a time limit is a good idea.

Work is love made visible. And if you cannot work with love but only with distaste, it is better that you should leave your work and sit at the gate of the temple and take alms of those who work with joy. For if you bake bread with indifference, you bake a bitter loaf that feeds but half a man's hunger.

KAHLIL GIBRAN
The Prophet

CHAPTER *9*

Commit Yourself

Going Deeper

ALTHOUGH YOU MAY HAVE DECIDED to let your shadow be your ally instead of treating it like an enemy, your ego will probably still want to lead, deciding when and how it will accept help from your shadow. This may sound like a good idea, but it will never really work. Your shadow is simply not that tame, and your ego is not that wise.

If you put your ego in charge, it will be far too easy to slide back into the old pattern of trying to keep your shadow underground until it's a good, safe, convenient time to deal with it, which is never. Your shadow will certainly get tired of waiting and will continue to make its presence known through lasting creative blocks and explosive shadow appearances when you least expect them.

But it's also clear that the shadow can't be in command either. So what part of you should be in charge?

Albert Einstein once said that a problem can never be solved on the same level it was created on, that we have to go to another level to find a solution. Until now, the problem has been that your ego- and shadow-self have been adversaries. So, the solution cannot be found at the level of ego and shadow. We have to go to a higher or deeper level; we have to leave the ego center behind and turn our attention and intention to the Creative Center, the True Center of our True Self.

Remember that Carl Jung said our Creative Center is our Moral Center, where our values and principles lie. When you commit yourself to live from the True Center of your psyche, you commit yourself to being fully yourself, fully creative, fully alive. When you do this, your creativity becomes your life, and all your life is creative.

In practical terms, this means you will no longer blindly follow either ego demands or shadow outbursts. Instead, you take the time to recognize the values and principles you hold most dear and then choose actions that reflect those values. Of course, it takes a long time to develop and refine your ability to follow the lead of your True Center—years of practice. But then, Jung did say that developing the ego is the task of childhood and early adulthood, and that integrating the shadow is the task of middle adulthood. Learning to live from our True Center, according to Jung, is the apprentice work that will lead us to become the masterpieces we are born to become.

What is important right now, today, is to make the commitment to begin this practice.

✍ Exercise: Discover Your Values

It can be surprisingly difficult to identify which values you consider most significant. Because they are so very important to us, we tend to take our values for granted. We lose awareness of them until we are jarred when someone else doesn't respect what we value or until we regretfully realize that we have sacrificed our own values for the sake of convenience. Subtle as they may be, it is vital that we identify our values.

Here is a three-step value identification process I've adopted from my personal coach, Valerie Olson. First, list ten to fifteen principles you value. This is just a first draft, so it's okay if you aren't clear yet exactly how to phrase things or what order to put the values in. It is also okay to combine values that seem to fit together. For instance, one of my values is "Spiritual connection/nature/beauty/recognizing the Divine," which reflects how my spirituality is connected to being in nature and recognizing beauty in the natural world. Be sure to include what really is important to you, not just what you think you're "supposed" to value.

Keep asking yourself, "What do I value most? If I were moving to an alien planet, what values would be most important for me to bring?" Or, "If I could set up a perfect society, what values would I have the members of that society share?" These values should reflect the essence of who you are.

Such a man knows that whatever is wrong in the world is in himself, and if he only learns to deal with his own shadow he has done something real for the world. He has succeeded in shouldering at least an infinitesimal part of the gigantic, unsolved social problems of our day.
CARL JUNG

You'll need a friend (or personal coach) to help you with the second step. Tell your friend about three to five experiences when you felt deeply moved. They might be peak creative experiences, peak spiritual experiences, or times when you felt deep love, pride and satisfaction, or extreme anger. As you describe what happened and how you felt, both you and your friend should be listening for how these situations reflect your values. For example, describing a time you were very angry will suggest which of your values were violated. Describing a time when you were in the creative flow will highlight what makes you feel fulfilled and how you were able to express your values. Your descriptions will reveal how the values you previously listed are connected and which values are most important to you. They may even reveal values that are so much a part of you, you couldn't see them before. Values are the lenses we see the world through, and, as anyone who wears glasses can tell you, it can be difficult to really see your glasses because you are so used to seeing *through* them.

Finally, with the help of your friend, list your top ten values, in no particular order. Both you and your friend should feel that this list reflects the essence of who you really are.

When you are satisfied that your top values are included, take a few minutes by yourself to rank the values, starting with most crucial as number one. Don't be surprised if ranking your values is difficult; after all, these values are all essential to you.

Make copies of your values to keep in your date book or planner, on a wall in your work space, and in your bedroom or bathroom. Remember, you are making a commitment to live your life in accordance with these values.

The world will little note nor long remember what we say here.

ABRAHAM LINCOLN in his address at Gettysburg

Fulfilling Your Creative Purpose

The "Desiderata" assures us, "You are a child of the universe, no less than the trees and the stars. You have a right to be here." Let me assure you, you have a reason to be here too. Whether you realize it yet or not, you have a purpose, a creative purpose, to fulfill. There is a reason you are here on planet Earth at this time. There is a reason you have had the experiences you've had, met the people you've met, lived the life you've lived. Your purpose is the reason you were created and the reason you, in turn, create. Each one of us has a creative gift to give.

Spaceship Earth carries no passengers, only crew members. Each and every one of us has a unique set of skills and abilities, and each of us has unique gifts to bring forth. When we delay sharing what we came to share, we degrade the quality of life for everyone and everything that shares our little blue spaceship.

There aren't just a few special people in the world who get to make a difference; we are all special and everything we do matters. Recognizing that you have a creative purpose is both lofty and humbling at the same time. You're special, just like everyone else.

You knew why you were coming to Earth before you arrived, but your ego had to struggle so to get born, get fed, get warm, get loved, and get recognized. The ego struggle of getting those survival needs met drove the memory of your real mission from your awareness. Still, there were and are moments of clear, passionate knowing that, "Oh my God, this is it!" Those thrilling moments, those peak creative experiences when you feel most alive, are vital clues. This passion is a message from your Creator, encoded in emotion so it will be noticed again and again. The message is, "This is it! Remember this. This is what you are here for!"

I know not what you believe in God, but I believe He gave yearnings and longings to be filled, and that He did not mean all our time should be devoted to feeding and clothing the body.
LUCY STONE

✍ Exercise: Remember Your Purpose

At a deep level, you *know* what your creative purpose is. You don't have to invent it, you only have to remember it. Take some time to write a draft of your creative purpose, what Stephen Covey would call a personal mission statement. You might write one or two sentences or a paragraph or two—whatever it takes to clearly state the reason you're here, what you are meant to do, who you are meant to be. Read this every day and revise it as your memory of your purpose becomes clearer and clearer.

Saving the World

When you follow your creative dreams and live in accordance with your values, you make a commitment to fulfilling this creative purpose. It's surprisingly simple: Commit to doing what you love in ways that reflect your values. This commitment will give you a path to follow. As you follow this path, you will find many places where your creative purpose intersects with the needs of others. True success is taking advantage of these opportunities to provide service while remaining true to your own journey. For example, Jacques Cousteau didn't start diving because he was guaranteed fame and fortune; he started diving because he loved the ocean. Because he followed his passion, he was able to share the beauty of the oceans with millions of people, develop new oceanographic research techniques and equipment, and alert the world to the crisis in our oceans. On a less publicized but equally important level, Dr. Glen Booth, a general practitioner, focused on how his own fascination with meditation and visualization intersected with the needs of his patients. In doing so, he has discovered satisfaction and joy in assisting some of his patients as they participate in their own healing through guided visualization.

Of course, as you follow your path, you will have to explore and embrace your creativity and your shadow. This commitment will naturally reveal the deep truth about the significance of shadow in creative work and bring the joy of creative play to shadow work. Your commitment to do your creative work and your shadow work is essential to your soul, to your spiritual growth. It is also absolutely vital to your family, your local community, and our larger global community.

It is abundantly clear that our world is in crisis—and our creative and shadow work are necessary to resolve the crisis. In the preface to *Shadow in America*, Jeremiah Abrams quotes Anthony Stevens:

> At this very moment in the history of humankind, evolution has put us on the spot. There is an urgent biological imperative to make the shadow conscious. The moral burden of this immense task is greater than any previous generation could have even conceived: the destiny of the planet and our entire solar system. Only by coming to terms with our nature—and the nature of the Shadow—can we hope to avert total catastrophe.

Being reminded again about the environmental, financial, and social crises facing not just our local communities but also our entire planet can make us throw up our hands and say, "What I can do about it? If the world is in such rough shape, who am I to express my little creativity?"

The bottom line is not how fast you make your dream come true, but how steadily you pursue it.

SARAH BAN BREATHNACH
Simple Abundance

The only thing that any of us can do about the crisis brought on by our shared "collective shadow" is our own work. That means our own shadow work and our own creative work. Both are the work of the soul. Fortunately, doing our own work is all we really need to do.

Later in the preface to *Shadow in America*, Abrams writes,

> *Every year I resolve*
> *to be a little less*
> *the me I know*
> *and leave a little room*
> *for the me I could be.*
> WENDY WASSERSTEIN

If enough of us carry our share of the darkness and open ourselves compassionately to the world around us, then—as a nation and as individuals—we add to the critical mass of awareness that is helping to create a compassionate culture, one that can tolerate paradox and ambiguity, one that allows these qualities to coexist with order and clarity.... Shadow work *is* soul work. And the frontier where we confront the shadow is, as it has always been, within one's own sphere of influence, within one's personal sense of joy and suffering, within the individual soul.

I can't speak for Jacques Cousteau, but Glen Booth is a friend (and former student) of mine, so I know he has done and continues to do his creative shadow work. Following his passion and facing his shadow empowers him to be of service to the world.

Making a commitment to live from your own True Center and to do your creative shadow work is the greatest gift you can give the world. It is both your divine right and your divine responsibility to fulfill your creative purpose by honoring this commitment. As Julia Cameron writes in *The Artist's Way*, "Creativity is God's gift to us. Using our creativity is our gift back to God."

✍ Exercise: Make the Commitment

Your commitment is just that: *your* commitment. I encourage you to write a statement of your commitment. You can use the following Commitment Statement and Alternative Commitment Statement that I share with students as a guide.

Commitment Statement

I, _____, commit myself to exploring and embracing my True Self, the larger Self that encompasses not only my usual ego consciousness, but also the bright light of my full creativity and the depth of my shadow. Just for today, I accept the fullness of my humanity, my imperfections and mistakes as well as my innate creativity and divine nature. Just for today, I acknowledge that there is more to me than I imagine or am usually aware of, and I am willing to know and embrace all parts of me that are revealed. Just for today, I will choose my actions from my Moral Center, not my ego desires or shadow demands. I, _____, make this commitment for my own ultimate benefit and for the greater good of all the people I connect with.

Alternative Commitment Statement

(to be read when the Commitment Statement feels overwhelming)
Today, I, _____, ask for a reprieve. Today, I am unwilling to face the overwhelming, unending task of self-knowledge and self-acceptance. I want to focus instead on the small details: to savor my food or my friends, to contemplate the movement of clouds or a leaf in the wind, to notice the feel of a rock or the sound of water. Today, I notice the small, light gifts of grace I receive. And I know this awareness of the light and the small is also for my ultimate growth and the benefit of all those I connect with.

After drafting your Commitment Statement or an Alternative Commitment Statement, make a copy on colored or parchment paper and hang it someplace where you will see it often. Use a gold calligraphy pen (or other special colors) to illuminate your Commitment Statement with lines or drawings. You may want to illuminate your list of values (from pages 162–163) in a similar way.

For at least three weeks, read your values list and your Commitment Statement once a day.

The Significance of the Small

Many of us have been trained to give ourselves away in small and meaningless ways that leave us without the time, energy, or permission to create the larger gifts we came here to give. That's why it is absolutely

Shoot for the moon.
Even if you miss it
you will land
among the stars.
LES BROWN

imperative that we choose our priorities and learn how to hold boundaries that will preserve our time and energy so we can fulfill our purpose in life.

Many of us have tried using deadlines to hold our boundaries. "I will finish the first draft by April 15," or, "I will finish five full-size paintings by May 1." But that doesn't seem to work. We know our self-imposed deadlines aren't as "real" as the ones our boss or family or whoever gives us. We find ourselves saying, "I want to work on my project sometime, but I really have to work on this report today (or clean the house before Bill's birthday party, or whatever)." We think it will only be a small delay, but the net result of all those small delays is that self-imposed deadlines tend to be in perpetual slide. "Okay, I'll do the taxes this weekend, and I'll get the first draft done by May 15." If we're honest, we recognize that May 15 is another way of saying "sometime later."

Not only does "sometime" never come, but deadlines make our creativity feel like just another onerous task we *have* to do instead of an opportunity to follow the direction of our Creative Center. We don't need more deadlines; we need to adjust our attitude to acknowledge, "Yes, I'd rather work on this report than try to explain to my boss why it isn't finished, *and* I want to ensure I have two hours to work on my own priorities today. That is, after all, my commitment to myself. So what alternatives do I have?"

> *I long to accomplish a great and noble task, but it is my chief duty to accomplish small tasks as if they were great and noble.*
> HELEN KELLER

Daily Do-ables

The best method I've found for me and my students to honor our priorities and fulfill our creative purpose is a practice of taking at least one action—large or small—every day. I call it the "daily do-able": What can I do today to further my journey to where I want to be and honor my commitment to myself?

It is vital to focus on your commitment every day. Ten minutes every day will have far more impact than a three-hour chunk every month or so. You need to remind yourself that you have made a commitment to yourself and take time to honor that commitment. If you don't, other people's desires and demands will take over your life. The best way to give credibility to your commitment is to invest time every day.

Taking action on a daily basis also keeps fear from immobilizing you. Just keep moving a little bit—taking baby steps—day after day. Take small, regular risks. Push on the edge of your comfort zone regularly, until pushing on the edge becomes a habit and you start to call that funny feeling in your gut "excitement" instead of "terror."

Some of your daily do-ables will be things you do every day or nearly every day. For example, to support my long-range goal of exploring my shadow and becoming fully creative, I journal every morning, record my dreams, and walk my dog in the park nearly every afternoon. Daily do-ables like these become habits that sustain us on the days we feel scattered or discouraged. We can remind ourselves, "Well, at least I did my journaling today."

The big advantage in developing a habit is that you just do it. I don't go through the debate every morning about whether or not I'm going to do my pages; I just do them. Habits short-circuit the whole will-I-or-won't-I debate, which frees up a lot of time and mental energy. I suggest you select one small daily do-able to make into a habit. For at least three weeks, do this task without any question or debate. Just do it because this is now what you do.

Some do-ables are regular, but not daily. I worked on this book three or four days a week. You might meet with a friend for coffee and writing exercises on Saturday mornings. Or take a watercolor or a pottery class once a week. Or meet with a therapist or support group once every week or two.

Other do-ables change from day to day. We do them and they're done. One day you'll do research, another day you'll buy supplies, another day you'll complete a project.

The point is to commit to doing something every day that you recognize as furthering your journey and then honoring that commitment. One or two steps every day is what it takes.

One does not discover new lands without consenting to lose sight of the shore for a very long time.
ANDRÉ GIDE

Recording Your Steps

An excellent way to ensure you take daily action is to record the highlights in a pocket notebook or in your planner. Recording what you've done reinforces and rewards you in this new habit. It also provides solace when you feel discouraged; you can take a look at all you've done to honor your commitment so far. Outcomes are often beyond our control, but we do have an obligation to do our "footwork," that is, to take the steps we can. Here are a few sample notebook entries:

2/6/99 What I did to honor my commitment to exploring my
Self today:
- ► bought this notebook
- ► read my Commitment Statement out loud
- ► went to library during lunch—read about Viktor Frankl
- ► journaled in the morning
- ► freewrote about how my life will look when I've finished my play

2/7/99 What I did to explore my Creative Center today:
- ► read yesterday's entry
- ► read my Commitment Statement out loud
- ► bought new canvas, brushes, and other supplies
NOTE: grant application deadline coming up

2/8/99 What I did today for my creativity:
- ► journaled this morning—got a great idea there
- ► painted for an hour

As you can see, the daily steps don't need to be huge. They just need
to be regular.

Action Mapping

When you have a large project, you may want to give more direction to
your daily do-ables. This is when I recommend action mapping, a practice I learned from my best friend, Claudia, who uses this process to
help organizations develop strategic plans.

You begin this process by identifying the priority, results, participants, resources, critical success factors, and the scope of the project.
Use the following questions to help you identify these factors:

PRIORITY STATEMENT: State your priority. Remind yourself why this is
important to you.

RESULTS: How will you know when you have accomplished this priority?
Express the outcome in noun-verb format. For example: quilt completed, contest entry submitted, garden planted, contract signed.

*The ultimate measure
of a man is not
where he stands
in moments of comfort
and convenience,
but where he stands
at times of challenge
and controversy.*

MARTIN LUTHER KING JR.

What other qualities are important in the result? For example: have fun, feel more confident, fits my personal mission statement, feel satisfied and proud.

PARTICIPANTS: Besides yourself, who will be involved with this priority? Who will be affected by the actions you take in moving toward this priority? List the people and how they participate.

RESOURCES NEEDED: List the materials, equipment, space, people, and financial and time resources you'll need.

CRITICAL SUCCESS FACTORS: What has to happen for this priority to be accomplished? What do you need to do well? What do you need to be sure to consider? If you have an audience or customers, what are their requirements?

SCOPE OF ACTION: What is the first step you'll take? What is the last step you'll take?

Once you've answered these questions, begin the action mapping by putting the first and last action steps on separate Post-it Notes. Place them at the beginning and end of an action map area, which is any large open space like a door, a wall, or a large, blank piece of paper.

Ask yourself, "What do I need to do before the last step?" or, "What do I need to do next?" or simply, "What else will I need to do?" Write other action steps on Post-it Notes as they occur to you and place them on the map area. The action map needs to be flexible and open to change as you add to the plan and begin the process itself. You will probably need to move the action steps around as you go, which is why they're written on separate Post-it Notes rather than on the mapping surface.

A primary action step may have substeps or details you want to remember. You can write these substeps or details on smaller Post-it Notes and attach them to the primary action step's note.

To make the action map more appealing and functional, add color, size, and dimension to your separate action step Post-it Notes by using different color notepads, writing with colored markers, making the size of the writing different, adding stickers to illustrate ideas, or making your own simple drawings on the Post-it Notes.

Vision without action is simply hallucination.
CHRISTOPHER HAGERTY

Keep It Simple

At its essence, the formula is really very simple. Do what you are passionate about doing in ways that reflect your values and allow you to be of service. Everything else is detail. And when you're on the path you're meant to travel, details have a way of falling into place.

But most women are not aware of their tremendous power for good. We are asleep to our Divinity. . . . Aren't you shaping unseen forces with your creativity and soulcrafts, bringing into the physical world through passion what has only existed in the spiritual realm? If you can do this unconsciously, how much more could you accomplish if you were fully aware of your powers?

SARAH BAN BREATHNACH
Simple Abundance

※ *Guided Imagery*

As you've done in earlier guided imageries, find a place and time when you can be relaxed and uninterrupted. Lie or sit comfortably and begin to relax. Close your eyes. Take several deep breaths, noticing and following the breath in and out of your body.

Consciously tighten the muscles in your feet and ankles. Notice the tension. . . . Feel the tension in all the muscles in your feet. . . . Hold the tension as long as you like . . . holding it until you're ready to let it go with a sigh. . . . Take a deep breath and notice how it feels to let go, to feel the warm relaxation in your feet. . . .

Now, consciously tighten the muscles in your calves and knees. Notice the tension. . . . Feel the tension in your calves and knees. . . . Hold the tension . . . until you're ready to let it go with a sigh. . . . Take a deep breath and notice how good it feels to let your calves and your knees relax and go slack. . . .

Consciously tighten the muscles in your thighs, buttocks, and pelvis. Notice the tension. . . . Feel the tension in your thighs and buttocks and pelvis. . . . Hold the tension . . . until you're ready to let it go with a sigh. . . . Take a deep breath and notice how good it feels to let the lower half of your body relax more and more with each breath you take. . . .

Take another deep breath and consciously tighten the muscles in your stomach, chest, and back. Feel the tension in your torso. . . . Notice what it feels like to hold tension in this part of your body. . . . Hold that tension . . . until you're ready to let it go with a sigh. . . . Take a deep, slow breath and notice how good it feels to breathe all the way down to your belly . . . how good it feels to let your belly go soft and round with each breath. . . .

Now, consciously tighten your hands into fists. Feel the tension move from your hands to your wrists, your forearms, elbows, upper arms, into your shoulders, and the base of your neck. . . . Notice that tension, what it feels like . . . holding it until you're ready to let it go with a sigh. . . . Take a deep breath and notice how good it feels to let any remaining tension ooze out of your fingertips . . . notice how good it feels to let your shoulders drop and let your arms relax more and more. . . .

Now, consciously tighten the muscles in your jaw and neck; scrunch up the muscles around your eyes and forehead. . . . Notice the tension in your face and neck . . . holding it until you're ready to let it go with a sigh. . . . Notice how good it feels to let your whole body become more and more relaxed . . . more and more relaxed with every breath. . . .

Continue to breathe deeply. If worries or thoughts about other things come to you, simply remind yourself, "Not this, not now," set the thought aside, and return your attention to your breathing. Allow your breath to assume a slow, natural rhythm.

Experience your whole body now as relaxed . . . your mind as quiet and still . . . your emotions as calm and clear . . . your spirit as peaceful and serene. . . .

From this place of inner serenity, harmony, and relaxation, begin to allow images to occur in your mind. . . . Imagine a sacred place . . . a church or a temple . . . a place where people gather to celebrate sacred rituals. . . . You slowly and reverently enter this sacred space. . . . Notice the colors, shapes, and textures all around you . . . notice the sounds . . . the smells of incense or candles or sacred herbs. . . . Take some time to explore this sacred place, allowing it to become more and more vivid in your mind. . . .

As you explore this place, you notice it has been prepared for a special ceremony . . . there are flowers and candles and other symbols you recognize as important when celebrating a wedding . . . and you notice you are dressed for a wedding, for your wedding. . . . You walk slowly down a long aisle to the altar, wondering where your beloved is . . . you walk up to the altar, dressed for your wedding, waiting for your beloved. . . . You see your betrothed moving toward you. . . . You realize that your beloved, your betrothed, is your own shadow-self. . . . You are finally ready to accept your shadow as your partner . . . ready to embrace your shadow as your beloved. . . . So when your shadow comes close, you hold hands. . . .

You look up to see that the person officiating at this special wedding is your Higher Self. . . . Your True Self beams with love and appreciation . . .

Each time a man stands up for an ideal, or the lot of others, or strikes out against injustice, he sends forth a tiny ripple of hope.
ROBERT F. KENNEDY

honored to finally join you in a holy sacrament that symbolizes the union within....

Take some time now to listen to the vows your shadow makes to you ... to love ... to cherish.... (pause)

Listen to yourself as you offer your own vows to your shadow ... to love ... to cherish.... (pause)

Finally you listen to your True Self offer words of wisdom to sanctify this most profound union.... (pause)

Take all the time you need now to experience this ritual of union.... (pause)

When your True Self concludes the wedding ritual, you embrace your shadow ... you close your eyes and sigh ... feeling safe and warm in your beloved's arms ... holding your beloved safe and warm in your arms.... Feel yourself merging with your beloved, melding with your beloved ... truly the two become one ... until you can no longer distinguish which parts of yourself you had sent away ... until you are embracing yourself, all of yourself ... feeling a profound love that will now allow you to truly love others....

When you walk from the altar, you are transformed; you are whole and holy ... and filled with joy and inner peace....

In a few moments, you're going to leave this sacred space to return to the ordinary world ... but you won't be ordinary anymore.... When you're ready, still feeling yourself filled with joy, leave this sacred place and slowly return your attention to this room.... Remembering the wholeness of who you can be, slowly return your attention to your body lying on the floor or sitting in the chair, and slowly open your eyes.... Move slowly and gently to find a marker or crayon and draw your wedding. After drawing, write any other impressions you want to remember.

❀ *Creative Shadow Play*

Take yourself on a one-day, in-town honeymoon—just you and your shadow. Treat yourself to some romance. Indulge in the kinds of things your shadow would really like to do. Take yourself someplace special. Splurge on yourself!

It is written in your "job description" that at some point you must have the courage to come out and be your Self as our great Teacher has done.

JACQUELYN SMALL
Living Your Bigger Story

◎ **EXERCISE CHOICES**

1. Consider the Possibilities. Make a list of the little steps you can take that honor your commitment or move you toward your creative goals. You aren't committing to do all or any of these; for now, just consider and list the possibilities. Keep this list available for future reference.

2. Map Your Journey. Using the steps described earlier in this chapter, make an action map for a project you want to commit to finishing. Use this action map to list possible daily do-ables.

3. Highlight the Intersections. Notice the places on your action map where your passion could intersect with the needs of others. Make a list of possible service opportunities.

4. Select Your Daily Do-able Habits. From the lists you made in exercises 1, 2, and 3, select which item(s) you want to make a daily do-able habit. Do it (or them).

Select others that you want to make regular do-ables that you could do once a week or once a month. Do these too.

5. Record Your Progress. Use a small notebook or your date book to record what daily do-ables you do each day. Refer to previous entries when you feel you aren't "doing anything." Noticing what you're doing to honor your commitments and move closer to a creative goal is as important as doing it.

6. Celebrate Your Small Steps. Find ways to celebrate the small steps. Take yourself to lunch. Buy yourself a treat. Ask a friend to give you an enthusiastic, "All right! Good for you!" Make a list of ways you can honor the small steps. Use these whenever appropriate. Don't wait to celebrate.

7. Make Appointments with Yourself. Mark off time in your calendar or date book to do your daily do-ables. Don't schedule other things in these times.

8. Go Back to Moodling. Go back to Creative Shadow Play in chapter 4 and review what Brenda Ueland means by moodling. To bal-

If you listen when a certain creative impulse comes and follow through *with it, you are pleasantly surprised at how utterly talented you are—at anything! Our commitment is the key that activates this process. We commit through our Intention to "the work" and then the work enlightens us.*
JACQUELYN SMALL
Becoming A Practical Mystic

ance all the activity of your daily do-ables and action mapping this week and in the weeks to come, make time to do nothing.

By now, you may have discovered some of your own favorite ways to moodle. For example, I like to take long hot baths, especially during the long, cold Minnesota winters. I get some of my best ideas just hanging out in my own tub or the hot tub at the YWCA. Make a list of your favorite ways to do nothing and make sure you get time to do nothing on a very regular basis. If you feel at all guilty about this, remind yourself it's part of your "homework."

9. Go Back to the Do-able List. When you don't know what to do with yourself, when you feel scattered or lost or aimless or bored, go back to the lists you made in exercises 1 through 4. Do something new from the lists.

10. Read Habit One in Stephen Covey's *The Seven Habits of Highly Effective People.* Notice your own language, especially how you talk about your commitment to your creativity. Is it proactive or reactive? Practice replacing reactive phrases and attitudes with proactive ones.

✴ ✴ ✴ ✴ ✴ ✴ ✴ ✴ ✴ ✴

CHAPTER **10**

Walk Through Your Fears

BY NOW IT SHOULD BE CLEAR that fear is part of the creative process, indeed, part of the human experience. It is completely natural and normal to feel fear. The significant question is not whether you'll feel afraid from time to time (you will) but how you're going to respond to fear.

In chapter 4, we discovered that fear always accompanies growth, since growth means moving beyond what is comfortable and familiar. Just knowing that we are going to feel afraid, that our fear isn't a sign we should turn back but an indicator that we're on the right track, makes it easier to move through the fear.

Of course, you don't have to decide how to respond to fear if you aren't clear that you're feeling afraid, which is partially why many of us disguise our fear.

Fear Disguised

Although some people are well aware of their fear most of the time, many of us find it is sometimes difficult to pinpoint exactly what we're afraid of or even to acknowledge that we're afraid at all. Many of us have learned different ways to disguise our fear behind other emotions.

This is where knowing your Enneagram type and the tendencies of your type is useful (see chapter 5). Sixes on the Enneagram are the people mostly likely to be clear about their fears. If you're a Six, take comfort in knowing that your heightened awareness of fear can serve you as long as you don't allow it to immobilize you. While other types are working to discover what disguise their fear is hiding behind, you can skip ahead to practicing how to handle your fear. In fact, you can be an excellent role model and mentor for others, helping them to identify and be honest about fear.

Fives and Sevens are the other two types likely to be aware of their fear, once they stop giving in to their tendency to defuse anxiety through acquiring knowledge (Fives) or overfocusing on the light side (Sevens). Fives need to be wary of their tendency to withdraw and isolate themselves when they really need to reach out for support to name their fear and move through it. Fives need to overcome both their inertia and their discomfort in asking directly for help. Sevens, on the other hand, need to be aware that others may not recognize their anxiety, confusing it with aggression or anger because of the Seven's expansive, energetic, and sometimes impersonal manner of dealing with anxiety. Sevens are sometimes surprised when others don't recognize how anxious they feel; it seems overwhelmingly obvious to them. They need to learn to openly acknowledge their fear, even though this might wreck their image as the life of the party. Sevens should also be aware that the shadow flip side of their almost ever-present optimism is a hopelessness that may feel overwhelming when they first acknowledge their fear.

Eights, Nines, and Ones tend to disguise their fear behind their "anger habit." Even though these three types express their anger very differently, they all tend to interpret most emotional discomfort as anger. Wrapped up in what they assume is anger, they don't recognize when the anger originates from feeling threatened in some way. Because anger is familiar, it is easier to use the anger-coping mechanism common to their type, rather than identify what fears might be associated with the anger.

The coping technique Ones tend to rely on is to outwardly deny they feel angry and inwardly seethe with resentment, which is a wonderful way to distract themselves from realizing what they're afraid of. Nines also tend to deny their anger, withdrawing inward to avoid any possibility of conflict. Nines need to beware of their tendency to express anger passive-aggressively, which makes the conflict they want to avoid even more likely. All that drama of avoiding conflict is another excellent way to distract themselves from recognizing the fears that underlie their anger. Eights, on the other hand, are quite direct about their anger. Like Sevens, Eights need to keep in mind that their expansive, energetic ap-

You gain strength, courage and confidence by every experience in which you really stop to look fear in the face.... You must do the thing you think you cannot do.
ELEANOR ROOSEVELT

I had to get over my fear of running through the world naked and learn to say "Take me or leave me."
STEVEN SPIELBERG

proach, combined with a willingness to "let it rip," can overwhelm others who have a hard time seeing how the Eight could be afraid of anything. This unfortunately reinforces Eights' difficulty in separating fear from anger and makes it harder for them to acknowledge that they feel afraid even when they do recognize it.

Anger is always a call to action. Anger energizes us; the trick is to use that energy properly. Since all three of these types—Eights, Nines, and Ones—often respond with spontaneous action, it is important for them to remember that they can't determine what action is appropriate if they haven't admitted exactly how they feel.

Twos, Threes, and Fours are likely to be confused about fear. Like anger for Eights, Nines, and Ones, confusion for Twos, Threes, and Fours can be a handy distraction that keeps the discomfort of really experiencing fear at a safe distance. And just as Eights, Nines, and Ones have different patterns for allowing anger to disguise their fear, Twos, Threes, and Fours use the confusion disguise in different ways. Twos focus their attention on the needs of others, which ensures they can avoid noticing their own needs and feelings, including fear or anxiety. Twos would much rather talk about you and reassure you about your fears. If pressed to disclose their own fears, Twos are likely to change the subject, unobtrusively turning the conversation back to the other person's emotions. Threes focus their attention on their own image of success. Since emotions like fear could interfere with achieving the results they demand of themselves, Threes would just as soon ignore fear. If pressed to disclose their fear, Threes are likely to say whatever they perceive the other person expects to hear. In their own minds, Threes believe experiencing fear is something to avoid whenever possible, and it is usually possible if they keep themselves busy enough. In fact, Threes sometimes walk through their fear by default, rather than intention, simply because they stay on the move. Fours, on the other hand, are willing to explore their own emotions, fear included. They are willing to admit being confused and may see their confusion as evidence of how emotionally complex they are. However, Fours are likely to become lost in the jungle of their tangled emotions and hence have no clear concept of what they're afraid of or how to deal with it.

When we're confused, we need to stop and seek clarity—something that is often easier said than done. When Twos, Threes, or Fours

And the day came when the risk to remain tight in the bud was more painful than the risk it took to blossom.
ANAÏS NIN

recognize their uncertainty or confusion, they need to pay attention. Twos and Threes especially need to notice how they feel, not what others might feel or expect them to feel. Fours need to get off the emotional merry-go-round of questioning how they feel and how they feel about what they feel, and so on. Fours can benefit from forcing themselves to state how they feel in ten words or less.

Remember that you don't have to be an Eight, Nine, or One to disguise fear with anger. Nor do you have to be a Two, Three, or Four to use confusion to distract you from fear. These are tendencies, not absolutes.

There are other emotions that can disguise fear, among them shame and jealousy. Being consumed by jealousy is often a signal that it's time to walk through fear to expand your comfort zone. It's frightening to consider leaving your comfort zone, so naturally you'd rather focus on someone else. Jealousy is the illusion that you can't have what you want because someone else has it. It might be nice if that were true because then you would be justified in not facing your fear. Jealousy, like anger, is a call to action.

Shame is the illusion that you don't deserve to get what you want. Like the illusion of jealousy, the illusion of shame simply isn't true. Shame can distract us from the fear of taking action on our own behalf. Shame is never comfortable, but it can be familiar. People who struggle with shame usually learned it as very young children. Ultimately the shame belongs to the adult who damaged the child. As damaging as shame is, as miserable as it makes us feel, we can work to move beyond it. If you feel shame occasionally, ask yourself what rising fear might be triggering the shame. If you feel shame often, find a good therapist to guide you in deeper explorations.

Not every emotion you feel should be simplistically assumed to be fear in disguise. Even Freud acknowledged that sometimes a cigar is just a cigar. Sometimes feeling angry might mean you're afraid and not admitting it to yourself, but sometimes it means you have a reason to be angry. Sometimes anger is just anger, sometimes confusion is just confusion, and sometimes jealousy is just plain jealousy. Being aware of how you tend to disguise your fear empowers you. Once you strip away any disguises you might be laying over your fear, once you identify the fear clearly, you're ready to consider how you will respond to your fear.

By far the best response to fear is to trust yourself to handle whatever happens.

Flops are part of life's menu and I'm never a girl to miss out on a course.
ROSALIND RUSSELL

✍ *Exercise: Promise Yourself, "I'll Handle It."*

Read your response to the first exercise in chapter 4 (on page 65) and recall the fears you listed about exploring your creativity. Make a new list, rephrasing those and any new fears this way: "I'm afraid that if I _____, then _____." List as many fears as you can think of, even the ones that seem silly. Leave two blank lines between each of these statements. For example, Carol, who finds creative joy in preparing gourmet meals, might write, "I'm afraid that if I started my own catering business, I'd never have time to spend with my friends."

When you've finished this new list of fears, write under each statement, "If _____, I'll handle it." In Carol's case, she would write, "If I never have time to spend with my friends, I'll handle it."

Next, identify your three most significant fears, the three that are the biggest obstacles for you. Rewrite each fear and an "I'll handle it" statement. Then make a list of options, of ways you can handle those three fears. So, Carol might write, "If I never have time to spend with my friends, I'll handle it. I could work part time at catering and part time at my other job. I could ask my friends to help me with the business. I can make sure I schedule time off to be with my friends. I could hire a cleaning person to take care of my house, so I would have more free time. I could lower my standards and let the house be messier for a while. I could give up watching TV so I would have time for what's really important to me, like my friends."

When you finish listing optional ways you can handle your fears, write, "_____ is important to me. I acknowledge my fears and commit myself to taking action anyway." Carol would write, "Exploring how to start my own catering business is important to me. I acknowledge my fears and commit myself to taking action anyway."

But one day, all those small but indelible moments of private courage will burst through. And both you and your world will have changed in an authentic moment.

SARAH BAN BREATHNACH
Simple Abundance

Comfort Zone Expansion Principles

Remember these four basic principles as you take action to expand your comfort zone: (1) play, don't push, (2) welcome mistakes, (3) take baby steps, and (4) don't try to go it alone.

1. PLAY, DON'T PUSH. A common misunderstanding is that brave people don't feel afraid. Bravery isn't the absence of fear; it is a willingness to move through fear for the sake of something or someone worth the effort. Your creativity is worth being brave for. Becoming more fully creative, more fully your True Self, is worth the effort.

Another misunderstanding is that once we've gathered up our courage and decided to be brave, we should rush headlong into whatever frightens us. Or that we have to discipline ourselves, driving ourselves forward by sheer force of will. It is just as important not to run through your fear as it is to not run away from it. The key is to walk, or maybe even dance, through the fear.

You see, enthusiasm and a playful sense of adventure will take you through the fear of leaving your comfort zone far more easily and effectively than some misguided attempts to force yourself. The line between excitement and fear is a fine one, and what you call the emotion is significant. Saying, "I'm really excited and a little nervous" acknowledges how you feel and frames it in a positive way. Putting a positive frame on your fear makes it easier for you to believe it when you remind yourself, "I can handle it."

Learn to play with your fear, dancing on the edge of your comfort zone. Experiment. Allow yourself to laugh and squeal and scream like a child on a sled or a midway ride.

2. WELCOME MISTAKES. You may be able to do something familiar without a hitch, but when you try something new, you will almost certainly make mistakes. Like fear, making a mistake is a reliable indicator that you have ventured into the unknown. Therefore, mistakes are permissible, even desirable. If you must be perfectionistic, save the demand for an error-free performance for the things that are solidly inside your comfort zone, like tying your shoes or signing your name.

Remember that naming is significant. What one person calls a mistake, another person calls a surprise. Or perhaps more accurately, what the ego calls a mistake, the psyche recognizes as an opportunity.

A hallmark of creativity is the flexibility to make the most of so-called mistakes. "Oops, I spilled the cinnamon" can turn into a new cookie recipe. "Sorry, we're out of that" combined with the willingness to experiment with different materials can lead to a breakthrough tech-

Keeping our creativity no big deal is what lets us do it in the first place. Making something a big deal creates obsession, and obsession gobbles time. Even when we are here, we are really there.

JULIA CAMERON
The Vein of Gold

Success often comes from taking a misstep in the right direction
ANONYMOUS

nique. "Uh-oh, I smudged the paint" can lead to a whole new style as it did for Deborah Koff-Chapin, who discovered what she calls Touch Drawing by "accident" when helping a friend clean inked glass plates in a print shop. (Koff-Chapin used the Touch Drawing technique to create the *Soul Cards* recommended in chapter 7. She describes how to use this technique in *Drawing Out Your Soul.*)

When you keep your mind and your heart open, a "mistake" or a "misstep" can lead you in surprising directions. Learn to recognize that what your ego resists may be Divine intervention. Watch for unexpected payoffs when you welcome these synchronistic opportunities to expand your comfort zone.

3. TAKE BABY STEPS. Take lots of small, manageable steps as you expand your comfort zone. Keep in mind that the edge of your comfort zone is never static. It fluctuates a little from day to day. When you take a small step outside your comfort zone, you have time to get comfortable with the expanded sense of yourself before you move on to the next step.

Remember Rachel (from chapter 4), who decided to step outside her comfort zone to take a dance class? She did it by taking small steps. She called to get information about classes—one small step. She signed up—another small, manageable step. She went to the first class and participated a little—yet another small step. At the next class, she participated a little more and then tried other new steps in the following classes. Each of these steps stretched Rachel's comfort zone. She started to feel comfortable in this expanded zone until another student made a comment that reminded Rachel of a painful situation in her past. Naturally, she pulled back from the pain of those memories, thus constricting her creative comfort zone. What had come into her comfort zone—being in the class—was outside again. It was enough of a challenge for her to finish the class. If the class had been scheduled to give a small public performance at the end, it would have been too much of a risk for Rachel at that time.

Like Rachel, we all need to recognize and respect our limitations. We serve ourselves best by expanding our creative comfort zones slowly in small, manageable stages. Eventually we reach the goal that was once far outside the comfort zone. A little fear, or excitement, if you prefer, is a good sign. Terror is also a sign—that you're taking on too much at once.

Do not fear mistakes—there are none.
MILES DAVIS

If you try to reach a goal far outside your comfort zone in one giant leap, you will feel a great deal of fear. There would be no way you could convince yourself you're feeling excitement when the emotion is that strong. You'd be focused on your fear of "failing," which almost guarantees that's what you'd get. Attention equals direction; where you look is where you go. If you're staring at the ditch while driving a car, you'll end up swerving toward it.

When we move beyond our comfort zone and get a result we define as failure, we experience pain and we naturally pull back from that pain. We constrict our comfort zone instead of expanding it. Moreover, there is a kind of pendulum principle that applies to the comfort zone. When we pull back, we constrict our comfort zone to the extent that we stepped beyond it. If we could measure our comfort zone in inches, it would work like this: If you step a half inch outside your comfort zone and get a painful result, you will not only retreat the half inch back to where your comfort zone was when you started, you will constrict another half inch as well.

> *Take a risk a day—one small or bold stroke that will make you feel great once you have done it.*
>
> **SUSAN JEFFERS**
> *Feel the Fear and Do It Anyway*

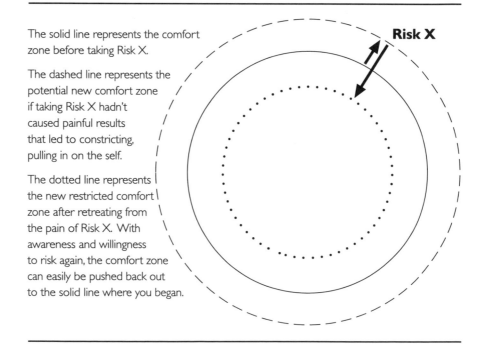

The solid line represents the comfort zone before taking Risk X.

The dashed line represents the potential new comfort zone if taking Risk X hadn't caused painful results that led to constricting, pulling in on the self.

The dotted line represents the new restricted comfort zone after retreating from the pain of Risk X. With awareness and willingness to risk again, the comfort zone can easily be pushed back out to the solid line where you began.

Risk X

This isn't bad; it's just a fact of life. It happens all the time. Remember that the outer edge of the comfort zone is never static. We are constantly adjusting and redefining our comfort zone. The first trick is to take small steps so that when you do occasionally pendulum back in, you won't lose as much ground and won't need as long to recover. The other trick is to keep pushing on the outer edge of your comfort zone so that you maintain an expansive momentum instead of allowing a constrictive spiral to take hold.

Remember that mythic Greek bird mentioned in chapter 4—the one that flew in ever smaller circles until it flew up its own tail feathers and disappeared. This is your choice—walk through your fears or fly up your own tail feathers!

4. DON'T TRY TO GO IT ALONE. Hand-in-hand with the insidious misunderstanding that brave people don't feel fear is the mistaken belief that when we are afraid, we had better put on a brave front. We'd better not let on that we're afraid, and we certainly can't ask for help. Hogwash!

Remember everyone feels afraid when expanding their comfort zone; fear isn't something to be ashamed of. The only people who never feel fear are the ones with their beaks up their own tail feathers.

Follow the wisdom of childhood: practice the buddy system and hold hands. Any fear is easier to handle when there is someone you trust to hold your hand, literally or figuratively. Take the risk of letting a trusted friend know when you're afraid, and you'll gain not only support right then, but also a deeper friendship that makes it easier for your friend to reach out to you when he or she is afraid.

Reach out to the allies you identified in chapter 7 when you're scared. You'll find that, as you talk about it, the fear begins to subside a little. You still have to go out and do whatever it is you need to do, but it helps to know you've got a friend cheering you on. Make a commitment to check in with a friend after you take the step outside your comfort zone. Besides holding your hand and helping you find your way through the dark, your allies will pat you on the back and remind you to celebrate the small successes along the way.

If you're not failing every now and again, it's a sign that you're not doing anything very innovative.
WOODY ALLEN

※ *Guided Imagery*

As you've done in earlier guided imageries, find a place and time when you can be relaxed and uninterrupted. Lie or sit comfortably and begin to relax. Close your eyes. Take several deep breaths, noticing and following the breath in and out of your body.

Consciously tighten the muscles in your feet and ankles. Notice the tension. . . . Feel the tension in all the muscles in your feet. . . . Hold the tension as long as you like . . . holding it until you're ready to let it go with a sigh. . . . Take a deep breath and notice how it feels to let go, to feel the warm relaxation in your feet. . . .

Now, consciously tighten the muscles in your calves and knees. Notice the tension. . . . Feel the tension in your calves and knees. . . . Hold the tension . . . until you're ready to let it go with a sigh. . . . Take a deep breath and notice how good it feels to let your calves and your knees relax and go slack. . . .

Consciously tighten the muscles in your thighs, buttocks, and pelvis. Notice the tension. . . . Feel the tension in your thighs and buttocks and pelvis. . . . Hold the tension . . . until you're ready to let it go with a sigh. . . . Take a deep breath and notice how good it feels to let the lower half of your body relax more and more with each breath you take. . . .

Take another deep breath and consciously tighten the muscles in your stomach, chest, and back. Feel the tension in your torso. . . . Notice what it feels like to hold tension in this part of your body. . . . Hold that tension . . . until you're ready to let it go with a sigh. . . . Take a deep, slow breath and notice how good it feels to breathe all the way down to your belly . . . how good it feels to let your belly go soft and round with each breath. . . .

Now, consciously tighten your hands into fists. Feel the tension move from your hands to your wrists, your forearms, elbows, upper arms, into your shoulders, and the base of your neck. . . . Notice that tension, what it feels like . . . holding it until you're ready to let it go with a sigh. . . . Take a deep breath and notice how good it feels to let any remaining tension ooze out of your fingertips. . . . Notice how good it feels to let your shoulders drop and let your arms relax more and more. . . .

Now, consciously tighten the muscles in your jaw and neck; scrunch up the muscles around your eyes and forehead. . . . Notice the tension in your face and neck . . . holding it until you're ready to let it go with a sigh. . . .

Notice how good it feels to let your whole body become more and more relaxed . . . more and more relaxed with every breath. . . .

Continue to breathe deeply. If worries or thoughts about other things come to you, simply remind yourself, "Not this, not now," set the thought aside, and return your attention to your breathing. Allow your breath to assume a slow, natural rhythm.

Experience your whole body now as relaxed . . . your mind as quiet and still . . . your emotions as calm and clear . . . your spirit as peaceful and serene. . . .

From this place of inner serenity, harmony, and relaxation, begin to allow images to occur in your mind. . . . Imagine a time in the future when you have expanded your comfort zone so much that the hopes and dreams of today are within your reach. . . . See yourself expanding your creativity in tangible ways. . . . Notice how you feel. . . . Explore the expanded sense of yourself. . . . Take some time to reflect on all that you have accomplished. . . . Listen to the compliments and praise of the people whose opinions matter to you. . . .

(pause for a minute or two)

Notice how you feel about yourself and the world. . . . Notice how you stand, how you hold your body now that you have made your dreams come true. . . . Revel in this experience. . . .

(pause for a minute or two)

Now, imagine an old friend comes up to you, and after congratulating you, asks you how you did it, how you got through all the obstacles to this glorious feeling of accomplishment and grace. . . . You think about it and you start to tell your friend about those obstacles. You remember that you thought you were beat when you hit the first big problem, but then you found a way to handle it. . . . Take some time now to tell your friend about that problem and how you solved it. . . .

(pause for a minute or two)

You can tell this friend really wants to hear more, so you talk about other problems, other obstacles, and the solutions you found along the way. . . .

Finally, your friend asks you how you found the courage to keep going through all that. You tell your friend about knowing that whatever happened, you knew you could handle it. . . . Take some time to explain to your friend how important achieving this dream was and how you always knew you could handle it, even when you weren't quite sure how. . . .

When nothing is sure, everything is possible.

MARGARET DRABBLE

(pause for a minute or two)

As you explain the source of your courage and faith to your friend, you realize that your friend really needed to hear this. . . . You realize that even though you didn't plan it, you've succeeded at your dream and become a living example of courage and commitment. . . . Notice how you feel about this. . . .

And now, take some time to thank the people and forces that have assisted you in this long journey. . . . Notice how you feel now. . . .

Remember what it feels like to have faced the challenges to make this dream a reality, and remember how it feels to have done this. . . . Treasure this memory. . . . Find a symbol or image that will help you remember this feeling. . . . Hold it in your heart and mind. . . .

When you're ready, remembering the symbol or image of this experience, slowly return your attention to this room. . . . Remembering what it feels like to face the challenges of your dream, slowly return your attention to your body lying on the floor or sitting in the chair, and slowly open your eyes. . . . Move slowly and gently to find a marker or crayon and draw the symbol or image you found. After drawing, write any other impressions you want to remember.

> The death of fear
> is in doing what
> you fear to do.
> SEQUICHIE
> COMINGDEER

❋ Creative Shadow Play

When we were children, we usually enjoyed the thrill and excitement of pushing on the edge of our comfort zone. That thrill is what encouraged us to move through the fear to grow up.

Make a list of things that both excited and frightened you when you were a child. Sledding down a big hill, going to kindergarten the first day, attending summer camp, moving from grade school to junior high, learning to drive, and so on.

For creative shadow play this week, return to the mix of thrill and fear you knew so well as a child. Remind yourself what it feels like to play with fear. Do something fun that scared you when you were a kid. Visit your kindergarten or junior-high school or take another trip down memory lane. Try something fun that still scares you enough to be exciting. Go sledding or rolling down a big hill, or ride a roller coaster, or sleep out under the stars, or . . .

◉ **EXERCISE CHOICES**

1. Identify Your Comfort Zone—Now and Then. Draw a large circle on a large piece of paper. This will represent your current comfort zone, so leave some space outside the circle. Think about what is comfortable or familiar to you now that was uncomfortable or downright scary a year or two ago. Write these just inside your circle, then draw a smaller circle inside your large circle so that what you wrote is between the two circles. Now think about and write what was comfortable two years ago, but uncomfortable three or four years ago. Write these just inside the second circle. Continue back for five or ten years, so that you make a series of circles representing your comfort zones over time.

Now take a step back and notice how much you've grown. Notice all the fears you've moved through in the past ten years or so. Congratulate yourself. As more things occur to you this week, add them to these comfort zone time-maps.

Alternatively, you may have a sense that in the past few years your comfort zone has been shrinking. If so, draw larger circles to represent previous comfort zones and note the things that you were once comfortable doing, being, or having. Highlight the ones you want to reclaim.

2. Identify Your Comfort Zone—Now and Coming. Outside the largest circle that represents the current comfort zone you drew in exercise 1, list some of the things that you are at least a little afraid of, but still want to do or be or have. Draw in future comfort zones with dotted lines. Remember: you've moved beyond your comfort zone in the past; you can do it again.

3. Take One a Day. List some small risks you could take this week. Sometimes taking just a tiny step outside your comfort zone breaks a long-standing block. Each morning, choose one small risk and do it that day. Remember the wisdom contained in the title of Susan Jeffers' book *Feel the Fear and Do It Anyway*. Also remember the old saying: Ships are safe in the harbor, but that's not what ships are built for.

Courage—fear that has said its prayers.
DOROTHY BERNARD

4. Map the Unclaimed Territory. Review the creative comfort zone you drew in chapter 4 or list the creative activities that you are not comfortable or familiar with now. Choose one or two that appeal to you and list some ways you can explore each new creative outlet. For example, I'm interested in play writing, although I've never tried it and don't feel particularly knowledgeable or competent in it. So I could take a class in play writing at the local playwright's center, or I could read a few books about it, or get season tickets to one of the local theaters, or just begin writing a play and see what happens, or volunteer at a theater, or offer myself as an unpaid intern to a playwright, or interview playwrights, or read several plays and analyze the structure, or . . .

5. Move into the Unclaimed Territory. Once you've made a list of ways to explore a new mode of creativity, choose one or two actions and take them. If an action feels too big and too frightening, break it down into smaller steps, and take one small step at a time. For example, if approaching a playwright for an internship seems too frightening, I can begin by getting the names of several playwrights and drafting a letter (letters are less frightening for me than phone calls or face-to-face meetings). One day I get the names and address from local theaters. Another day I write the letter. Another day I address and stuff the envelopes. Another day I actually mail the letters. A week later, I might be willing to call one person to confirm that she got my letter.

In other words, make daily do-ables out of your fears.

6. Ask Yourself, "What If I Couldn't Fail?" Freewrite for five minutes or so completing the phrase, "If I knew I couldn't fail, I would _____."

Do this exercise a couple of times this week. Once you've written as much as you can think of for this, read the following paragraphs:

DON'T READ THIS UNTIL YOU'VE DONE THE FIRST PART OF THIS EXERCISE
Remember all those things you said you would do if you knew you couldn't fail? Go out and do them. Because you cannot fail. There is no failure. There are only results. Some results you'll like, and

> *I just say to myself, "Just give it another hour. Just plod along, one foot in front of the other" and then six months later I see it's a beautiful piece.*
> **VIRGINIA CARTWRIGHT**

you've been trained to call those results "success." Some results you won't like, and you've been taught to call those results "failures." But all results are equally valuable. You tried something, you got a result, you learn from it and go on. There is no failure.

Even the "failure to try" isn't a failure; it's just another result you can learn from. What you've probably learned from not pursuing your dreams is that the result of not trying is not terribly satisfying. Great! Use that information. You know, you can't start doing something you don't know how to do until you stop doing what you do know how to do. You may want to read that last sentence again.

Stop doing what is giving you results you're not satisfied with.

You cannot fail. You may have setbacks, rejections, disappointments, mistakes—what you used to call "failure"—but if you commit yourself to taking action toward your dreams, you cannot fail. Remember, the passion you feel for your dreams is a message from your Creator, encoded in emotion. The message is "Do it." So-called failure is just a lesson that what you tried isn't quite the way to do it.

This is a frightening truth. Nothing is more frightening than possibility. Just as ships aren't built to remain safe in the harbor, you weren't created to wallow in fear of failure. You were created to follow your dreams.

A small minded man weighs what can hinder him and fearful, dares not set to work. Difficulties cause the average man to leave off what he has begun. A truly great man does not slacken in carrying out what he has begun although obstacles tower thousand fold until he has succeeded.

INDIAN WISDOM

※ ※ ※ ※ ※ ※ ※ ※ ※ ※

CHAPTER **11**

Balance Your Creativity and Your Shadow

We Need Them Both

WHEN A DANCING IN THE DRAGON'S DEN CLASS comes to
an end, I tell the story of "How Grandmother Spider Brought
the Light" as our closing ceremony. The participants each receive
a piece of air-drying clay to make a small candle-holding pot as they
listen to the story. Before you read the story, you may want to get a
piece of clay yourself. Let your fingers shape the clay as you read.
Your fingers have their own wisdom and may appreciate having your
brain busy with something else so they can craft the clay without
interruption.

This is one of the Cherokee creation stories. I first heard it on an audiocassette collection of Native American stories told by January
(Janet) Kiefer called *Bringing the Light* (produced by StoryPerformances,
St. Louis, MO, 314-647-1070). Like every storyteller, I have added elements that resonate for me. I've abbreviated the story here, telling the
parts that seem most significant.

Long, long ago, when the world was new, there was no light.
The animal people lived in darkness. And though the dark was
less intense at times, more gray than black, the animal people
were unhappy. Especially Fox, for he believed that the Creator
made nothing without purpose. Fox had ears to hear with, a
nose to smell with, a tongue to taste with, and whiskers to feel
with. But he could smell no purpose to having eyes. He wondered about that and wondered about that, until one night he
had a dream.

Fox dreamed of a Lake of Light, far to the east. The Light was so beautiful, Fox said, that the Animal Council should send a mighty warrior to bring back the Light. The Council asked Fox to go, and Fox was honored. He started out immediately, running as fast as he could to the east, running in the dark. He ran and ran and ran until at last he came to the Lake of Light. It was even more beautiful than in his dream! Fox jumped in the lake and grabbed a big mouthful of Light to carry home, but that Light was hot! It burned Fox's feet and muzzle black and turned the rest of Fox's fur bright red, except the tip of his tail, which stayed the white color Fox had always been until then. You know, Fox still carries those colors in honor of trying to carry the Light.

So Fox came home from the long, perilous journey wounded, burned, and empty-jawed. But he had seen the Light, and it was glorious. So the council sent Buzzard, another fine warrior. Buzzard set out immediately and flew as fast as he could until he reached the Lake of Light. Buzzard tried to carry a ball of Light home in his fine top feathers, but that Light was so hot, it burned all Buzzard's top feathers off. And you know, Buzzard is bald with a red head to this very day. So Buzzard, too, came home burned and in darkness. One by one, the animal warriors journeyed to the east, and one by one, they all came home, hurt and without the Light.

"Maybe what we should learn from this is that we are not meant to have the Light," one warrior said. "Maybe we are meant to live in darkness and be content."

"Maybe," a quavering old voice replied, "what we should learn from this is that it is not the task of a warrior to bring the Light." The voice belonged to Grandmother Spider. "Send me. I am an old woman, and I cannot run or fly fast like the young warriors, but send me and I will bring the Light."

The council was honored with Grandmother Spider's offer and asked her to make the journey. Grandmother Spider didn't set off at once, running as fast as she could, like the warriors had done. Instead, she went down to the river. She gathered clay with her long fingers, and singing a little clay-shaping song,

It is in darkness that we can learn to be transformed in a deep way. When our hearts break, the cosmos opens up.

MATTHEW FOX
Stories That Need Telling Today

she made a small pot. Then, holding her pot in front of her and singing a little walking song, she began to walk slowly i̶ the dark to the east.

Maybe you know that if you put a clay thing in the fire too soon, it will explode. But if you let the clay dry completely, it will not break but will become stronger when you put it in the fire.

This is what Grandmother Spider did, walking slowly and patiently through the darkness. When she reached the Lake of Light, she dipped her pot in. She held up the pot, and it glowed with the Light within. Grandmother Spider smiled and said, "Ah, you are beautiful." And then she returned home, carrying the Light before her.

When she returned to the Animal Council, Grandmother Spider took a big ball of the Light and put it high in the sky so all the animals could see it. This she called the sun. Then she took a smaller ball of Light and put it at the other end of the sky, and this she called the moon. Then she shook out the last drops of Light across the sky, and these she called the stars. Then Grandmother Spider taught the sun, the moon, and the stars to move in right rhythm, so that there would be day and night, light and dark.

"Because," she said, "we need them both. It is in the Darkness that we are prepared to carry the Light."

In a dark time, the eye begins to see.
THEODORE ROETHKE

Preparing Yourself to Carry the Light

Working through the first ten chapters, you have made steady, patient progress. Even when it seemed that you were lost and alone in the dark, you have been like Grandmother Spider.

You have seen how your creativity and your shadow are woven together. You have begun to recognize how much creative potential is locked in your shadow. The challenge you face as you complete this long journey is to discover how you will balance and blend your creativity and your shadow.

As you continue to explore your shadow, you will receive enormous payoffs in your creativity. As you continue to express your creativity, you will receive more information about your shadow. You learn to balance the dark and the light. You learn that you need both the light and the dark, that you need all aspects of yourself. You learn to value the dark for its own sake. You give yourself opportunities to become whole. You give yourself opportunities to be your genuine self. You prepare yourself to carry the light.

Like Grandmother Spider's clay pot, you have begun to shine from within. Like Grandmother Spider's clay pot, you are beautiful!

But this integration cannot take place and be put to a useful purpose unless one can admit the tendencies bound up with the shadow and allow them some measure of realization—tempered, of course, with the necessary criticism. This leads to disobedience and self-disgust, but also to self-reliance, without which individuation is unthinkable.

CARL JUNG

Exercise: Find Your Balance

Draw a symbol that represents balance to you. I think of a scale with two pans on either end when I think of balance. For you, it might be a person on a tightrope, the yin-yang symbol, or something else. Draw whatever symbolizes balance to you.

Draw this symbol again, this time drawing it to represent the degree of balance you have in your life right now. When my life has been out of balance, I've drawn the scale with one pan high in the air and the other hitting the table. At other times, I've drawn the scale with the pans level with each other.

Identify the factors that contribute to your sense of balance or imbalance. Add these to your drawing. If you have a regular practice of making time for yourself that helps you stay centered, you could draw that as the balancing stick a tightrope walker carries. Or, if your job seems to be taking all your time and leaving you feeling stressed out, you could draw that as a heavy weight throwing the scale off.

Indicate where your creativity is in your drawing. Do you have enough time for your creativity, or is it on the side that's too light? Or are you sacrificing time with friends for the sake of your creative efforts?

Where is your shadow work? Is it something that feels too heavy, perhaps because you've focused on it these past ten weeks? Or does it seem like something that needs continuing attention?

Balance Is an Illusion

Don't worry if you feel out of balance from time to time. Life is nearly always in a state of imbalance. Thermostats don't maintain the same temperature every minute. Instead, they allow temperatures to rise and fall within a range so that, over time, the average is the temperature requested.

I once read a detailed description of how humans walk that helped me realize that balance is mainly illusion. Because we stand precariously on two feet, we humans have to continuously throw ourselves off balance. To walk, we throw our weight forward, making ourselves unbalanced, then bring one foot forward to catch ourselves just before we fall on our faces. If we were never willing to be off balance, we could never walk, never move forward.

Consider how sailboats move against the wind. They use a maneuver called tacking, moving in large zigzags that eventually bring the boat four miles east by first moving two miles northeast, then two miles southeast, then two more miles northeast, and finally two miles southeast.

As another example, consider what a straight line means on a heart monitor—it means death. Your life's balance is like the line a monitor draws of a healthy heart's rhythm—up, down, up, down. The reason your heart can keep working night and day for eighty years or more is because your heart doesn't work nonstop. It beats, it pauses. Beat, rest, beat, rest. Your heart may be the hardest-working muscle in your body, but only because it is also the wisest-resting muscle.

Many of us think that balance is a virtue we should always hold on to, but in reality, it is a virtue only when we are striving for it. Like a heart constantly opening and closing, beating and resting, we gain our balance, lose it, gain it, lose it. As soon as we regain our balance, we have to throw it away. While you're walking or moving through your life in a larger sense, you have to be willing to sacrifice your balance as soon as you get it. Throwing yourself off balance is the only way to keep moving.

Balance is only achieved in the long run.

When nothing seems to help, I go and look at a stonecutter hammering away at his rock perhaps a hundred times without as much as a crack showing in it. Yet at the hundred and first blow it will split in two, and I know it was not that blow that did it—but all that had gone before.
JACOB RIIS

✐ Exercise: Identify Next Steps

Although balance is something we can hold on to only momentarily, your drawing of how balanced you feel provides important insight. It reveals what you need to do next to achieve that long-term balance called equilibrium. If your drawing shows that you're feeling greatly off balance, you need to restore your balance. If, on the other hand, you were feeling a little smug because your drawing shows how balanced you are, it's time to throw yourself forward again.

Look at what you identified as factors contributing to your state of balance or imbalance. Use these as a starting point to make a list of possible next steps. Get specific. What do you need or want to do next? What would help you achieve equilibrium?

Be really whole and all things will come to you.

LAO TZU
Tao Te Ching

Blending Is Reality

There are two basic kinds of creative expression: creating for process and creating for product. Creating for process is doing morning pages, freewriting, dream journaling, doodling, or playing with paints just to see what comes out and to enjoy yourself. It is any kind of creative activity you do just for the sake of doing it. It gives you insight and helps you work on your life as you explore your shadow and creativity.

Creating for product is writing a poem, short story, or novel that you intend others to read, painting a picture you intend others to view, or making a quilt you intend to use or display. It is any kind of creative activity you do for the sake of the result you'll achieve. It gives a tangible creation you can share with others.

Creating for process always supports and develops your ability to create a product. Creating a product often gives you insight, supporting and developing your process. We need to balance and blend creating for process and creating for product. As Grandmother Spider said, we need them both. So we have to value and make time for both.

Do you tend to favor one kind of creating over the other? Do you spend so much time creating for process that you rarely have to face the challenge of creating for product? Or is it the other way around for you? Which way do you need to lean your balancing act to achieve equilibrium here? Add this to the list of possible next steps you just made.

Avoiding the Siren's Call

Whether we are creating for process or for product, we can experience a tremendously blissful state of being when we are in the creative flow. In the flow, we open ourselves to a state of consciousness that takes us beyond our usual ego perspective. These peak experiences give us a profound sense of ecstasy. When we are in the flow, we no longer struggle to be creative; we recognize that creativity surrounds us and fills us and flows from us without effort. We experience work as play. There is a sense of timelessness. We are no longer bothered by the ego's concerns.

It is your work in life that is the ultimate seduction.
PABLO PICASSO

Naturally, we yearn to have more of these peak experiences where we feel energized, alive, whole, filled with grace. Indeed, being in the flow is a state of grace. It is also a spiritual state, and since we are spirit embodied, spirit in body, we can stay too long in the spiritual realm. After all, who wants to a take a break when the work is going so well? Who wants to stop in the middle of ecstasy? Who cares about Greek myths of sirens luring sailors to their deaths on the rocks? Why would anyone want to steer the ship away when the singing we hear is so sweet?

We need to be wary of the siren's call of creativity. We can stay so long enjoying the creative flow that we lose track of our bodies and our bodies' needs. Composing at the keyboard (computer or piano) too long, we strain our arms and backs, developing carpal tunnel symptoms and lower back pain. Singing too long, we can injure our voices. Playing a musical instrument too long, we can ruin our embouchure. Sculpting or painting or sewing too long, we strain our neck and shoulder muscles. Following the urge to dance or skate or ride despite the nagging little pain in an ankle or hip, we can deepen a little pain into an injury that could take months to heal. We can forget to take a break to eat, stretch, or even go to the bathroom. We forget to go to sleep, or we wake up in the middle of the night burning with an idea when we need to sleep. Occasionally, it can be good to follow the idea that wakes you in the middle of the night, but as a regular practice, you wear out the very body you need to do your creative work.

If the effects of following the siren's call of creativity don't appear in physical discomfort, they might appear in a general sense of being disconnected from life. You've checked out from ordinary reality. Your family and friends may start complaining that you aren't paying enough attention or that even when you're physically there, there's no one home. Of course, you need uninterrupted time to work on and play with your creativity, but it cannot become the whole of your existence. Your creativity comes from your life, so you had better have a life.

Part of the balancing act we do is blending our time in the flow with time in ordinary, mundane, everyday life. I am blessed with dogs that need walking and a housemate who comes home from her job and expects me to engage in dinner conversation. When I'm "on a roll" with my writing, I resist leaving the keyboard, but even though I'm my own boss now, quittin' time is still quittin' time.

As long as we are in physical bodies, we need to take care of our bodies. And since we are social creatures, we need to take care of our relationships. This is the ego's job. Sometimes our egos get in the way of the surrender process we need to go through to enter the creative flow, but we need our egos to protect us from following the siren's call until we crash on the rocks. Remember, our task is not to get rid of ego, but to find ways for our ego to work in concert with our spirit.

✍ Exercise: Blend Idealism and Practicality

Be idealistic. Review the list of values you made in chapter 9. These probably represent your most idealistic sense of how you want to live. But if they don't, make a list of your ideals. Do you think the Golden Rule is still a good one? Do you agree with the tenants of the Ten Commandments? Make a list of your most ideal principles.

Next, be practical. Make a practical principles list. This is a list of the principles you actually live by, the criteria that determine your everyday, mundane decisions. Do your unspoken mottos include something like "Don't get caught" or "You have to go along to get along"?

For example, even though it's not on my list of top ten values, I had to admit one of the most basic principles that guided my life was "Avoid pain." Not terribly heroic or noble, but true. I've been in healing and recovery circles long enough to know that we sometimes have to endure short-term discomfort and pain to bring ourselves greater freedom and joy. Still, it wasn't until I started working with a massage therapist who did deep-tissue work to alleviate

It is not the critic who counts; not the man who points out how the strong man stumbled, or where the doer of deeds could have done them better. The credit belongs to the man who is actually in the arena, whose face is marred by dust and sweat and blood; who strives valiantly; who errs and comes short again and again; who knows the great enthusiasms, the great devotions; who spends himself in a worthy cause; who, at the best, knows in the end the triumph of high achievement; and who, at the worst, if he fails, at least fails while daring greatly, so that his place shall never be with those timid souls who know neither victory nor defeat.

THEODORE ROOSEVELT

carpal tunnel symptoms that I really embraced the idea of accepting pain in the present for the sake of a pain-free future.

Most of the practical principles we live by are valid. But when we think we *should* be one thing and know in our heart of hearts that we *really are* a different thing, we feel unsettled, uneasy, incomplete. I decided that avoiding pain is not a bad principle to live by; after all, avoiding pain tends to keep my body intact. I just need to make sure I don't get shortsighted about it and do things to avoid pain now that will only cause me more grief later. We can take what is valid from our practical side and blend it with our idealism to develop solid, workable guidelines.

Examine your own ideal principles and practical principles lists. Do some of the items on your lists seem incompatible? Do you want to change some principles you live by to match your ideals? Do you need to scale back on some of your ideals so they fit a human, not a demigod? Are there some values you're willing to sacrifice for other values? Can you identify one guiding principle that encompasses the others?

Decide whether you want to revise the top-ten value list you made in chapter 9 to reflect this blend of idealism and practicality. Remember, these are your values, a reflection of how you blend your ideals with the practical difficulties of life. There are no wrong choices. They either work for you or they don't. If they don't work for you, revise them until they do.

Your thorns are the best part of you.
MARIANNE MOORE

❋ *Guided Imagery*

As you've done in earlier guided imageries, find a place and time when you can be relaxed and uninterrupted. Lie or sit comfortably and begin to relax. Close your eyes. Take several deep breaths, noticing and following the breath in and out of your body.

Consciously tighten the muscles in your feet and ankles. Notice the tension. . . . Feel the tension in all the muscles in your feet. . . . Hold the tension as long as you like . . . holding it until you're ready to let it go with a sigh. . . . Take a deep breath and notice how it feels to let go, to feel the warm relaxation in your feet. . . .

Now, consciously tighten the muscles in your calves and knees. Notice the tension. . . . Feel the tension in your calves and knees. . . . Hold the tension . . . until you're ready to let it go with a sigh. . . . Take a deep breath and notice how good it feels to let your calves and your knees relax and go slack. . . .

Consciously tighten the muscles in your thighs, buttocks, and pelvis. Notice the tension. . . . Feel the tension in your thighs and buttocks and pelvis. . . . Hold the tension . . . until you're ready to let it go with a sigh. . . . Take a deep breath and notice how good it feels to let the lower half of your body relax more and more with each breath you take. . . .

Take another deep breath and consciously tighten the muscles in your stomach, chest, and back. Feel the tension in your torso. . . . Notice what it feels like to hold tension in this part of your body. . . . Hold that tension . . . until you're ready to let it go with a sigh. . . . Take a deep, slow breath and notice how good it feels to breathe all the way down to your belly . . . how good it feels to let your belly go soft and round with each breath. . . .

Now, consciously tighten your hands into fists. Feel the tension move from your hands to your wrists, your forearms, elbows, upper arms, into your shoulders and the base of your neck. . . . Notice that tension, what it feels like . . . holding it until you're ready to let it go with a sigh. . . . Take a deep breath and notice how good it feels to let any remaining tension ooze out of your fingertips. . . . Notice how good it feels to let your shoulders drop and let your arms relax more and more. . . .

Now, consciously tighten the muscles in your jaw and neck: scrunch up the muscles around your eyes and forehead. . . . Notice the tension in your face and neck . . . holding it until you're ready to let it go with a sigh. . . . Notice how good it feels to let your whole body become more and more relaxed . . . more and more relaxed with every breath. . . .

Continue to breathe deeply. If worries or thoughts about other things come to you, simply remind yourself, "Not this, not now," set the thought aside, and return your attention to your breathing. Allow your breath to assume a slow, natural rhythm.

Experience your whole body now as relaxed . . . your mind as quiet and still . . . your emotions as calm and clear . . . your spirit as peaceful and serene. . . .

From this place of inner serenity, harmony, and relaxation, begin to allow images to occur in your mind. . . . Imagine a symbol of balance. . . . See it clearly in your mind's eye. . . . Notice the colors, shapes, textures.

There is a time for everything, And a season for every activity under heaven.

ECCLESIASTES 3:1

. . . Hear the sounds this symbol makes. . . . See it moving, changing, transforming. . . .

Begin to imagine your body as this symbol of balance. . . . See your arms and legs and torso become parts of this symbol of balance. . . . Feel yourself becoming a living symbol. . . . Take some time now to notice how this symbol fits your body. . . .

Notice the natural rhythms and balances in your body . . . the moving in and out of your breath . . . the rising and falling of your chest . . . the opening and closing of your heart . . . the pulse of blood moving through your veins. . . . Begin to see with your mind's eye how the blood flows through your body, bringing oxygen from your lungs to the cells in your fingers and toes, bringing carbon dioxide from your cells back to your lungs. . . . Listen for the sound of your heart and the sound of your pulse. . . . Allow images and colors to arise in your mind . . . see the color of your breath, the color of your blood. . . . Notice on a deep level how all the cells in your body feel . . . notice the muscle groups in your body . . . notice if there is any pain or distress anywhere in your body, and if there is, allow an image or a metaphor of that distress to arise. . . . Is there a weight on your shoulders or do you feel itchy because someone or something has gotten under your skin? . . .

Notice how this image or metaphor fits the image of your body as a symbol of balance. . . . Spend some time now listening to what your body has to tell you about balance, about blending, about equilibrium. . . . Take all the time you need to listen to your body. . . .

(long pause)

When you're ready, remembering the balance symbol your body became and the images or metaphors your body gave you, slowly return your attention to this room. . . . Slowly allow your awareness of your body to return to normal. . . . Wiggle your toes and become aware of the feel of your body lying on the floor or sitting in the chair. . . . Open your eyes and move slowly to find a marker or crayon and draw your body as a symbol of balance. Add any other images or metaphors that came to you. After drawing, write any other impressions you want to remember.

There are some things you learn best in calm, and some in storm.
WILLA CATHER

⊛ *Creative Shadow Play*

Play around with the following moving meditation to help you gain an intuitive awareness of your next steps. In a moving meditation, you should move slowly, gently, and always with intent. Only you know what is an appropriate stretch for your body. Move in ways that are comfortable for your body. For the purposes of this moving meditation, no pain means lots of gain. It is the focus you bring to the movement that makes this form of meditation effective.

Begin to notice your breathing. Allow your body to relax into a standing position. Gently bend your knees and rock back and forth to find your balance point. Imagine your head is held up by a string. Roll your shoulders back and let your body relax. Breathe deeply and slowly.

Drop your head slowly toward the floor, and begin to bend from your waist. Bend very slowly, stretching your back one vertebra at a time. Let your arms dangle, your shoulders dangle, your head dangle. Hold the stretch as long as it is comfortable for you, then slowly straighten up, straightening one vertebra at a time.

Become more and more aware of your breathing as you relax again into the standing position with bent knees and loose arms. Experience your whole body as relaxed, your mind as quiet and still, your emotions as calm and clear, and your spirit as peaceful and serene. Now find your center. For some people it is in the solar plexus, for others it is an inch or two below the navel. Breathe all the way down into your belly. Notice the center of your body and breathe into it. Become more and more aware of the true center of your body.

Begin to walk very slowly. Walk mindfully, meditatively. Notice each tiny movement of your foot as you shift your weight, slowly raise your foot, and place it on the ground. Walk slowly. Walk consciously. Be aware of each movement before you make it and as you make it. Allow your true center to lead your body. Allow your eyes to close halfway. Remain aware of your breathing.

Before each step, ask yourself, "What is my next step?" Allow your body to answer without words. Know, "This is my step" with each slow, conscious step you take. Walk in this way, asking, "What

You already have the precious mixture that will make you well. Use it.

RUMI

is my next step?" and noticing the answer with each step you take, for about ten minutes or as long as it feels good.

Then take one more meditative step and stop. Become aware of your stance. Be aware of your feet, your legs, your hips, your back, your shoulders, your arms, your neck, and your head. Be aware of your body standing here now. Know that all moments are contained in the Eternal Now. And know that, here and now, you make a stand for your creativity.

Walk meditatively to a chair and sit down. Slowly and easily write, "This is where I stand for my creativity" on the left half of a piece of paper and, "These are the next steps on my creative journey" on the right half. Continue to write slowly, easily, meditatively. There is no need to rush or to try to force the writing. Write about what it means to you to take a stand for your creativity and describe the next steps you need to take. These will probably be related. One will lead to the other and back again, that's why I suggest you write about them side by side.

You can use this writing to make a list of things you want to do during future Creative Shadow Playtimes. Put these possibilities in a small notebook for future reference. Record what you do for shadow and creative play and how you felt about it in the notebook too, if you wish.

⊙ **EXERCISE CHOICES**

1. Try a Tai Ji or Chi Kung Class. These Taoist Chinese dance meditation and movement practices will develop your sense of balance. Or try yoga. Practicing one of these fluid movement disciplines will have a profound impact on your ability to integrate your body, mind, and spirit.

2. Brainstorm the Blending Possibilities. Make a list of ways you could blend your creativity and shadow exploration into your life. Make this list as long and inclusive as possible—shoot for at least one hundred ideas. This means you'll write down many things you may never get around to doing. This is a list of possibilities, so include a couple of crazy ideas. They'll seed the list, helping you find

If cleanliness is next to godliness, then messiness is next to goddessness. God creates order, gives us ten neat rules carved with no crossing out in a stone tablet. The Great Goddess, on the other hand, gives us life. . . . The Goddess wants us to create, to enjoy the fruits of the earth, not to make perfect order, but to make full and whole lives.

JOHN BOE
Life Itself

possibilities you wouldn't have noticed if you hadn't stretched yourself a little.

3. Select Your Next Steps. From the list of possibilities you made in exercise 2 and the writing you did in the Creative Shadow Play and for the exercise on identifying next steps (page 198), select a few steps you want to commit to putting into action in the next couple of weeks.

4. Stop Telling Yourself There Are More Than Twenty-four Hours in a Day. To maintain your equilibrium, it is necessary to recognize that your time is a limited resource. If we promise ourselves we'll add a new commitment, for example, to exercise for an hour every day, we either have to have seven hours of free time a week or be willing to delete something that is already taking that seven hours.

Most of us have already committed, or overcommitted, our time and energy. If you don't agree that your life is already full, if not overfull, check it out for yourself. Make a list of all the activities you have in a week and the time it takes for each one. Be sure to include the time you need to sleep, prepare and eat meals, spend time with friends, clean your house, maintain your car, pay your bills, exercise, go to classes, watch TV, read books, and so on. Count the hours you really work and the time it takes to commute, not just the hours you're scheduled to work. Add all these hours up and divide by seven. How many hours of activity are you trying to stuff into a twenty-four-hour day? (I first discovered this insightful exercise in Carol Orsborn's book *Enough Is Enough.* If this exercise was particularly painful or powerful for you, I suggest reading Orsborn's entire book.)

Believing we can add something new without giving up something else is delusion. If you've committed yourself for twenty-eight hours' worth of activity a day, you cannot possibly honor all those commitments. That just sets you up to feel frenzied and guilty. Stop lying to yourself about this. If you decide to add something new, decide first what you'll give up.

5. Decide What You Will Give Up. Decide what activities you are willing to give up so that you will have the time and energy to put the next steps you chose in exercise 3 into practice. Will you sacrifice watching TV for practicing a musical instrument? Will you give up reading the equivalent of mental popcorn to give yourself time and impetus to write your own stories? How about skimping on the cleaning so you have the energy to take a workshop on dyeing silk?

6. Plan for Spontaneity. Leave an hour a day unscheduled and uncommitted to accommodate the unexpected. The payoff for this exercise will probably be that you actually get the amount of sleep you want and need and still have time for spontaneous play.

7. Consult a Balance Barometer. Make a drawing of your balance symbol, then cut it into two equal parts. For example, if your symbol of balance is a scale, cut it in the middle; if your symbol is the yin-yang symbol, cut along the curve separating the two colors. Overlap the two pieces of your symbol slightly and place them on a new piece of paper. Punch a hole through all three pieces of paper and connect them with a brad (or, if necessary, with two holes and two brads). When you're finished, you should be able to move the parts of the balance symbol to represent your current state of balance. Use Post-it Notes to indicate which aspects of your life are on which side of the balance. For example, you might be putting in overtime at work and not having enough time to relax with family and friends. The side of the balance barometer that is showing more would have *work* on the Post-it Note.

Sometimes all we have to do to restore our balance is notice where we're overdoing one thing and where we're underdoing something else. The balance barometer is a visual reminder. If your balance barometer is consistently tilted, take another look at exercises 4 and 5.

8. Prioritize Your Next Steps. Review the values you identified in the Blending Idealism and Practicality exercise (pages 200–201). Then list (in any order) nine activities or goals you are already working on or want to add as next steps. Number the choices 1 through 9. Then use the form below to compare choice 1 to all eight other choices, circling your choice for each separate comparison.

I think of it like I'm a car . . . broken down on the highway. But I realize, 'It's cool, the tow truck is gonna come, and I'm gonna be back on the road.' You just gotta ride through it.
WILL SMITH

For example, if choice 1 is "write a screenplay" and choice 2 is "audition for community theater production," and you prefer writing a screenplay to auditioning, then circle 1 over 2. Then compare choice 1 to choice 3, let's say "take an acting class," and circle your preference in that comparison, and so on for all other choices.

1   1   1   1   1   1   1   1
2   3   4   5   6   7   8   9

Next, compare choice 2 to all other choices.
2   2   2   2   2   2   2
3   4   5   6   7   8   9

And so on.
3   3   3   3   3   3
4   5   6   7   8   9

4   4   4   4   4
5   6   7   8   9

5   5   5   5
6   7   8   9

6   6   6
7   8   9

7   7
8   9

8
9

Next, count the number of times you circled each choice. The choice with the highest score is your top priority. Or if the choices all tie with scores of three or four, you can see why you feel so confused—you just plain want it all. Then you may just have to either randomly choose what to focus on so you don't get scattered and ineffective, or work out ways to schedule time for all your choices.

9. Live Your Priorities. Schedule your day to accommodate the priorities you've identified in exercise 8 and the other priorities in your life like being a parent, a friend, or a home owner. Define daily do-ables for your top priorities. Check to see whether adding these daily do-ables sets you up for days where you're trying to cram twenty-six hours of activity into twenty-four hours. If so, you'll need to eliminate some of your lower priorities.

These can be extremely difficult choices, but ignoring the reality is like closing your eyes when you're about to be in a traffic accident—you may feel safer, but you're not. If you don't make these choices for yourself, someone else will, and the likelihood of the choices supporting your priorities is dramatically reduced.

THREE

SURRENDERING TO THE
CREATIVE SHADOW PROCESS

CHAPTER **12**

Stories of the Descent

PART 1 gave you information about the connections between your creativity and your shadow. Part 2 challenged you to put this information into action, to consciously begin the long journey to being fully creative and fully yourself, your True Self.

Part 3 will introduce you to the sometimes uncomfortable truth that there will be times when collecting more information isn't going to do any good, when there is no conscious action you can take that will yield results. There will be times when all you can do is surrender to the process. When is that? You might not like it—I know I don't like it—but the time to surrender is often the time when you feel most resistant to surrendering.

Resistance May Be Futile, But It Is Persistent

You know what resistance feels like: someone says, "You're really good at this; why don't you . . . ?" But what he or she suggests feels too big, too grandiose, too risky, too impossible to even consider. Why don't you send slides of your art to the art-fair jury, enter a quilting contest at the state fair, apply to graduate school, submit the proposal? Of course there is fear, but there is something more. Why do you get your back up when someone suggests something? Why do you feel so snappy when someone tries to help? Because you are resistant. You've been saying the same thing to yourself and haven't really been hearing it; why should you listen to someone else? Who do they think they are, telling you what to do? This is a road you suspect you should investigate, but you have no intention of following it, no matter how much your friend raves about what a great idea it is. And of course, the more good-natured nudging your friend does, the more you dig in your heels.

We often feel resistance when a new road is beckoning or when we need to change the one we're on. We are particularly resistant when the new path requires abandoning something that has provided short-term relief, even if it provided that relief at the expense of long-term results. Give up eating chocolate, watching late-night TV, acting codependent, playing the victim? Are you nuts? Resistance will attack ideas offered by good friends. Resistance will discount the advice of gifted instructors. Resistance will ignore the recommendations of wise therapists and insightful coaches.

And what makes it even more difficult is that we know we're being resistant. We can feel the nasty comments welling up in our throat, ready to snap and snipe at anyone who has the audacity to express honest concern or enthusiasm for us. We can see what needs to change, and for the most part, we want to make the change, but the resistance just keeps getting in the way.

Take heart. The hardest part of the transformational journey is when you see clearly how much you don't like what you're doing and aren't quite ready to change it yet. This is the resistance phase, emphasis on the word *phase*. It does pass. No matter how much resistance you feel, if you can hold on to the smallest iota of willingness, the phase will pass and you will move into the part of the journey where willingness overcomes resistance and change overcomes inertia.

Take heart: the resistance phase is one stage of the creative process. As with fear, feeling resistance is a sign that you're on your way. Another way to say that the time to surrender is when you resist the surrender, is to say that the time to surrender is halfway through the creative process.

> *The strength of the aversion means that there is something just beneath the surface, thinly disguised, ready to emerge. Resistance is a reminder to probe your inner fears and defenses.*
> MICHELL CASSOU
> and
> STEWART CUBLEY
> *Life, Paint and Passion*

✍ Exercise: Describe Your Creative Process

Remember a time when you did something creative. It can be a big creative project or a quick spurt of creativity, but a creative episode that was of medium duration will probably be the easiest to describe. Either write or talk to a friend to describe what you did and how you felt. Pay particular attention to any part of the process when you felt resistant or needed to surrender.

Creativity Comes in Stages

In her book *Drawing on the Artist Within,* Betty Edwards defines five stages in the creative process. She calls these stages First Insight, Saturation, Incubation, Illumination, and Verification. First Insight is the first glimmering of an idea or a creative possibility. It is when we see the whole picture, see the holes within the whole, and recognize that those holes are creative opportunities. It is a stage marked by open-ended "What if?" questions. Edwards points out that in First Insight we should try to maintain (or pretend) our innocence as long as possible. Assuming we know answers at this stage can prematurely close our minds to considering and exploring what could have been worthwhile concepts and possibilities.

Once we have generated lots of open-ended questions, it's time to begin gathering information. This is the second stage, what Edwards calls Saturation for reasons that will become apparent. This is the time to be looking for answers and investigating what others have said, done, thought, and written. It's when we start conducting our own research through introspection, interviews, observing data, calculating, and so on. In the second stage we gather more and more information, inundating ourselves with data. Eventually we gather so much information, we are saturated. This Saturation leads naturally to the next stage, Incubation.

At the end of the Saturation stage, our minds begin to bog down. We have so many facts, so much data, so many studies, and so much research that we can't keep it all straight anymore. Logical thought begins to falter, yet the solution eludes us. We often feel frustrated or anxious that we can't force a solution. We try harder and still nothing happens. Nothing except increasing our frustration and anxiety. We need to set the problem aside, give up consciously trying to solve it, and let our unconscious have a whack at it. We need to incubate.

When we stop trying so hard to find it, we gain insight after a while. Sometimes it's a long while, sometimes a short while, but sooner or later, the incubation pays off. We hatch an idea. We have the satisfaction of exclaiming, "Aha! I see it now!" This is the fourth stage, Illumination, where everything falls into place and we see how to solve the problem.

Then it is a matter of taking action to put the solution into practice, to create what we have seen. In the fifth stage, Verification, we make the creative possibility a tangible reality. Often, in the process of Verification, we recognize a related creative opportunity, another

During periods of relaxation after concentrated intellectual activity, the intuitive mind seems to take over and can produce the sudden clarifying insights which give so much joy and delight.

FRITJOF CAPRA

hole in the whole. And this starts the creative process all over again at First Insight.

At other times, we finish the Verification stage of putting our inspiration into tangible form and then move into Hibernation, which I identify as the sixth stage of the creative process. As its name implies, Hibernation is the stage when our creativity sleeps. It is the fallow time. Think of First Insight as the early spring, when we get wonderful ideas for how our garden will look. Saturation is later spring, when we gather seeds and prepare the ground. Incubation is early summer, while the seeds are sprouting unseen in the dark earth. Illumination is the joy of seeing the seedlings rise and grow in full summer, and Verification is the autumn harvest. And then the winter Hibernation follows, giving us time to go inward and prepare ourselves for the new growth that will come round again.

Edwards explains that each of these stages can take varying amounts of time with the exception of Illumination, which tends to be a brief flash of inspiration. For one project, you may spend days getting the First Insight, weeks gathering information, an evening incubating, and then a couple of hours implementing the idea, followed by a few days of Hibernation before the next insight comes along. Or you might recognize a creative opportunity in an hour of quiet contemplation, spend fifteen minutes confirming facts you had gathered weeks ago for an entirely different reason, but then not be able to figure out quite what to do with the information and spend days incubating the idea.

✍ Exercise: Identify Your Stages

For the creative experience you described in the first exercise in this chapter, identify each of the six stages in your creative process. If you don't remember all the details, make your best guess. Either write or tell a friend what you did (or probably did) and how you felt (or probably felt) in each of the six stages. Notice which of the stages you are most comfortable with, which ones you prefer.

The great majority of artists are throwing themselves in with life-preservers around their necks, and more often than not it is the life-preserver which sinks them.

HENRY MILLER

Creativity Comes in Modalities

Edwards associates each of her five stages with one of two styles of mental processing, what she calls R-mode and L-mode. These modes refer to the kinds of thinking that were called "right-brain" and "left-brain" when researchers thought we could plot brain processing by identifying which hemisphere it occurred in. Acknowledging recent research that indicates that the brain and its functioning is much more complex but still retaining the value of identifying different kinds of mental processing, Edwards coined the terms *R-mode* and *L-mode*. L-mode is associated with sequential and linear processing; rational, logical thinking; language; mathematics; and definite, precise distinctions and categories. L-Mode thinking is marked by a preference for verifiable facts, details, and data. R-mode, on the other hand, is associated with holistic processing that relies on patterns and associations; visual images and metaphors; simultaneous or random processing; intuition; imagination; and emotional nuances. R-mode is undaunted by ambiguity and paradox.

> *If we hope to live not just from moment to moment but in true consciousness of our existence, then our greatest need and most difficult achievement is to find meaning in our lives.*
>
> **BRUNO BETTELHEIM**
> *The Uses of Enchantment*

The old right-brain versus left-brain discussions were based on the recognition that we all tend to prefer one style of processing over the other. While we're not left-brained or right-brained in the same way that we are left-handed or right-handed, we do tend to prefer one mode. Make a note of which modality you tend to prefer and how strong your preference is.

Edwards associates First Insight with R-mode (relying on patterns, seeing the whole), Saturation with L-mode (gathering data and facts), Incubation with R-mode (setting aside logical thought, waiting for random or simultaneous solutions to arise from the unconscious), Illumination with R-mode, and Verification with L-mode (step-by-step implementation of the inspiration received in Illumination). I'm certain that Hibernation is another R-mode stage (waiting for random or simultaneous insights to arise from the unconscious as we do in Incubation). Moving through the creative process, Edwards points out, relies on our ability to make transitions between the two modalities.

Notice whether there is a correlation between what you identified as your preferred mode (L-mode or R-mode) and the modality of the creative stage(s) you said you prefer. For many people, but not everyone, there is an interesting connection.

I disagree, however, with Edwards in defining Illumination as R-mode. I believe Illumination is both modes. It is a delightful experience of all your mental capabilities working in concert. This would explain why most people list Illumination as one of their preferred stages regardless of whether they prefer L-mode or R-mode. It also explains why Illumination tends to be brief; our preference for and reliance on one modality makes it difficult to balance both modalities for a long time. It's like trying to balance with one foot in the boat and the other on the dock. It is also precisely the experience of being in the creative flow.

There are techniques we can use to develop our ability to sustain the balance and remain in the creative flow, among them journaling (L-mode) first thing in the morning when you tend to be in R-mode because of the lingering affects of sleep, and certain kinds of guided imagery and meditation. When we develop our ability to stay in the creative flow, the Illumination and Verification stages tend to meld together in a sustained period of simultaneous L-mode and R-mode processing. This is creative bliss.

Creativity Comes in Waves

The High Performance Mind by Anna Wise is an excellent resource for developing your ability to remain in the creative flow. In this book, Wise describes a state of consciousness her mentor, C. Maxwell Cade, a distinguished British psychobiologist and biophysicist, calls the Awakened Mind. Wise's description of the Awakened Mind is synonymous with what I've described in previous chapters as the creative flow. Wise's techniques for developing the Awakened Mind, therefore, improve our ability to enter and remain in the creative flow.

According to Wise and Cade, the Awakened Mind is a state where all four brain waves—beta, alpha, theta, and delta—are present and balanced. They base this theory on research that investigated whether there is a state common in people having peak creative or spiritual experiences. This research used a special EEG Cade developed, which uses spectral analysis to measure brain wave frequencies.

Beta waves, the fastest of the brain waves, are present during ordinary, waking thought. Wise associates these with the conscious mind. At the other end of the spectrum, the slowest brain waves, called delta waves, are present during deep, dreamless sleep and profoundly deep meditation. Delta waves are associated with intuition, deep empathy, and the unconscious mind. Theta waves, a little faster than delta, are present during REM (dreaming) sleep and meditation. They are particularly strong during creative or other peak experiences. Wise associates theta waves with the subconscious mind. Finally, alpha waves, which are slower than beta and faster than theta, are present during daydreaming, fantasizing, and visualizing. Alpha waves appear to be a bridge between the conscious and unconscious mind. For example, if alpha waves are not present while you sleep or meditate, you will not remember your dreams or meditation experience.

Although there hasn't been enough research to prove it, I think we can better understand the stages of the creative process by considering which brain wave(s) are dominant during each stage. I suspect that First Insight arises from either a predominantly theta state, a predominantly alpha state, or a mix of theta and alpha. (I think what Brenda Ueland calls moodling is a mix of theta and alpha brain waves.) Saturation is obviously a beta dominant stage. I see Incubation as a delta stage because it is the stage where we surrender conscious control and allow our unconscious mind to work with the problem. It is not surprising to me that so many famous inventions and discoveries have come from the developer's dreams (the sewing machine, the structure of the benzene ring, the double-helix structure of the DNA, for example). As suggested earlier, I believe Illumination is an Awakened Mind state where all four brain waves are present and balanced. Sometimes we sustain the Awakened Mind state into the Verification stage, and then creating is pure bliss; other times we complete Verification in a predominantly beta state or beta and alpha state, and then creating is more like work. I suspect the brain waves that dominate the Hibernation stage vary among individuals, but at least some part of a prolonged Hibernation includes the beta-dominant thinking of everyday life. Moving through Hibernation into First Insight requires slowing our beta-dominant thinking to open ourselves to the influence of alpha and theta waves.

Creativity Comes from Surrender

Just as most of us enjoy Illumination, many of us resist Incubation. And whether or not my hypothesis about which brain waves are dominant in the different stages of the creative process is ever studied, I know something significant happens in the Incubation stage. My assumption that the Incubation stage is dominated by delta waves partially explains why we are uncomfortable with it.

According to Edwards, the discomfort or difficulty we have when moving between any two stages in the creative process arises because the transition requires us to switch from one mode of thinking to the other. If Incubation relies on delta waves, then moving into Incubation is an even more difficult transition. It's not just moving from one style of conscious thinking to another; it is switching from conscious to unconscious.

And, opening to the unconscious is opening to your shadow. This switch is not one you can simply will yourself to make. How can you use your conscious mind to access your unconscious? You can't, which is precisely why Incubation is so frustrating. There is no point in gathering more information; there is nothing you can do to force a solution and muscle your way through to Verification. All you can do in Incubation is surrender and wait.

Those of us who have a preference for R-mode may have a slightly easier time with this surrender, but not by much. Personally, I rarely surrender without putting up a fight. It's pointless, and even more so because I know it's pointless, but it's true.

We struggle because we know that opening ourselves to the unconscious requires not willpower, but willingness—willingness to begin the descent. This descent into the unconscious shadow frightens our ego-self to the very core. We fear that if we make this journey into the underworld of our own Self, we shall never return. It's an old, old fear, perhaps as old as humanity itself. That's why there have always been stories of the descent to remind us the journey is worth making, to challenge us to become willing, and to reassure us that we will return.

Living is a form of not being sure, not knowing what next or how. The moment you know how, you begin to die a little. The artist never entirely knows. We guess. We may be wrong, but we take leap after leap in the dark.

AGNES de MILLE

Persephone's Descent

One of these stories is the tale of Persephone's descent into the underworld. As the Greeks told the story, Persephone was the daughter of
Demeter, the Earth Mother. Where Demeter walked, flowers sprouted
and grain grew. She was always pregnant, constantly giving birth, and always ready to nurse and give succor. The Greeks said that milk flowed
nonstop from Demeter's breasts, and this is what created the Milky
Way. Demeter was the fertile principle, responsible for all living and
growing things and for fertility, both present and potential.

Persephone was Demeter's beautiful and beloved daughter, the
maiden who was the delight of all who saw her. Young and innocent,
Persephone was always at play.

Now it came to pass that Hades, god of the underworld, saw
Persephone and began to lust for her. He talked to his brother Zeus,
who was running more of an old boys' club than a universe. Since Zeus
was Persephone's father, Hades needed Zeus's permission to make
Persephone his wife. Zeus gave Hades his permission and agreed to
look the other way when Hades abducted her. So when Persephone was
singing and walking alone, Hades, in his black chariot pulled by six black
stallions, burst through the crust of the Earth. He grabbed Persephone
and dragged her kicking and screaming into the underworld. Some say
Hades wooed Persephone, trying to talk her into marrying him and becoming queen of the underworld. Others say Hades ravished Persephone
immediately. Either way, Persephone resisted and wanted only to return
to her mother, Demeter, and the green and living earth.

Demeter searched everywhere for her daughter. As Demeter
searched, she grieved, and the earth showed the results of her grief.
Crops failed; the cattle and sheep were barren; streams dried up;
women could not conceive; babies were stillborn or died in the cradle.
The people of the earth appealed to Zeus again and again, asking him to
help. He cajoled Demeter, telling her to give up her mourning for one
child and offer her bounty to all the people again. But by then Hecate,
the crone goddess, had told Demeter she had heard Persephone's cry,
and Helios, the sun god, had told Demeter he had seen Hades steal
Persephone. So Demeter told Zeus she would not cooperate until her
daughter was returned from Hades.

*One must also
accept that one has
"uncreative" moments.
The more honestly one
can accept that,
the quicker these
moments will pass.
One must have the
courage to call a halt,
or feel empty and
discouraged.*
ETTY HILLESUM

Zeus was the chief god, but he had no choice. He sent Hermes, the messenger, to tell Hades to return Persephone. Hermes told Hades that Zeus had decreed that if Persephone hadn't eaten any food in the underworld, she would have to be returned to her mother forever. Some say Persephone was forced, some say she consented, but one way or the other, wily old Hades got Persephone to swallow six pomegranate seeds.

Persephone was delighted to see her mother again, but when Zeus discovered that she had swallowed the pomegranate seeds, he decreed she would be Hades' wife for half the year. Hecate comforted mother and daughter and became Persephone's companion for the six months she was queen of the underworld. Demeter released her bounty again, but when her daughter returns to Hades every year, the earth becomes barren again and winter comes. When Persephone returns, she brings spring with her.

Finding Meaning in Persephone's Tale

In her audiocassette *Creative Fire,* Clarissa Pinkola Estés reveals layers of meaning in this story of Persephone. Primarily, it is a symbol of the cycles of life in general and the cycles of creativity in particular. Estés explains, "That cycle is this: one of quickening, birth, rising of energy to a zenith, gradual entropy, decline, and death. Ah, but it doesn't end there. Then incubation, again quickening, a rising of energy to a zenith, the beginning of entropy, decline, and then again a death, and then again incubation. And it is this cycle that, unmolested at the center of the psyche, accounts for the creative acts and works we put out into the world."

Incubation is part of the cycle. If we descend in season, at times that our Self recognizes as appropriate (even though our ego-self feels like Persephone being dragged kicking and screaming), and then feel rejuvenated and transformed when we ascend again, then the descent and the incubation are right and proper. At times we will all feel like Demeter mourning the lost creative joy and searching to bring it home. Every creative person experiences times of creative drought, usually without being able to explain why. As long as these times are not too protracted, then they, too, are part of the Incubation stage (or sometimes Hibernation).

But Estés cautions, the cycle is sometimes interfered with. One reading of Persephone's tale asks us to consider how our creativity is stolen from us. All of us possess an aspect that is like Hades, that wants to steal our creative joy and keep it only for itself or even destroy it. This may be a part of our shadow or inner Destroyer. Every creative person struggles with a critical internal voice. If we can befriend it and allow it to guide us, we are strengthened. But if this Hades aspect of us is too powerful, becoming what Estés and other Jungians call a negative complex, then we need to find ways to bring it down to a manageable size. You will find the exercises and techniques suggested throughout this book helpful in doing that. Again, I recommend you enlist allies, particularly a personal creativity coach and a good therapist, especially if the Hades aspect won't budge.

From Incubation to Illumination

In *Creative Fire*, Estés also tells an earlier version of Persephone's story. In this version, Persephone is by herself playing when she hears people crying. She looks but can't find them. At the evening meal, she tells her mother, Demeter, about this. Demeter tells her to ignore the sound. But the next day, Persephone hears the crying again and finds a crack in the earth where the crying is coming from. She knows it is the souls of the dead, lost in the underworld, who weep. She tells her mother, and again Demeter tells her to pay no attention. But on the third day, Persephone hears the weeping and, moved by a deep compassion, crawls through the crack in the earth to find the lost souls and lead them.

When Persephone doesn't come home for the evening meal on the third day, Demeter searches for her. And when Demeter cannot find her daughter, she mourns. She asks Helios, the sun god, where her daughter is. Helios replies, "Your daughter is in the underworld, doing her work. Be ready to receive her when she returns." Demeter waits, but she still grieves and because she grieves, the earth is barren for a season.

As Persephone makes her descent through the dark earth to the underworld, her clothing is torn away from her. She struggles, and eventually she reaches the great World Tree at the center of the underworld. Here she is caught on a branch and hangs upside down until she dies. Then, an old crone (probably Hecate) and the good king of the underworld minister to Persephone for three days and three nights. After this time, Persephone is reborn.

Because of her compassion and because she has experienced death and rebirth herself, Persephone is able to lead the lost souls of the dead

A myth is far greater than a history, for a history only gives a story of the shadows, whereas a myth gives a story of the substances that cast the shadows.
ANNIE BESANT

out of the darkness and into the light. When the souls of the dead return to life, a crack opens in the earth again and Persephone is able to return to the upper world. Demeter and Hecate wait for her, and they clothe her in a white robe.

Personally, I prefer this version of the story. It tells us that we can choose our descent. Like Demeter, the ego insists we ignore this call, but another part of us is moved by compassion and by the creative impulse to begin the descent despite the ego's resistance. This ego resistance is appropriate since the function of the ego is to protect itself, particularly the playful and childlike aspects of the Self that Persephone represents.

When Persephone ignores the ego's resistance and heeds the inner call, she makes it possible to reclaim significant parts of the Self, to bring to consciousness what was lost in the unconscious. But a journey into the unconscious is not without peril. When Persephone goes exploring the underworld, she is lost. She loses her clothing, which symbolizes losing her defenses. Eventually she gets stuck in the unconscious and dies. The ego resists the descent because it instinctually knows that a part of it will die—not a literal death of the body, but a symbolic death of some aspect of the Self. Just as the ego is in charge of making sure we don't step in front of speeding cars or leap off cliffs, the ego resists this descent into the unconscious, where a different kind of death and loss will occur.

But if the ego resists too long, what happens? Then the unconscious aspects that have been crying out and ignored will come bursting through like Hades. The joy of creative play will be lost, and the ego will be dragged kicking and screaming into the unconscious. This can happen as a sudden shadow outburst, a creative drought that goes on and on, or a prolonged depression or illness.

The older version of the story promises us that we will be guided on this descent. It promises that the benevolent crone and king of the underworld (a balance of feminine and masculine) will nurture the creative child and bring her back to life. We can trust that even when it seems we have pulled our world down around our ears, there is a part of us deep inside that will care for us while we struggle in the descent.

But in the newer version of the story, it is the head god Zeus who demands Hades return Persephone, and only because there is so much suffering while she's gone. The older story promises that at the heart of our unconscious there are aspects that will guide and protect us through the death-rebirth transformation. The later tale suggests we will need intellectual intervention and willpower, because what lies in the unconscious is as jealous and malevolent as Hades.

The newer version threatens that the descent is inevitable, and we are powerless to initiate it or defend against it. It is true that for all our resistance and fear, we cannot avoid the descent. And that is fortunate, because it is only after we make the descent into Incubation that we can return to Illumination. But the older version promises us that if we make the descent by choice, we will be reborn and reemerge in the land of the light. Persephone returns, Estés points out, "no longer as a naïve, innocent young woman, but as a knowing young woman, who is attracted to the good and the deep and the compassionate in a way that she never could have realized before her descent."

Why have these changes in the story of Persephone's descent taken place over time? There is the historical-cultural explanation that Greek culture, in fact world culture, was profoundly changing at that time. Goddess worship was being changed, often by force and coercion, to god worship. The feminine, both sacred and secular, was denigrated more and more. The later version reveals a male chief god, Zeus, who was willing to deflate Demeter's power by cooperating in the abduction of her daughter. It also reveals an attitude that the kidnap and rape of young maidens was just what happened sometimes.

But myths reflect more than history; the differences in the two versions reflect profound differences in our psychological makeup. Some of us are blessed with a benevolent crone and king in our unconscious, but many of us are also cursed with the Hades aspect that wants to steal our creative joy and keep it all for itself, never letting it out into the light to be shared with others. What can we do about this Hades aspect? Even when Zeus, the head god, the intellect, orders Hades to return Persephone, Hades pulls a trick. Intellect alone is not sufficient to heal the Hades aspect.

For a fuller solution, let's take a look at a story older than Persephone's. You will notice elements that were carried through from this story of Inanna and Ereshkigal to the story of Persephone, which shows how the stories are related.

In a way winter is the real spring, the time when the inner things happen, the resurge of nature.
EDNA O'BRIEN

Inanna's Descent

I heard this story of Inanna and Ereshkigal in the spring of 1994 at a weekend workshop Linda Star Wolf led on exploring the feminine aspects of the Divine. Linda Star Wolf is one of my mentors. She has facilitated my process with compassion, has carried my white shadow projections with grace and handed them back to me with even more grace, and has challenged me again and again with relentless love. An ancient myth like this one has many variations, all of them colored by the individual and culture relating the story. One of Linda's gifts is the ability to add her own style to a myth in a way that reveals the essential truth and empowers the listeners to apply what they hear to their own lives. Those of us who were favored to hear Linda's drumming and telling of the story will never forget special aspects of it. I can't duplicate Linda's style, but I am going to retain some of her additions as I share the story with you in my own way.

Inanna was the Queen of Heaven and Earth. She was the Evening Star, the Bright of Dawn, and the Wayward Moon. She was queen of the birds and the beasts. When she stepped upon the clouds, lightning flashed and the rains fell, and where her footsteps touched the earth, plants sprouted and the animals quickened with new life.

Inanna's sister, her dark sister, Ereshkigal, was the Queen of the Underworld. She was the Dark of the Moon, the Deep Cave without End, and the Keeper of the House of the Dead. She was Queen of the Snakes, which symbolize death and rebirth by the shedding of their skins. And yet it was Ereshkigal who gave birth to infancy and Inanna herself who was fallow.

Inanna decided to visit her sister in the underworld. Why? Perhaps because she was fallow and recognized she needed Ereshkigal's power of transformation. Perhaps Inanna was bored. Perhaps she thought that as Queen of Heaven and Earth, she could go anywhere as she pleased, even to the House of No Deposit, No Return. Goddesses are like that.

So Inanna ignored the pleas and advice of her servant Ninshubar, who begged Inanna not to go. But Inanna did follow the advice given to those who trek in the wilderness; she told Ninshubar where she was going and when Ninshubar should send out a search party if she didn't re-

We all have to take our own responsibility when it comes to being creative. We have to find ways of protecting the special place inside that enables us to create. If anything were to kill my creativity, it would be my fault, not other people's.
NICHOLAS CAGE

turn. Then Ninshubar helped Inanna prepare for her journey, dressing her in all her finery—her crown, her jewels, her cloak of stars, her diamond belt and flowing skirt. Inanna was going to the House of the Dead dressed for a party. Goddesses are like that.

Now Ereshkigal, Queen of the Underworld, had invented something that is still used in some parts of the world like Illinois and New Jersey. She had set up toll gates and guards on the road into her realm. I don't know why Ereshkigal did this. After all, there aren't a lot of people trying to sneak into the Underworld, although I suspect quite a few would like to sneak out. Well, like I said, goddesses are like that.

After she passed through heaven and passed through earth, Inanna came to the first gate, where she told the guard, "I am Inanna, Queen of Heaven and Earth. Let me pass."

To which the guard replied, "This ain't heaven and this ain't earth, and there ain't no queen here but my boss Ereshkigal. So if you don't have exact change for the gate, hand over the gold crown or turn around and go home."

Well, you know goddesses, they never have exact change and they never change their minds. So Inanna handed over her crown, the guard raised the gate, and Inanna, looking a little less regal, went on her way in the dark.

At the next toll gate, Inanna, who still didn't have exact change, said, "I am Inanna, Queen of Heaven and Earth and a guest of my sister Ereshkigal. Let me pass."

To which the guard replied, "This ain't heaven and this ain't earth, and there ain't no guests here. If you don't have exact change for the gate, hand over your lapis earrings and we'll call it even."

So Inanna handed over her earrings, the guard raised the gate, and Inanna, looking a little less radiant, went on her way in the dark.

At the third gate, Inanna told the guard, "I am Inanna, Queen of Heaven and Earth and Ereshkigal's sister. Let me pass."

To which the guard replied, "This is ain't heaven and this ain't earth, and if you insist on going to visit your sister and you don't have change for the gate, hand over the six-pointed necklace."

So Inanna gave up her jewels, the guard raised the gate, and Inanna, looking a little more diminished, went on her way in the dark.

At the fourth gate, the guard demanded Inanna's star cloak, and she began to feel the cold upon her body. At the fifth, the guard demanded Inanna's jeweled shoes, and she began to feel the cold upon her feet. At the sixth gate, the guard demanded Inanna's breastplate, and she began to feel vulnerable. At the seventh and final gate, the guard demanded Inanna's diamond belt and flowing skirt, and now naked and alone in the dark, Inanna began to feel the cold upon her spirit.

And so Inanna came, shivering and feeling fear for the first time, to stand before her sister's throne in the underworld.

"I am Inanna," she began, but before she could finish, Ereshkigal interrupted.

"I know who you are, Sister. I wonder why you have come to see me here. Did you come to gloat about your glories? Or to bring tidings of the overworld that I couldn't possibly care about? Or did you come to ask me to do you a favor? It doesn't matter. Whatever your reasons, you have come into my realm, into the House of No Return, and so, Sister, you have come to die." (Goddesses always talk like this. Goddesses are like that.)

And Ereshkigal turned her cold eyes and her skeletal face on Inanna. Along with all her crown and her jewels, along with all her finery, Inanna had given up her immortality. And when Ereshkigal's eyes fell upon her, Inanna dropped dead.

Ereshkigal picked up her sister's body and hung it on a meat hook to rot. And then Ereshkigal sat on her throne, wailing and feeling sorry for herself. "My sister is dead. And so I am dead too." There's just no accounting for goddesses, but they're like that.

As time passed, plants withered, streams dried up, and animals became barren. The moon never showed its face and the evening star was never seen. And so Ninshubar knew her mistress was having trouble in the underworld.

Ninshubar asked the other gods to help Inanna, but they all said, "We told her not to go. Now she's in Ereshkigal's realm, and no one can save her."

Ninshubar asked Inanna's lover and consort Dumuzi to help, but he said, "I asked her not to go. Now she's in Ereshkigal's realm and I can't help her."

Finally Ninshubar asked for help from Enki, who was a bit of a clown and a bit of a trickster, usurping the power of other gods and goddesses.

Enki thought about how he could help Inanna and what it would get him if he did. He thought about how Inanna and Ereshkigal were sisters and how Ereshkigal would mourn Inanna even if she herself had harmed her. As he thought, Enki picked his nose, and from the dirt under his fingernails, he shaped two small demons. He gave one booger a small vial of the water of life and the other booger a small vial of the food of life. Then Enki sent his booger-demons to the underworld.

Now those boogers flew right past the seven gates and the seven guards without being seen. They flew into Ereshkigal's throne room and saw Inanna rotting on the meat hook.

"Oh, her insides," the one booger said, shuddering.

"Oh, her outsides," the other booger replied, shaking.

Then those boogers flew up to Ereshkigal and listened to her wailing and moaning. "Oooh, my insides," Ereshkigal wailed.

"Oooh, your insides," one booger whispered sympathetically in Ereshkigal's ear.

"Oooh, my outsides," Ereshkigal moaned.

"Oooh, your outsides," the other booger echoed empathically in Ereshkigal's other ear.

"My sister Inanna is dead and rotting, and it pains me so," Ereshkigal cried.

"Then let us take her away," the boogers said.

Ereshkigal agreed and the boogers lifted Inanna down from the meat hook. They sprinkled her body with the water of life and the food of life from the vials Enki had given them.

"Take her away," Ereshkigal said, "but she must send someone to take her place so I am not all alone."

So the boogers took Inanna back through the seven gates, collecting her skirt and cloak and jewels and crown along the way. They dressed her and restored her to heaven, where they revived her and told her what Ereshkigal said.

So Inanna began her search for who to send to keep Ereshkigal company. She searched heaven, and when she spied a brother god who had not helped her when she was held in Ereshkigal's realm, she thought of sending him. But she saw her brother weeping and heard him call for the return of the Queen of Heaven. So she looked elsewhere.

She searched the earth and spied a man in a field. Because he was not in her temple, she thought of sending him. But then she saw that the man mourned his failing crops and cried out for the return of the Queen of Earth. So Inanna looked elsewhere.

She went inside her temple and saw her lover Dumuzi. He wasn't weeping or calling for her return. Instead he was sitting on the altar-throne made for her. He smiled and winked at the priestesses and called for more wine and music.

Inanna remembered how she had longed for Dumuzi and his sweet caresses as she neared her death. She realized that while she was in the underworld yearning for Dumuzi, he had gotten drunk and made passes at her priestesses. So Inanna said, "Dumuzi, my lover, you're the one I choose." Dumuzi, who had been understandably a little worried at Inanna's sudden return, smiled with relief. That is, until Inanna said, "You're the one I choose to keep my sister company."

Some people say Dumuzi had a sister who begged for mercy on her brother's behalf. There is no accounting for some people's sisters, either. And so Dumuzi spends half the year in the underworld with Ereshkigal, and his sister, Geshtinanna, spends the other half-year there on his behalf. And while this can't explain goddesses or sisters, it does explain the passing of the seasons.

Passing Through Our Own Seasons

What do you do when your shadow has captured your creativity, when the descent reaches a depth from which there seems no escape? Detached intellectualizing that offers no compassion and hence holds no true understanding won't change anything. Stern marshaling of the forces of willpower won't change anything. There is no point in the ego trying to assert itself over the shadow—you may be Queen of Heaven and Earth, but you're in the underworld now. Ereshkigal isn't going to listen to Inanna or Enki or any other god or goddess in the overworld ordering her about. (Even Hades pulled a fast one so he wouldn't have to fully obey Zeus.) In other words, ordering "All right now, enough of this nonsense and self-indulgence. I'm just going to march myself into my studio today and produce something, by God!" isn't going to work. It never has and it never will.

But something must. There must be something that can return our

---

We are healed of our suffering only by experiencing it to the full.

MARCEL PROUST

creative joy, our Persephone. What helps is earthy and basic. Enki sent boogers made from the dirt of his nose and from under his fingernails. And because these boogers had no dignity to preserve, because they felt no need to be defensive, they were willing and able to be with Ereshkigal in a way that was truly healing. They attended to Ereshkigal's misery. They empathized with her suffering. They paid attention to her struggle. Because they were able to listen to and be with her in this way, Ereshkigal became willing to let her sister go.

A rare reference in the Persephone story echoes this truth that help will come from a surprisingly crude source. Most modern recordings of the myth have sanitized this reference out of existence, but Estés remembers. Estés remembers Balbo, the goddess of obscenity (meaning outside of accepted practice) who appeared when Demeter was about to give up hope. Balbo was able to break Demeter's depression by dancing and raising her skirt to reveal herself to Demeter. In *Creative Fire*, Estés tells us that Balbo has no head, her nipples are her eyes, and her genitals are her mouth. Balbo told ribald jokes, and it was this earthy humor that broke Demeter out of her hopeless despair. Laughing loosened Demeter enough to hear the significance of Balbo's question, "Who do you think took your daughter?" Demeter then gave up her desperate, haphazard search and instead moved with purpose, asking Hecate what she heard and Helios what he saw. Laughter empowered Demeter to seek out allies.

So what can you do when your shadow has hung your ego-self out to dry (or die)? Give your shadow empathy, attention, and love. Be a booger, tossing away dignity and self-importance and crooning, "Oh my insides, oh my outsides." Find allies who can give you insight about where your creative joy and juice might have gone and who are also willing to croon, "Oh your insides, oh your outsides."

Take a good look around to identify what habit or personality quirk is your Dumuzi. What part of you revels rather than grieves when you experience creative dry spells? Do you spend too much time reading junk and not enough time journaling? Do you use TV or food or sex to forget about the discomfort of what's not happening in your creative life? Do you have a friend who encourages you to give up when you need someone to help you hang in? You need to make a sacrifice to your shadow, and guess who or what is the number one choice. Making a sacrifice

Everyone has talent. What is rare is the courage to follow the talent to the dark place where it leads.

ERICA JONG

doesn't mean indiscriminate shadow-blasting. Remember to choose your action from your Moral Center, based on your own values. But do take a good long look at what needs to "die" so you can fully surrender to the process.

And get some dirt under your fingernails. Squish wet, yielding clay (modeling or air-dry) between your fingers just to see what comes out. Notice how your hands have a wisdom of their own; how, if you will stop paying attention to your ego's endless chatter, the wisdom of the body creates without conscious willing. Or mix flour, sugar, and yeast, knead it with your hands and shoulders, and bake bread. Notice the time you have to leave it alone to rise and the time you leave it in the hot, dark oven; both of these are excellent metaphors for Incubation. Break up soil with your hands in your garden and bury seeds underground. If Ereshkigal or Hades take over during the winter (as they are wont to do), use potting soil and indoor planters. Pay attention to those seeds you buried, how they cease to be seeds and are reborn as tiny, green sprouts.

Guided Imagery Preparation

You need to make a few extra preparations before you start this guided imagery. Set out some modeling or air-drying clay, a glass of water to keep the clay moist as you work with it, and some clay shaping tools like a nail, nutpick, garlic press, and plastic knife, fork, and spoon. Place these materials on a piece of clean paper or a piece of canvas. Keep the clay wrapped so it will stay moist.

You will also need to read the following list of seven important items to take on a trip to a foreign country. Change the list as necessary to reflect what you would take. You must take seven items and no more than seven items. So if you want to add something to the list, you'll either have to delete something or combine two items. For example, you might consider your identification papers to be part of your wallet.

- Passport or other identification papers
- Wallet with money, traveler's checks, and credit cards
- Purse, briefcase, or carry-on bag with miscellaneous items, books, and magazines
- Tickets and boarding passes

- Suitcase full of clothes
- Toilet kit with toothbrush and other necessities
- Nice clothes to wear on the plane

The items on this list will be referred to in the guided imagery. So if you alter this list, ask the person who will read the guided imagery to you to read through it in advance and make any necessary changes.

✳ Guided Imagery

As you've done in earlier guided imageries, find a place and time when you can be relaxed and uninterrupted. Lie or sit comfortably and begin to relax. Close your eyes. Take several deep breaths, noticing and following the breath in and out of your body.

Consciously tighten the muscles in your feet and ankles. Notice the tension. . . . Feel the tension in all the muscles in your feet. . . . Hold the tension as long as you like . . . holding it until you're ready to let it go with a sigh. . . . Take a deep breath and notice how it feels to let go, to feel the warm relaxation in your feet. . . .

Now, consciously tighten the muscles in your calves and knees. Notice the tension. . . . Feel the tension in your calves and knees. . . . Hold the tension . . . until you're ready to let it go with a sigh. . . . Take a deep breath and notice how good it feels to let your calves and your knees relax and go slack. . . .

Consciously tighten the muscles in your thighs, buttocks, and pelvis. Notice the tension. . . . Feel the tension in your thighs and buttocks and pelvis. . . . Hold the tension . . . until you're ready to let it go with a sigh. . . . Take a deep breath and notice how good it feels to let the lower half of your body relax more and more with each breath you take. . . .

Take another deep breath and consciously tighten the muscles in your stomach, chest, and back. Feel the tension in your torso. . . . Notice what it feels like to hold tension in this part of your body. . . . Hold that tension . . . until you're ready to let it go with a sigh. . . . Take a deep, slow breath and notice how good it feels to breathe all the way down to your belly . . . how good it feels to let your belly go soft and round with each breath. . . .

Now, consciously tighten your hands into fists. Feel the tension move from your hands to your wrists, your forearms, elbows, upper arms, into your shoulders and the base of your neck. . . . Notice that tension, what it feels like . . . holding it until you're ready to let it go with a sigh. . . . Take a deep breath and notice how good it feels to let any remaining tension ooze out of your fingertips. . . . Notice how good it feels to let your shoulders drop and let your arms relax more and more. . . .

Now, consciously tighten the muscles in your jaw and neck; scrunch up the muscles around your eyes and forehead. . . . Notice the tension in your face and neck . . . holding it until you're ready to let it go with a sigh. . . . Notice how good it feels to let your whole body become more and more relaxed . . . more and more relaxed with every breath. . . .

Continue to breathe deeply. If worries or thoughts about other things come to you, simply remind yourself, "Not this, not now," set the thought aside, and return your attention to your breathing. Allow your breath to assume a slow, natural rhythm.

Experience your whole body now as relaxed . . . your mind as quiet and still . . . your emotions as calm and clear . . . your spirit as peaceful and serene. . . .

From this place of inner serenity, harmony, and relaxation, begin to allow images to occur in your mind. . . . Imagine yourself getting ready to go on a journey. . . . See yourself gathering all the things you will need on this journey . . . notice your picture on your passport . . . notice the color and feel of the traveler's checks and credit cards in your wallet . . . feel how heavy your purse, briefcase, or carry-on bag is getting . . . check to make sure you have your tickets . . . see yourself closing your suitcase filled with traveling clothes . . . smell the toothpaste and the other toiletries you've packed . . . and notice what clothes you're wearing to start your journey. . . . Take some time to prepare yourself to start your journey. . . .

And now see yourself leaving your house . . . bringing all the essential things with you to the airport. . . . Notice the sights and sounds of the airport. . . . You go to the gate to sign in and the person there checks your name . . . and tells you there's been a change in plans. . . . You're going to make a different journey . . . a journey to meet your dark sister or brother, your dark sibling. . . . The person leads you to a quiet room, where you set down your suitcase and your carry-on bag. . . . The person invites you to relax on a couch and wait. . . . You sit or lie down on the couch and close your eyes . . . alone . . . waiting for your journey to begin. . . .

You feel yourself begin to move through darkness . . . walking slowly, carrying your heavy suitcase and carry-on bag and all the other essential items you packed . . . you walk slowly in the dark . . . until you come to a gate. . . . You tell the guard your name and that you've come to see your sibling. . . . The guard checks your passport and identification papers and then waves you through. . . . You pass through the gate and reach for your passport, but the guard glares at you and won't give it to you, no matter how much you argue and gesture. . . . Notice how you feel about losing your passport . . . about losing your identity. . . .

You continue to walk slowly through the dark, carrying your heavy suitcase and carry-on and all the other essentials . . . until you come to a second gate and a second guard. . . . You tell the guard your name and that you've come to see your dark sibling. . . . This guard takes your wallet and all your money, your traveler's checks and credit cards. . . . The guard waves you through the gate, but no matter how much you argue and gesture, the guard refuses to return your wallet. . . . Notice how you feel about losing your wallet . . . about losing your value and power. . . .

You continue walking slowly in the dark, carrying your heavy suitcase and carry-on and your other essentials . . . until you come to a third gate and a third guard. . . . You tell the guard your name and that you've come to see your dark sibling. . . . This guard takes your carry-on bag with all the important little things you packed inside. . . . The guard waves you through the gate, but refuses to give your carry-on bag back to you. . . . Notice how you feel about losing your carry-on and all those important little things. . . .

You continue walking slowly in the dark, carrying your heavy suitcase and your other essentials . . . until you come to a fourth gate and a fourth guard. . . . You tell the guard who you are and why you've come. . . . The guard takes your tickets and refuses to give them back. . . . Notice how you feel about losing your tickets . . . how will you get back without your tickets? . . .

You continue walking, carrying your heavy suitcase and a few other essentials . . . until you come to a fifth gate and a fifth guard. . . . You tell the guard who you are and why you've come. . . . The guard takes your suitcase and everything in it except your toilet kit. . . . No matter how much you plead, the guard won't return your suitcase. . . . Notice how you feel about losing your suitcase and all your clothes, all your protection against the cold.... Notice how cold it is walking alone in the dark, carrying nothing but your toilet kit....

You come to a sixth gate and a sixth guard.... You tell the guard who you are and why you've come.... The guard takes your toilet kit and refuses to give it back.... Notice how you feel about losing your own toothbrush and all your other personal items....

You continue walking, carrying nothing ... until you come to a seventh gate and a seventh guard.... You tell the guard your name and that you've come to see your dark sibling.... You tell the guard you have nothing left ... and the guard rips the clothes from your body.... You stand alone, naked, shivering in the cold and the dark....

You walk until you come to a throne.... Sitting on the throne, dressed up fine and surrounded by riches, is your dark sibling.... The one you've come to see.... Your dark sibling, your shadow, stares at you.... She (or he) raises an arm and points a finger at you.... Take time now to listen well to what your dark sibling has to say about what needs to change in your life, about what needs to pass away, die, and be reborn....

As your dark sibling speaks, keep asking, "What do you see more clearly than I?" ... until you realize your sibling's eyes are your eyes....

Take time now to pay attention to your dark sibling's complaints and laments.... As your dark sibling speaks, keep crooning over and over, "Oh, your insides. Oh, your outsides," while comforting, holding, rocking your dark sibling in your arms ... until you realize that your sibling's complaints are your complaints ... that you are comforting, holding, rocking yourself, crooning over and over, "Oh, my insides. Oh, my outsides."...

Take time now to recognize what your dark sibling has kept safe here in the underworld.... Notice that parts of yourself you thought you had lost forever are safe here, where your dark sibling has treated them as the treasures they are....

When you're ready and when your dark sibling is ready, make an agreement about what you will send as a sacrifice to your dark sibling ... maybe you know what that sacrifice will be ... maybe you don't know yet.... And when you're ready, look around to see that the aspects of yourself you had lost are ready to return to the light, are ready to be reborn as you return to the light ... maybe you understand what these aspects are ... maybe you can't see them clearly yet....

Gathering these aspects of yourself that are ready to be reborn, bid

Among indigenous peoples, it is understood that we give away the things we value most; whether or not we can see it at the time, we will get something we need in return.

RICHARD KATZ
The Wisdom of Ancient Healers

farewell to your dark sibling . . . and begin walking back up the road through the seventh gate . . . through the sixth gate . . . through the fifth gate . . . back through the fourth gate . . . through the third gate . . . back through the second gate . . . back through the first gate . . . back up the road toward the light. . . .

And when you're ready, remembering the sacrifice you promised and the aspects returning with you, slowly return your attention to this room. . . . Slowly allow your awareness of your body to return to normal. . . . Wiggle your toes and become aware of the feel of your body lying on the floor or sitting in the chair. . . . Open your eyes and move slowly to where you left the clay. Allow your hands to work the clay without thinking about it too much. See what emerges. After playing with clay, write any other impressions you want to remember.

⊛ *Creative Shadow Play*

Working with modeling clay or air-drying clay, shape a pair of boogers. Give them wings so they can fly to the underworld. Make the meat hook Inanna hung on. Make the crone and the king who brought Persephone back to life. Make the chariot Hades drove and other shapes from the stories. Make a shape that represents the sacrifice you promised and then smash it. Make a shape that represents an aspect of you that is being reborn. Keep this in a sacred and safe place.

⊙ **EXERCISE CHOICES**

1. Honor the Dirt under Your Nails. Use the suggestions offered earlier to get your hands dirty working with clay or bread dough or potting soil. Or be Cinderella and sweep ashes from a fireplace. Or play with papier-mâché or finger paints or a glue gun. Get your hands dirty one way or another. As you do, ponder the sacred nature of mundane things like clay, dirt, ashes to ashes . . .

2. Listen to Clarissa Pinkola Estés's Stories. Listen to the audiocassette *Creative Fire.* You can get a copy from your local library or from *Sounds True* (800-333-9185).

There is a time to let go of even the things that are most precious to you—segments of your life, your feelings, affiliations, old and new relationships, ideas and affinities. Sometimes you simply outgrow them. In either case, they no longer serve you. They prevent life from going forward in any bountiful or useful manner.

CLARISSA PINKOLA ESTÉS
Women Who Run With the
Wolves

3. Read about Inanna and Persephone. Borrow a couple of books about mythology from your library to read different accounts of the stories. Decide which version you resonate with, that is, which one makes the most sense to you and seems most satisfying.

4. Share the Story. Find a couple of friends and tell them a version of Inanna or Persephone that you like best. Begin with a few written notes about the elements that seem most important to you and allow yourself to embellish as you tell the story. Then talk with your friends about what the story means to each of you, how it relates to your creativity, your shadows, your lives.

5. Read All about Her or Him. Make a list of creative people you admire. Read a bibliography or autobiography of some of these people. Pay attention to the times in their lives when they went through a descent and came back up. Notice how they responded during these times.

6. Make Up Your Own Story. Think about the major descents you've experienced in your life. These might be times of loss—the death of a loved one, a divorce or other significant relationship change, a job loss, a midlife crisis. Select one and make up a story about that time. As in a myth, have most of the major characters in the story be different aspects of yourself.

7. Tell Your Own Future. Think about the descents you have been called to take and have resisted so far. These might be creative opportunities or personal challenges—starting a new major project like a new sculpture, screenplay, painting commission; exploring a new kind of creative media; quitting your job and going back to school; leaving school and starting a new career; and so on. Select one of these future descents and spend some time mulling over possible ways you could tell a story about it. What characters will you use? Are there important props? What will the plot be? What will happen to you on this journey?

✳ ✳ ✳ ✳ ✳ ✳ ✳ ✳ ✳ ✳

CHAPTER 13

Re-storying Ourselves

YOU MAY NOT REALIZE IT, but you are a storyteller. It's part of being human. Storytelling is the most ancient and universal art. Humans have always told stories to explain the world, to entertain each other, and to educate our young. Sometimes we even use stories to explain ourselves to ourselves.

We all tell our stories all the time. We dream elaborate plots each night, we tell jokes, we share what happened during our day around the dinner table, we vent our complaints to a sympathetic friend, and it always comes out as a story. "And then she said . . ."

✍ *Exercise: Complete the Story*

Complete the story started in each of the three scenarios below. You can sit down and write with pen and paper or with your computer, or simply sit in a comfy chair, close your eyes, and let the story unfold in your imagination. You can tell the story as it might really happen in your life, as an exaggeration, or as a complete fantasy. Include as many vivid and concrete details as you can think of for each story.

Scenario 1: A Change in Plans A good friend calls to tell you that the two of you won't be going to the movies as you planned because . . .

Scenario 2: Important News Your boss (or an important client) asks you to step inside his or her office, invites you to sit down, and says, "I have important news that will affect you. Starting next week . . ."

Scenario 3: The Midnight Call A close family member (a child, sibling, spouse, or parent) wakes you from a sound sleep at midnight on a Saturday night and says, "You won't believe what happened . . ."

✍ Exercise: Explore the Stories You Tell

> *The events in our lives happen in a sequence in time, but in their significance to ourselves they find their own order.*
>
> EUDORA WELTY

Consider each of the three stories you completed in the first exercise. What do they have in common? How are they different? How would you classify the stories—as drama, comedy, tragedy, romance? Are they fairy tales, murder mysteries, science fiction, true confessions, or something else? If they were TV shows or movies, what kind would they be—sitcoms; doctor, cop, or lawyer stories; soap operas; romantic comedies; action-adventures; science fiction; Westerns?

Is there a particular kind of story you often or usually tell about yourself? What kinds of stories do you find yourself in the middle of? Are you surrounded by tragedy or comedy?

The Pattern of Your Life Story

The story that dominates your life probably arises from patterns that were imprinted on your psyche early, patterns that have a way of repeating throughout your life. That's how and why we find ourselves in the same kind of situation again and again ("This kind of thing always happens to me!"). It's why we find ourselves in significant relationships with the same kind of person time after time ("I can't believe I found another boss just like my father!"). The funny thing isn't that this happens, it's that it takes us so long to realize that changing the supporting cast doesn't make much difference if we never change the script.

We can become so immersed in the details of our life stories that we fail to see other plot possibilities. Like the solution to a maze that can only be seen when you're above it, identifying the exact nature of the pattern can be difficult when you're standing in the middle of it. Fortunately, there are ways to get the distance we need to identify the primary patterns of our life stories. And it is vital that we do so.

Our Stories Determine Our Reality

The stories we tell about ourselves are highly significant. Clearly, the kind of story we tell about the events in our lives determines our perceptions of reality. We all know someone who always makes a big, dramatic production out of what seems to us minor things. Or someone who takes every bump in the road of everyday existence as a personal affront.

On the other hand, my best friend and heart-sister, Claudia, has the marvelous life skill of telling most of the stories she's in as comedies. Claudia has had her share of tough moments and feels the whole range of human emotions including anger, anxiety, frustration and disappointment, as well as joy and satisfaction. But she has a talent for reframing her experiences. Usually within a day or two, longer for major disturbances, Claudia has changed the story to make it one that other people will laugh at with her. She restores her own sense of equanimity as she re-stories the tale. To listen to some of Claudia's stories, you'd think she's had a charmed life. She hasn't. Better than having than a charmed life, Claudia has the charm to make most of her life stories interesting, amusing, and uplifting.

Or maybe it's more than that.

Contemporary research in the field of physics has proven again and again that, at a subatomic level, it is impossible to observe a particle without affecting that particle. It's called the "observer effect." So much for Newtonian-based science that assumes we can discover truth by posing a hypothesis, running a series of experiments from an objective and detached stance where we control and alter the variables, and then interpret truth by observing the data the experiments produce. According to the latest research, there is no objective and detached stance where we can control the variables because the attempt to control the variables is itself a variable. As soon as someone tries to observe a phenomenon—any phenomenon—that phenomenon is changed!

If subatomic particles are so affected by being observed, how much can our perceptions of reality be affected by our perceptual habits? In other words, how does our habit of seeing events as another chapter in the kind of story we expect to live affect what happens to us? Claudia, for example, expects to be able to see the funny and positive side of most everything that happens to her. I know someone else who expects to

It is only when people begin to shake loose from their preconceptions, from the ideas that have dominated them, that we begin to receive a sense of opening, a sense of vision.

BARBARA WARD

have always bad luck—*sigh*—another difficult day in a difficult life haunted by tragedies large and small. Is it really coincidence that they both seem to get what they expect? Perhaps the stories we tell about ourselves don't just affect our perceptions of our reality. Perhaps they affect our reality itself! Let me tell you a story about Claudia as an example.

Claudia was trying to squeeze the last few months out of her old car before her new one arrived. Driving early in the morning to Monticello, Minnesota, a very small town, to present a training program for her employer, Claudia noticed ominous noises coming from her car. Claudia started praying, "Please, just let me make it five more miles into town. Please, just let me make it into town." And she did. (The car had to be towed back to Minneapolis, where the mechanic determined the transmission was shot.)

Claudia pulled into a gas station and used the pay phone to make frantic phone calls to her co-workers and boss. Someone had to inform the engineers and plant operators she was supposed to train that she would be late. Someone had to get the training materials out on the tables. And somehow she had to find a way to get to the training center. Just as she was explaining this, a cab pulled up to get gas. Claudia rushed over to the woman filling the cab's tank. Yes, she could take Claudia where she needed to go. Problem solved.

The "coincidence" gets better. The tiny town of Monticello has only one cab. And the woman who runs the cab service doesn't answer her phone early in the morning because she has a standing order to drive some senior citizens to another small town. Who else but Claudia would have the good luck to have the only cab within twenty miles pull up just when and where she needed it? Maybe things like this happen to Claudia because she expects everything will work out in the end and make for a great story to laugh about later. Maybe anyone who has perceptual habits similar to Claudia's can have Claudia's kind of "luck."

🖎 Exercise: Examine Your Story Habit

What kind of perceptual habits do you have? What kinds of stories have you told about yourself in the past? How might that have affected not only your perceptions of what happened, but also what happened?

Consider this essential truth Salman Rushdie offers: "Those who do not have power over the story that dominates their lives, power to retell it, to rethink it, deconstruct it, joke about it, and change it as times change, truly are powerless, because they cannot think new thoughts."

If you could retell the story of your life, changing any event as you wish, how would you retell it? How would you re-story yourself? Spend some time pondering and playing with these questions.

The Central Figure

Most of us see myths as outdated stories about gods we don't believe in and naive attempts of prescientific people to examine the natural world. We think fairy tales are only for children, and maybe not even for them since they're so violent and nasty. But myths and fairy tales take on new significance when we view them from a Jungian perspective, recognizing the figures in a myth or fairy tale as aspects of one person's psyche, just as the figures in a dream often represent different aspects of the dreamer. With this perspective, myths and fairy tales are very relevant to our lives.

These old stories hold the wisdom of the ages about the human condition, about the struggles all humans face. Identifying which myth or fairy tale you resonate with will provide excellent insight. Who is the central figure you see in yourself? Which stories are home to your spirit? Are you Cinderella waiting to go to the ball? Are you Goldilocks trying things out to see what is "just right" for you? Are you the Little Engine That Could? Parzival seeking the Holy Grail? Which stories were your childhood favorites?

When you see yourself in a myth or fairy tale, you can use that story to guide you, not in a literal sense, but with psychological truths. In *Women Who Run With the Wolves*, Clarissa Pinkola Estés writes, "the guiding myth or fairy tale contains all the instruction a woman [or man] needs for her [his] current psychic development. . . . Stories are medicine. . . . They have such power; they do not require that we do, be, act anything—we need only listen."

Of course, to recognize that significant aspects of your life have been described in a myth or fairy tale, you have to be familiar with those tales.

The real stories that will sustain us will only come out of a community where we tell and listen to other stories. The act of telling a story creates community and, at the same time, elicits more stories.
SAM KEEN
Our Mythic Stories

Women Who Run With the Wolves is an excellent resource, as is *The Brothers Grimm* by Jack Zipes. You can also browse through the children's section of your local library. I had wonderful discussions in a class on fairy tales at the Minnesota Jung Association. Check if there is a similar organization in your area or if a college near you offers similar classes.

You also need to be aware of how the tales have been changed, altered over time by the cultures telling them. Remember the way Persephone's story was changed over time. In *Women Who Run With the Wolves,* Estés explains: "We also suspect the famous brothers [the Brothers Grimm] continued the tradition of old pagan symbols overlaid with Christian ones, so that an old healer in a tale became an evil witch, a spirit became an angel, an initiation veil or caul became a handkerchief. . . . Sexual elements were omitted. Helping creatures and animals were changed into demons and boogeys."

Since we define ourselves and live our lives to fit the patterns crystallized in the stories we resonate with, it is vital that we tell the truth with those stories. Sometimes that is difficult because we've lost so much of the ancient truth. As Estés highlights, "many women's teaching stories about sex, love, money, marriage, birthing, death, and transformation were lost. It is how fairy tales and myths that explicate ancient women's mysteries have been covered over too. Most old collections of fairy tales and mythos existent today have been scoured clean of the scatological, the sexual, the perverse, the pre-Christian, the feminine, the Goddesses, the initiatory, the medicines for various psychological malaises, and the directions for spiritual raptures."

This loss of ancient story truth affects both women and men. But not all is lost. As Estés affirms, "they are not lost forever. In every story fragment is the shape of the entire story . . . there is a strong pattern that still shines forth." This is a loss we can at least partially restore by re-storying ourselves, by rewriting the stories, both individually and collectively.

Not Just What, But How

It is important to identify not only what story we tell about ourselves, but also how we tell that story.

Many myths and fairy tales include a hero who is at first reluctant to

---

The best way out is always through.
ROBERT FROST

What's on its way up is on its way out. And the only way out is through.
LINDA STAR WOLF

take the journey he or she is called to make. Like the reluctant hero, many of us resist moving forward with the story. We work hard to keep ourselves stuck in one part of the story.

For example, Colleen sees herself as Cinderella, always doing the dirty work for everyone else and never getting to go to the ball. Colleen has frozen the story in the first chapter, replaying that theme over and over with many situations in her life. Without admitting it consciously, Colleen prefers playing the noble, long-suffering sister who always baby-sits her sister's kids to risking the possible rejection of going on a date herself. And this reluctance to take risks seems evident in other parts of her life, including her long-standing painter's block. Colleen needs to move on with the story.

Consider Andy, who secretly sees himself as the Cowardly Lion. Afraid to become who he is meant to be, Andy forgets the part of the story where the Lion leads the charge into the witch's castle. He needs to move on to the next chapter and win his own medals of valor.

Shadow work begins when we are willing, on a soul level if not on the conscious ego level, to move on with the story of our lives. Significant growth occurs only when we become willing to begin the descent we fear. Only when we are willing to die to the old can we be reborn to the new, to the whole person we are meant to be. People in Alcoholics Anonymous talk about how important it is to hit bottom so that a new life can begin. Scary as it is, we need to be willing to move on with the story, to take the whole journey. We can't reach the top again until we have made the descent and hit bottom.

The following stories—Robin Hood Retires!, Oedipus Opens His Eyes, and Humpty Dumpty Does What the Kings' Horses and Men Couldn't—are stories from three people who had the courage to endure the descent and move on with the story of their lives. They all partici-pated in one of my Dancing in the Dragon's Den classes. All of them talk about how the class helped initiate some of the changes in their lives, but the class wasn't the only impetus for any of them to begin the journey, nor the sole source of support. The three people featured here and the other participants in the classes have learned to identify the pat-terns in their stories and to re-story themselves. I trust you will find their stories as inspiring and restorative as I do.

I didn't understand that I needed management and publicity and all those things that were anathema to the old me in order to be efficient and have people hear what I create.

JOAN BAEZ

Robin Hood Retires!

Robin Hood is a hero from British mythology. He was a displaced noble who protested the excessive taxes levied by Prince John while good King Richard was away fighting in the Crusades. Robin Hood and his band of outlaws, the Merry Men, roamed Sherwood Forest, poaching game and eluding the dubious Sheriff of Nottingham. They were famous for robbing from the rich to give to the poor.

Theresa (not her real name) was an upper-level manager for fourteen years. She enjoyed her work, the sense of esteem it gave her, and the accolades she got from her colleagues and employees. She saw herself as a kind of corporate Robin Hood, using her power and influence to undermine executives who abused their power (robbing from the rich) on behalf of employees who were lower in the hierarchy and power structure (and giving to the poor). The people who worked for and with Theresa appreciated and applauded her efforts. But Theresa had a growing sense that it was time to leave her powerful position—an awareness that would launch her on a transformational journey that would profoundly affect her and the people close to her.

"The longing to quit my job was a feeling I had fought for a long, long time. In one of the exercises we did in class, we talked about what we wanted and why we weren't doing it. I started with all the practical reasons I couldn't quit my job, but when it came right down to it, I was really afraid of losing my value. I was afraid of letting that part of my ego die. If I quit work, who would I be? I would lose my identity."

Theresa used her role as leader of a reorganization team to eliminate her own job. "I did it rather unconsciously, but then all of sudden when it worked, I thought, 'Well, okay.'" Offered another job with a similar title and equivalent pay, Theresa declined. "They pushed me to take the new position, so I came up with reasons, but I really didn't have a good reason to walk away. I wasn't leaving for another great job. People asked me what I was going to do, and I didn't know."

Theresa stayed on to help with the transition at her company and to ease her own transition. Rationalizing that her preschool daughter needed more time before leaving the corporate-sponsored day care, Theresa postponed leaving. "It was more for me than her, though. It was a grieving process, and I needed to do some of it there. I couldn't just walk away.

"When I finally faced being home all day, I was lost. I cried every day. I had told everyone I had decided to retire, so everyone was jealous. No one could really understand what I was feeling except one friend, who had taken the shadow class with me.

"It was hard for my whole family, and that was hard for me too, because I wanted to think this was happening only to me. I wanted to believe they should all support me, but they were all going through their own ordeals because of what I started. That was hard to accept. My husband was supportive, and now he sees some of the benefits of the change, but at the time it was easier to see what everyone was losing. Everyone was being forced to change because Mom changed. I did it. I initiated it. I went from being the hero to walking into a situation where I was clearly the bad guy. I didn't want to be the bad guy. I went from being Robin Hood to being the Sheriff, the one who goes around and takes care of business. Not the hero, not even the villain, just a nobody bad guy. The worst possible character for me. That's what I willingly walked into."

The changes included financial stress. The family sold their house and moved to a smaller one with a lower mortgage payment. There were also changes in family dynamics and relationships. Without a job to define who she was, Theresa fought being defined as a stay-at-home mom.

"When my two older children were home all day during the summer, there was a whole other adjustment. They all wanted to do different things and they all wanted my attention because having me at home was new. I really fought that. I would hire high-school girls to come over and then I would disappear. I was fighting being a mom so hard.

"I kept thinking of the parable of Moses and the burning bush. I kept ignoring the burning bush, which was telling me to stop running and to stop fighting. I kept ignoring the message that I should start to accept and enjoy who I am. When I started taking voice lessons, a friend gave me a wonderful book, *The Woman Who Found Her Voice* (by Susan O'Halloran and Susan Delattre). The woman in the story is changed into different creatures. When she is a turtle, she gets stuck on her back in the mud at the bottom of a pond. She fights and struggles

Only those who dare, truly live.
RUTH P. FREEMAN

until she realizes that if she stops fighting, the water can help free her. There is this quote, the only thing I highlighted in the whole book:

> To be alive, to save yourself, requires great effort. Keep fighting or you will die. Marina knew in her turtle bones that her fall to the bottom of the pond had changed the message to "If you keep fighting, you will die."

That spoke to me. The inner voice, the burning bush, was trying to tell me, 'Stop fighting or you will die. You have other things to do. You have to be who you are because no one else can be that. It is time now.' About midsummer I finally let go and let the kids take what they needed from me as their mom."

The other thing Theresa was fighting was her tendency to project her shadow onto her husband and especially her oldest daughter, twelve-year-old Stephanie. "Self-care was in my shadow. I didn't take care of myself. I was very angry and judgmental of people who took care of themselves, like my husband and daughter. I would say to myself, 'Can't they see that other people need them? They don't have a sympathetic bone in their bodies.' I was always trying to do things for other people and I would always come last. I neglected my own physical and emotional well-being. But I wasn't really there for other people. I would just get more crabby and stressed. I would have to fight harder and harder to contain my emotional outbursts.

"I had difficulty just going with the flow. I had to drive everything. I was like a moth, drawn to the fire and burning myself out. I remember a discussion we had in class about how people sometimes fear ego-death more than physical death. That was true for me. I had no fear of physical death in terms of burning myself out or in terms of what the stress was doing to me physically. That was just the way I was supposed to live and die. When I think of myself as a moth, I think of moths as coming on strong at night, doing what they need to do real fast, and not living long. A moth has muted colors; it has to be by the fire to be bright. A moth is nothing without the light. For me, the fire was all the recognition that came with my job. I could do it all. I could master anything. But without the recognition, I felt like nothing."

Theresa is transitioning from moth to butterfly, and her daughter Stephanie is her best teacher. "A butterfly is someone who is around all the time, not just at night. A butterfly is someone who isn't afraid to be bright and bold—someone who explores, tries one flower and then tries something else. A butterfly loves to experiment. I'm starting to feel okay with exploring who I really am instead of having to say I'm my job.

"In this transition, there's been a lot of turmoil with Stephanie. She is not a moth, she is definitely her own person, and she is very good at taking care of herself. My other two children are more like me, more pleasers. Stephanie is so different, it's hard for me to love her. I felt a lot of guilt and shame when I realized I have to learn how to love her, really love her the way she is. I felt a lot of guilt about trying to make her more like me and for not being there for her when she needed me, because I worked. I didn't want to admit to myself that I didn't really know her and that the way I dealt with her was to not be around. I tolerated Stephanie, but I didn't love her. And I was her mother! That was horrible!"

Theresa shows remarkable insight into her relationship with her daughter as she explains, "People told me it was just her age, but I knew it was more. I projected a lot of my stuff on her. She would bring out emotions in me that I brought out in my dad. She did things that made me want to be physical with her, the way I did things that my dad used to rationalize physically abusing me. My dad never abused my sisters, but he said I was as bad as my brothers, so he abused my brothers and me. I saw Stephanie becoming rebellious the way I had been. In some ways she is very like me, how I was when I was her age. But I felt I was past all that and judged her for it. She is so raw, and because I wasn't allowed to be raw as a child, I didn't want her to be—partly out of jealousy that I didn't get to be that way and partly because I wanted to protect her. I didn't want her to be hurt because she is so outspoken. She says what she thinks, she doesn't follow the norm, doesn't fit in the boxes. She's a butterfly in that way. In some ways, I want to be more like her. I want to recapture what I repressed, what was beaten out of me."

Most parents project some unclaimed aspect of themselves onto their children. It's so common that Carl Jung observed that nothing affects the life of a child as much as the unlived (shadow) life of the parent. But few parents have the courage to allow themselves to be consciously aware of the projections. Parents need to become consciously aware of projections so they can take the next step of withdrawing those projections.

The challenge, then, is to be the creative myth-maker that we are, to consciously choose our myth, lest it be chosen for us by the collective mind.

MARY ELIZABETH MARLOW

This gives their children the freedom to choose who they are, independent of who their parents are or aren't.

Theresa showed true heroic courage when she acknowledged her projections and began to express previously denied feelings as her own. "I started to allow myself to show Stephanie how I was feeling. I allowed myself to cry in front of her. I was afraid of being judged by her because she comes across as being judgmental. It seemed she liked the mom she had before and didn't like this wishy-washy mom who didn't know what she was doing. That was hard for Stephanie. Right when she needed me to be the same, I was a totally different person she didn't know and couldn't relate to. So we're getting to know each other. Letting her know how I feel has helped her balance herself a little too. I had taught her, by role modeling, that it wasn't okay to cry. Now she's learning balance by showing when she's hurt. And I learned to apologize to Stephanie."

When Theresa took that painful first step of recognizing she needed to love her daughter differently, she made it possible to do that—to truly love Stephanie. Theresa courageously applied what she had learned about what shadow is and how it works. Combining that awareness with meditation exercises, daily readings, creative play, and consulting with professionals at a leadership and outsourcing firm, Theresa has made significant progress in her relationships with herself and her family.

"Gradually, I've learned to take of myself. For example, when I walk in the door and the kids want something, I can say, 'Mom's really hungry right now. I need to eat.' Now I can say I'll be there in fifteen minutes and really be there. I never would have thought of saying that before. Before, I was working my life away, always doing, doing, doing. I couldn't go fast enough. I feel more comfortable. I know I'm going to do things for other people again, but right now I need a stronger foundation. I need to focus on me now. I feel good about that."

Theresa has also gained a deeper awareness of the dark shadow side of playing Robin Hood. "My calling in life was that I was the hero who took care of everybody else. That was the hardest thing to walk away from when I left my job. I loved being a hero; I loved being there for all those people. They loved it when I went after the high-level people who took advantage of other people.

"I was a go-getter; I was a driver, so it was easy for me to get into the

Remembering the past gives power to the present.

FAE MYENNE NG

inner circle. I infiltrated the brotherhood; I got accepted; I was knighted. Then I destroyed from within. I detested it even when I wasn't in it, but I did everything I could to become a part of it. And I justified being angry and judgmental as long as I was doing it to right a social injustice.

"Then I went to a session at a Zen meditation center when there was a discussion of equanimity, about how if you go after a social injustice in a negative or violent way, you're just as bad. That's when I realized what I had done was not okay. There are a lot injustices, but we can't deal with them in a violent way. And I had a narrow definition of what was violent. I didn't hit anyone like my dad did, so I thought what I did was okay. But I realized it was still violent. I went after people and exposed their behavior. I was proud that because of me people were fired. I thought that was good; that they deserved it. I was robbing from the rich for the benefit of the poor.

"And I enjoyed it. It gave me a high. When I was done with one person, I looked for the next person because I got off on that. Some of my close friends I've admitted this to were horrified I could actually be that way. I would do it with a smile—nice, thoughtful, always thinking of someone else; how could it possibly be that I would do that?

"I was trying to prove I wasn't going to be a victim. And if you're not the victim, then you have to be the perpetrator. It's one or the other and I certainly wasn't going to be a victim. So I found people who deserved it. Then not only could I accept being a perpetrator, I could enjoy it. I didn't have to deal with shame. I wasn't a criminal, I didn't have to break any laws. I created my own Sherwood Forest, an environment where it was not only socially acceptable to be the Robin Hood, but in many respects, it was glorified. I got a lot of recognition. A lot of people knew my name, knew me when I walked down the hall.

"I still identify with that Robin Hood character, but I've definitely let go of a lot of anger. I don't believe what I did was right. I've had to deal with that in meditation. Now I focus on my own backyard, myself and my family, instead of Sherwood Forest. I'm completing the Robin Hood story, going on to a new chapter, instead of repeating that one over and over again. I've decided to break that pattern."

Most versions of the Robin Hood story we know has Robin staying in the forest, ending his life as an outlaw. Theresa could have stayed in her job and continued to kill herself and alienate her family. But she had the courage to listen to the inner voice that told her it was time to change. She had the courage to make the change. She walked away from being the outlaw hero; she walked away from Sherwood Forest, the stolen gold, and the cheering crowds. She's retired from being the corporate Robin Hood and is learning to be a butterfly in her own backyard.

Oedipus Opens His Eyes

You need to claim the events of your life to make yourself yours. When you truly possess all you have been and done, which may take some time, you are fierce with reality.

FLONDA SCOTT MAXWELL

Before his son was born, King Laius of Thebes received a prophecy that his son, Oedipus, would usurp the kingdom, kill his father, and marry his mother. Desperate to keep this prophecy from coming true, King Laius ordered that the child be killed. But his wife, Queen Jocasta, countermanded the King's order and had her infant given to a shepherd to be raised as a commoner.

The shepherd gave the infant Oedipus to a servant of a foreign king, Polybus, who raised Oedipus as his own son. When an oracle told Oedipus he would kill his father, Oedipus left his father's country, determined to defy that fate. But in his exile, he met King Laius and fought with him. Not knowing Laius was his father, Oedipus killed him. Later Oedipus defeated the Sphinx that had besieged Thebes. A hero to the rescued city-state, Oedipus married Queen Jocasta, not knowing she was his mother. Thus Oedipus became king and fulfilled the prophecy.

After Oedipus and Jocasta had four children, Oedipus's true identity was discovered. Queen Jocasta, horrified by what she had done, killed herself. Oedipus, equally horrified and blaming the sin upon the lust he felt when he first saw Queen Jocasta's beauty, gouged out his eyes so that he would never be so moved again.

The work we do with our shadow takes many guises, conscious and unconscious, over the course of our lives. Because Glen and I have been traveling companions on many parts of our individual journeys, it was particularly gratifying that he participated in the first Creativity and Shadow class I taught. Before we started the interview for his story here, he showed me his latest artwork, which graces the walls of his home. Glen's beautiful mandalas remind me what a multitalented and multifaceted person he is, and how delighted I am that chance brought us together at the beginning of what would be a significant leg of the journey for both of us.

Back in 1992, Jacquelyn Small's business manager, Greg Zelonka, urged me to feature Small and her work in transpersonal psychology in *The Phoenix*, a recovery and personal growth newspaper I edited. I wrote the article, and my friend Claudia and I both accepted Greg's invitation to attend an Integrative Breathwork workshop Small led in Minneapolis.

Glen read that article just hours before the workshop was scheduled. Something in it prompted him to attend the workshop, despite his resistance. Glen was the last one in a circle of forty people to introduce himself. He talked about his work, both in his profession and in his recovery, about his attraction and resistance to being at the workshop, and about his awareness that he was deeply angry. At first I was rather pleased with myself—the article I had written had prompted someone to take action. But when Glen mentioned his anger, I could feel it across the room. The person I was then was far more interested in politely hiding anger than truthfully acknowledging it. Glen scared me.

But synchronicity wasn't done yet. Claudia and Glen became partners for the two-day workshop. Glen's ex-wife's name was Claudia, and the issues that Claudia had with her ex were the same issues that Glen had with his ex. Naturally, those issues came up in their breathwork experiences.

This workshop formed a community of breathworkers here in Minneapolis, and that core group attended many workshops together after that. Some of us had the good fortune to attend a weeklong shadow workshop with Jacquelyn Small and Jeremiah Abrams in Atlanta in the spring of 1993. What happened at that workshop was a turning point for all of us. I came home with the first glimmerings of this book in my mind. Glen came home with open eyes.

Glen recalls the shadow dance of that workshop as particularly significant. "We were supposed to bring a costume for our shadow. I thought that a leather jacket with a hood that I had recently bought would be part of the costume. The hood would be about being a holy man. I liked the symbolism that the jacket had cost several hundred dollars. I would be a yuppie monk wearing leather instead of cheap cotton. And somehow Oedipus was part of it. So as I was creating the costume, I decided to make my eyes look like they had been gouged out. I closed my eyes and painted them.

"As we were waiting to enter the room, I stood with my face to the wall, with my hood up, getting into the character of an ascetic monk.

Every person, all the events of your life are there because you have drawn them there. What you choose to do with them is up to you.
RICHARD BACH
Illusions

While everyone else was laughing and talking, I was getting into character, saying to myself, 'I'm holier than you guys; you're just a bunch of
heathens.' It was acting and I was getting into it. Someone came along
and saw me there with my eyes closed. This person said, 'Is this one of
us?' I whispered, 'No, I'm not one of you!' It was the perfect line for my
character.

"Then we were led into the party room, and I was blind. There was
music, noise, people shouting and dancing. I stayed in character, kept
my eyes closed, and hovered near the wall. Every now and then someone
would touch me, and I would move away. It went on like that for a
while. Then I thought, 'Oh God, what will happen if the whole thing is
all over and all I've done is act this isolated, blind person?' I really felt
the loneliness of being alone in my own dark world. But I kept on like
that—it was my role.

"Finally, I decided to touch someone. I tottered toward the middle of
the room like a little old blind man. I touched a couple who were dancing together. I tried to hug them both, but the man slipped away. A moment later, I found myself holding one of the most beautiful, sensuous
women in the group in my arms. We started to dance and pretty soon
we were snuggling like it was closing time at a single's bar.

"I wasn't playing an ascetic monk anymore. I was trying to figure out
how I could get closer to this woman. I had reached out, and what did I
find across a crowded room with my eyes closed? An attractive woman
acting out her Aphrodite role, the archetype that blinded Oedipus in
the first place.

"It took me a while to realize that, even with my eyes closed, I found
what I did not want to see that night. The intellectual, holier-than-thou
part of me secretly desires Aphrodite and is afraid to admit it. When the
sensual beauty I desire is in my arms, I condemn her as a slut. I think I
understand Arthur Miller and Marilyn Monroe. I can find Aphrodite
blindfolded; but when I hold her and she holds me, I'm afraid of dis-
honor or death. For my shadow, dancing with Aphrodite is a tragic
struggle instead of a love story or just a delightful dance."

Glen went to the shadow workshop as Oedipus and explored the
tragedy of remaining in that role. The shock of realizing, "Oh God, what
will happen if the whole thing is over and all I've done is act this isolated, blind person?" had a profound effect on Glen. He made a choice

to open his eyes to look at the role he was playing. He made a choice to tell a new story.

"I don't play Oedipus as much as I used to. It's still in my repertoire; I can still remember some of the lines," Glen laughs, "but I don't stay in character as long as I used to. A mentor of mine used to say, 'You're making it all up anyway, so you can decide to create life as a tragedy or a romantic-comedy. You can do *Hamlet* with dead bodies all over the stage, or you can star in *Twelfth Night* where couples dance off into the forest together. Which one do you want to make up?'

"I'm making up fewer tragedies. A few weeks ago, one of my cats got run over in the street. Friends across the street saw her just minutes after she got hit, and they came over and told me. I ran out and there she was. She was still warm. I brought her in and looked for any sign of life, but she was dead. I asked myself, 'What would I like to do right now?' And the answer came to turn on the Christmas tree lights and sit in my chair and just pet her for a while. So I did that.

"Some of the thoughts that went through my mind were, *What did I do wrong? Was I a bad master to let her go outside?* Then I thought, *No, she had gone to the door three times. The first time I opened the door, she just looked out. The second time, she decided she didn't want to go out. But the third time I opened the door, she went out. She wanted to go across the road, which she had done thousands of times before, and this time she didn't make it. In one way, she died with her boots on, so what was there to feel guilty about?*

"I did feel sad. I thought about how thankful I was for the time we had spent together. I used to joke that she was my design associate because when I'd sit in my chair and draw, she would lay on my lap for hours. While I was petting her, I was thinking how grateful I was for all the love and the gifts she brought. She looked exactly like the cat my sister and I grew up with, so when my sister came over, she loved to hold her. And that helped my sister and I appreciate each other more.

"And every once in a while I'd think about how I'd miss her, but most of the time I was entertaining thoughts about how grateful I was. I could have written a whole tragedy about how I would miss her and never see her again. Or I could write it as a love poem of thanksgiving. I'm thankful that I have the freedom to choose between making a tragedy or a love poem.

"Awareness of that choice is part of my shadow growth process.

Don't be afraid your life will end; be afraid it will never begin.
GRACE HANSEN

I want to make more romantic comedies and love poems and fewer tragedies."

Glen told me he still has tragic or resentful thoughts. "But the difference is that I don't entertain them as much as I used to. I don't waste my time, so I can do other things." The paintings lining the walls in Glen's home represent one of the other things he has opened his eyes to and made time for now. So does the loving relationship he and Peggy, the special woman in his life, are creating and defining for themselves. And so does what Glen calls the "special teaching" he offers as an additional way to heal to the patients in his medical practice.

"What I do is create a situation where someone can daydream. It's as simple as remembering when you were in third grade, and it was September, and it was just after lunch, and the teacher was up at the board talking. You were sitting in your seat, looking our the window, and your mind was out on the playground or in the trees or somewhere else. The teacher asks you what three times four is, and you answer twelve. Then you're back out on the playground.

"When I let people do that for a period of time—create a situation where they can get to a place where they are just calm, quiet, and peaceful—the results are amazing. A fourteen-year-old girl who had been in the emergency room the night before with a panic attack tried it. She looked over at me and said, 'I feel so good,' and then looked away for a while. Then she turned back and said, 'I can't even think about anything to worry about.' She had accessed that peaceful part of her mind.

"It usually takes an hour to an hour and a half. People who do it feel better than they thought they could. When they're done with the guided visualization part, I ask them if anything outside them has changed. Did they get a million dollars, did their boss change, did any of the things they thought were making them miserable change? They say no, and I ask, 'Then what changed?' They always point to themselves.

"I use the analogy that you can watch life on either of two channels— the one you were watching when you came in or the one you're watching now, where you feel calm and peaceful. And guess who's got the remote control. No one else has your remote. As I see other people do that and see them change before my very eyes, I have to believe that I, too, have my own remote. I can't convince myself that Peggy is making me miserable for very long. From time to time I can entertain those

It doesn't matter who my father was; it matters who I remember he was.

ANNE SEXTON

thoughts, and I do, but I can't entertain them for as long. It's like saying to those thoughts, 'Sorry, it's time for me to go to bed, so why don't you go home now?'"

Glen acknowledges that healing, change, and growth are not always comfortable. "I tell people in the special teaching that for a while, the more you do, the worse it's going to look. I use the analogy of moving. Before you start, things look okay in the place you're moving out of and the place you're moving into. But once you start, you get to a point where both places are totally a mess. There are boxes everywhere; there's dust and dirt; there's cleaning you need to do. And the more you do, the worse it looks in both places. If you could quit, you would, but you've got no place to stay. And you do more and it looks worse, but eventually it starts to looks better. So when a person is in the middle of that kind of thing with their healing or their personal growth, I say, 'Remember, I told you when you started that you could expect this. And remember, I also told you that what you really want to work on will happen. You will get "moved in," in a sense.'"

The process may not be comfortable, but Glen doesn't believe it always has to be traumatic. "From time to time in the daydreaming, people may encounter something they don't like. I don't ask about content, but when they tell me, it's usually some kind of shadow element. I encourage them to stand their ground peacefully and look for a glimmer of light somewhere in the picture of what's frightening them. I encourage them to let the picture change however it wants to change around that light. When people describe what happens then, it is something like being in the presence of God, or seeing the sacred heart of Jesus, or seeing a nonreligious, peaceful symbol. That experience seems to dissolve some jagged edge of the ego or make the ego more permeable.

"I've been studying a part of *A Course in Miracles* titled 'I Need Do Nothing.' We have the illusion that we are body. But we also have holy instants, moments when we forget that illusion and remember who we really are. After we have a holy instant, we come back to our illusion of who we think we are, but we see it differently. And in my eyes, that is part of the definition of healing—you see yourself differently. I know I see myself differently and that the shadow work has been a part of that healing.

"My maxim is this: It is complicated and difficult to learn how easy

When you think you've arrived, you realize you've come all this way just to prepare yourself to begin again.

SARAH BAN BREATHNACH
Simple Abundance

and simple life is. I'm at the part of the path where I know it is simple and easy, that life is designed to be simple and easy. I ask myself which channel I want to watch. One of the psychologists I worked with years ago said she had seen many people come to the edge of change, recognize they could change or stay in their misery, and then chose to stay miserable. I'm recognizing that, more than I want to admit, I choose to stay in my misery instead of trusting that the next stage of the change will be easier and more beneficial than what has already happened. Then I remember how complicated and difficult it can be to learn how easy and simple life really is."

Glen acknowledges he still struggles with shadow issues, that he hasn't "arrived" yet. But he has given up blinding himself and facing the wall alone. He has opened his eyes to beauty and love and healing. In that process he has learned to open his heart and create beauty, share love, and offer healing.

Humpty Dumpty Does What the King's Horses and Men Couldn't

> *Humpty Dumpty sat on a wall.*
> *Humpty Dumpty had a great fall.*
> *All the King's horses and all the King's men*
> *Couldn't put Humpty Dumpty back together again.*

Hope (not her real name) was in her early forties when she began to remember the systematic incest and abuse she had endured as a very young child. As a child, Hope had discovered a creative way of surviving; she sent parts of her psyche away, out of the room, away from her abusing parents. In her forties, Hope finally had the resources she needed to remember those now disparate parts of herself. She was shocked to discover she had MPD, multiple personality disorder.

"I believed I had this wonderful, happy childhood. I knew I felt like a broken person, but I didn't know why. Once I started remembering, once I saw the reality of how incredibly broken I had been, I felt like Humpty Dumpty pushed off the wall."

Hope believed she lay in so many pieces, no one could possibly restore her to wholeness. But with the help of caring and skilled therapists, Hope began the long, difficult work of identifying her alter personalities, reconciling herself to their existence and their diverse perspectives and values, and finally integrating them.

"Years ago, I had a recurring dream image when I was meditating. I would be on a roller coaster and I was very scared. There would be a big brick wall and it was obvious that I was going to crash into it. I would always jar myself out of meditation just before the crash because it was so terrifying. The image kept repeating itself. I knew that my path was to let myself hit the wall. I finally convinced myself to remember this was a dream state, it wasn't real, and I wasn't going to literally hit the wall. So then I could let it play out.

"In one version, I hit the wall and it turned out to be paper. I went through and there was a fairy-tale land on the other side. But in the other version, which was much more meaningful for me, I did hit the wall and smashed into smithereens, including my heart. I had been wearing a blue hat, a red shirt, yellow pants, and black shoes. Very clear, definite colors from one part of my body to another. All those colors, all those pieces were smashed everywhere. A piece of me got up and started looking for my heart. I thought, *I'll start with my heart, at least.* But I couldn't even find my heart. So that piece said, 'Well, I guess we start with me, with wherever I am.' And that piece started picking up other pieces. And when that piece was done, there was a beautiful rainbow of kaleidoscope colors because the colors were no longer clear, definite, rigid.

"I still see myself doing some of that reconstruction. I'm starting to let other people see the beauty a little bit. And I'm working up my courage to show more people. I've worked with the Humpty Dumpty rhyme, writing other verses where Humpty Dumpty gets up and says: 'I'll just have to put myself back together again. All the king's horses and the king's men can't do it, so I guess it's up to me.' That's how that story is changing for me."

Hope describes her life before her memories returned as a comforting illusion. "I did many things in professional capacities and never thought twice about feeling insecure. It was a false security, but it was nice. Since then, I've had to create my own security based on a more solid foundation of who I truly am. I've realized that I am not clearly defined, that life isn't clearly defined. Life isn't black and white; life is a kaleidoscope. I accept that and that's how I build my life now."

Hope's story is clearly a story of the descent. Her innocence was stolen, like Persephone, dragged into an underworld no child should have to endure. But Hope's story is also one of transformation and rebirth. Out of tragedy, Hope recreated a beautiful, intricate, kaleido-

In a very real sense, we are the authors of our own lives.

MANDY AFTEL
The Story of Your Life

scope self. With this transformational experience behind her, Hope was empowered to initiate changes in her life, changes she chose. One of those changes was to consciously explore the connections between her creative gifts and her shadow in the Dancing in the Dragon's Den class.

"The shadow collage I made in class was painfully revealing. I found a bunch of pieces of black construction paper that I had cut other things out of before. I didn't know what those black pieces stood for. All I knew was that they had to go on over the pictures and mess up everything and be in the way of everything else. I was mad that was the way it was supposed to be, but it was. Since then, the meaning of many of those pieces has come to light. I'm grateful because they were pieces I needed to clear out so my creativity could come forth more. They were shadow parts of my personality.

"It was fun to do the class with my partner and it helped our relationship. The class also made me more honest at work. For instance, now I'm more likely to notice when I'm crabby. Being crabby is a characteristic my father had, and the class helped me see that I had some of his characteristics that I detested the most. The light is shining on that now and I can see it, name it, acknowledge what's going on, and choose whether or not I'll continue the behavior.

"In the past, when I thought about my shadow or my dark side, I would always focus on my addiction to food. And I've done tons of work on 'my addict.' It was primarily through the class that I started to see that the shadow side of me that needs the light is my giftedness. That's what I'm looking at now: where my giftedness is and how I can learn to affirm my gifts and share them with the world. I'm learning to see myself as being able to give as much as other people do.

"The fact that I'm taking care of doing the dishes now, for instance, is a miracle because there was a time when I would just sit and let everyone else do all the work. Accepting that I need to be a responsible adult is one way I'm moving into my creativity."

As Hope has grown through therapy, through accepting responsibility in her relationships, and through experimenting with her writing and other creative outlets, she's learning to tell a new story about herself. It's no longer Humpty Dumpty that Hope resonates with, but the biblical parable that describes how a master gives three servants some of his money to invest while he goes away. The servants are given talents of

Secular stories talk of who you are; sacred stories playfully explore who you aren't.

ROBERT BLY
Story Food for Men and Women

money, "each according to his ability." (It's a wonderful bit of synchronicity that the word *talent*, which meant money then, now refers to our abilities.) The first servant is given five talents. He invested the five wisely, earning five more talents for his master, who praises him. The second servant is given two talents, which he invests wisely and earns two more for his master, who praises him. But the third servant is afraid and takes the one talent he is given and buries it and then gives it back to his master. Because he has not used what his master gave him wisely, he is scolded.

Hope explains how the story relates to where she is in her journey now. "It's time to stop struggling to shove my gifts away or to say I don't have any gifts. I'm very aware that so far I've been like the man who went to his backyard and very carefully buried his talent so it would be safe. As I think about that, I feel a deep sadness. Even if I believe I have only one talent, 1 percent of the creativity I believe other people have, that doesn't mean that I could not or should not or am not called to share what I have. Pretending the talent isn't there is going about life like a lie. If the man in the story would have just put his talent on his doorstep and shone a light on it, that would have been something. He might have helped other people recognize that if he has one talent, maybe they have one too."

Recognizing that the servant in the story buries the talent because he was afraid and didn't believe in himself helps Hope recognize her own reasons for burying her talents. "I think the man in the story was afraid that if he tried, he would fail and have nothing, whereas by burying it, he would at least still have the original talent. For me, it's difficult to believe in myself. It used to be impossible; now it's just difficult. I'm afraid of being hurt, or criticized, or not understood. I can see inside a tree or beyond a tree; a tree can tell me a wonderful thing about life, but what if I write about that and no one else gets it? If I write something and share it, I'm letting go, surrendering to the other person's process."

Hope isn't willing to let fear and the lies she was told bar her way anymore. "I used to think that I was just a mistake. I must have started out as a mistake because the rest of my family didn't seem to have any problems. When I started remembering the incest, I realized there was a reason for my difficulties. There is a reason I developed all those strategies to deal with life. There is a reason I cling to them so desper-

There is a vitality, a life force, an energy, a quickening, that is translated through you into action, and because there is only one of you in all time, this expression is unique. And if you block it, it will never exist through any other medium and will be lost.

MARTHA GRAHAM

ately even now, at times. There is a reason I feel like I'm a nothing. And I've learned to challenge that, to declare that I'm not a nothing. I do have something to give. I am worthwhile.

"I'm digging up my talents and taking them out to my private garage. I'm shining them up. I'm working on my creativity a little bit, sneaking around in the dark. Every once in a while, I let people I trust in to see it. Then I push them back out and sometimes I quit working on it for a long time. I leave it in the garage. That's the process I'm continuing to work on. I want more, not only to be willing to share more, but to be willing to create more and more. When I bring myself to enough clarity to write things that can be published and that are published, that will tell me I've come full circle. That will be my proof that the all the work and all the pain of recovery was worth it. I don't want to keep those garage doors shut, I really don't. I may have to start with a garage sale, but eventually I'll have a frontyard sale."

Hope is right when she affirms for herself, "I have been gifted with insight into a lot of things. I don't think that's supposed to be wasted. It's not just for me. People in Twelve Step groups have affirmed that for me. I need to take that affirmation from that sacred place, from that sacred garage, and say, 'Okay, I can apply this in my garage.' I can fling the doors open and say, 'This is who I am.'"

Who she is, is a woman of talent, a woman of hope. She is a Humpty Dumpty woman of scrambled, scattered colors transforming herself into a kaleidoscope woman who reflects the insight of pain transformed and the beauty of rebirth.

Does Your Story Need a Rewrite?

As Salman Rushdie points out, the ability to rewrite your life story is vital. Part of the reason the patterns repeat is so that we can complete them, transform them, and move on. The most healing thing we can do with a story is to change it.

Richard Stone, author of *The Healing Art of Storytelling*, advises,

> To transform your pain, you must become the author of your own story. Assuming authorship gives you complete literary license to do whatever you choose. It's your life and your story.

Imagination has always had powers of resurrection that no science can match.

INGRID BENGIS

As author, you are father and mother to yourself. Stories that enslave you in the here and now can be recrafted to empower a different outcome. And, like a nurturing parent, you can gently select new aspects of your story to emphasize, freeing you to experience new feelings and possibilities.

Return to the Examine Your Story Habit exercise (page 242) and reconsider how you can change your future by rewriting your life story. Identify the fairy tale or myth that reflects your life story. If you aren't sure what story that is, remember your favorite childhood stories and read these again. Read other myths and fairy tales. Then, considering the meaning and impact of these stories, rewrite them. Change them in any way that empowers you. Write the stories on paper, if you wish, or simply change the plot as you tell the story to yourself out loud or silently.

It's never too late — in fiction or in life — to revise.
NANCY THAYER

☀ Guided Imagery

Use the guided imagery descriptions in earlier chapters to write your own guided imagery script. After writing it, record it onto a cassette tape or ask a friend to read it to you.

Begin the guided imagery script with the same steps for relaxing your body and calming your mind. Then provide suggestions that will help you see and feel yourself in a fairy tale, myth, or other story that reflects your life. Use all your senses to make the imagery vivid in your mind. Incorporate pauses to allow the story to unfold in your imagination. During the imagery experience, allow yourself to transform the story and allow the story to transform you. You don't need to know beforehand how the story will change during the experience. Allow yourself to be surprised.

After the experience, draw, play with clay, or write to expand and record your impressions.

✸ Creative Shadow Play

Write and illustrate the new version of the story from your guided imagery experience. Read this out loud to yourself at bedtime.

⊙ **EXERCISE CHOICES**

1. Follow Your Dreams. The stories you create while you sleep can give you tremendous insight to the patterns you've been living and the changes you are moving through and toward. If you've been keeping a dream journal for a while, review your entries, looking for common themes and patterns. If you haven't kept a dream journal, start by recording your dreams for a week or so. Pay attention to what your dreams may be trying to tell you. (*Dream Thinking* by Alex Quenk and Naomi Quenk is an excellent resource.)

2. Pitch Your Life. When screenwriters try to get a screenplay made into a movie, they have to "pitch the script." That means they have a very short time, as little as five to ten minutes sometimes, to convince the people with money that this will be a movie worth investing in. To be successful, the pitch has to provide the highlights of the plot, insight to the major characters, and enough energy to get the people listening excited about the story.

Just for fun, create in writing or in your mind a ten- to fifteen-minute synopsis of your life story. You may want to make comparisons to movies: "It's a romantic-comedy cross between *French Kiss* and *The Full Monty*." You can even make suggestions for which actors could play the leading parts.

3. Edit Your Shadow Back In. Often our ego edits most or all of our shadow aspects out of the story, at least out of the story we tell others about ourselves. Make a list of some of the uncomfortable pictures of your shadow that have been edited out and left on the cutting room floor. How will your life story change when you edit those clips back in?

4. Review Your Progress. Take a look at your responses to the exercises you've done as you worked through this book. Read some of the highlights from your journals. Ask your friends, personal coach, and/or therapist to highlight some of the changes they've seen you make in the past few months.

5. Celebrate! Congratulations! You've come a long way since you began this book. It's time to celebrate. Take yourself out or throw a

> *A fairy tale's deepest meaning will be different for each person and different for the same person at different moments in his life.*
>
> BRUNO BETTELHEIM
> *The Uses of Enchantment*

party. Ask your friends to dress as their shadow and invite them to come dance with you in your own Dragon's Den.

6. Don't Stop Now. There are many ways to maintain the momentum you have achieved so far. Using the suggestions in chapter 7, start or keep meeting with a creativity and shadow support group. Keep exploring your creativity. Take a class in a new kind of creative play. Teach a class in the kind of creative play you're experienced in. Reread this book with a friend. Write your own book (that's what started this book, after all). Go back and try some of the exercises you skipped the first time through.

7. Let Me Know What Happens for You. Please let me know about your journey. You can write to me in care of my publisher, Nicolas-Hays, P. O. Box 2039, York Beach, ME 03910, or e-mail me at rosanne@dancinginthedragonsden.com, or see what's new at www.dancinginthedragonsden.com. I can't guarantee I'll be able to respond to every comment, but I'll try.

Learning is finding out what you already know.
Doing is demonstrating that you know it.
Teaching is reminding others that they know
  just as well as you.
You are all learners, doers and teachers.
RICHARD BACH
Illusions

Author's End Note

Even after writing this book and reading through it time after time
to prepare it for publication, I am surprised by what is on these pages.

In some places I thought, *Oh yeah, I need to do that again.* In some
places I thought, *What a great idea, wonder where that came from.* Then
I thought, *How is it possible that I wrote this really good book with all these
great ideas and I'm still struggling to get my life together?*

I know it's possible because, at its very best, my creativity, my writing
and teaching, comes through me, not from me. For the very best stuff,
I'm only the channel, not the creator.

The last thing I want to say to you is this: You and I are different in a
whole lot of ways, but at our most basic level, we're the same. We're both
human and share all human limitations and gifts. So it follows then, that
since the Creator is willing to work through me, to share the joy of creativity with me, the Creator is willing to work through you. All you have to
do to share the joy of creativity is to open yourself up to it, open yourself
to your True Self, open yourself to the Divine in you. If I can do it, so
can you.

Namaste
—Rosanne Bane

APPENDIX A

The Shadow

By Hans Christian Andersen

In *hot* countries the sun burns fiercely, so that the inhabitants become as brown as mahogany, and in the very *hottest* they are burnt to Negroes. But it was only to a *hot* country that a learned man once came from the cold climates. There, he thought, he could roam about just as he had done at home, but this he had to give up very soon. He, like all sensible people, had to stay at home during the whole day, with doors and shutters closed. The houses looked as if all the people were asleep or away. The house in which he lived was so built that the sun shone on it from morning till night—it was really unbearable! The learned man from the cold country, who was young as well as clever, felt as if he were sitting in a glowing oven, which had such an effect upon him that he grew quite thin, and even his shadow shriveled and became much smaller than it had been at home. Then the sun took away almost all of it. But after sunset, when the lights were brought into the room, it was really a pleasure to see how the shadow stretched itself across the wall, and up to the ceiling, so tall did the learned man make himself, for he needed a good stretch indeed in order to regain strength.

In the hot countries every window has a balcony, and as soon as the stars shone forth in the clear, beautiful sky, the learned man would go out on his balcony to stretch himself and would feel revived. At this hour, on all the balconies people began to make their appearance, for one must have fresh air even when one is accustomed to burning. Above and below now all was alive. Shoemakers and tailors—all the people—filled the street beneath; chairs and tables were brought out, and lights were kindled—above a thousand lights. Some talked and others sang and people strolled to and fro, with carriages driving by and mules trotting along with a dingle-dingle-dong: for they had bells on their harnesses. Street boys, screaming and hooting, set off squibbs and fire-crackers, and the dead were carried to the graves by hooded corpse bearers, to the sound of psalms and hymns and the tolling of church bells. Yes, it was, in truth, lively enough down in the street.

Only in one house, exactly opposite the one where the foreign scholar lived, all was quiet; and yet someone certainly dwelt there, for on the balcony flowers were growing luxuriantly in the hot sun; and this could not have been unless they had been watered carefully. That must be done by someone, and so it was evident that people lived there. Also, the door leading to the balcony was half open in the evening; and, although it was dark within, at least in the front room, one could hear the sound of music. The learned man thought this music was quite marvelous; but perhaps he fancied it only; for everything in the hot countries pleased him, if only there had been no sun. The foreigner's landlord said he did not know who had rented the opposite house—nobody was ever seen there; and as for the music, he deemed it terribly tedious. "It is just as if someone were practicing over and over again a piece that he could not master—always the same piece. He must think that he will be able to master it at last; yet he cannot, however long he plays."

One night the learned foreigner awoke; he slept with the door to his balcony open, and as the curtain before it was raised by the wind, it seemed to him as if a wonderful glow came from the balcony of the opposite house. The flowers shone like flames, in the most gorgeous colors, and amongst them stood a slender, graceful maiden. It seemed to him as if light streamed from her too and dazzled his eyes; but then he had only just opened them, as he awoke from his sleep. With one leap he was out of bed, and gently stole behind the curtain. But the maiden was gone; the glow had disappeared. The flowers no longer looked like flames, although still as beautiful as ever. The door stood ajar, and from an inner room sounded music so sweet and so lovely that one could melt away in enchanting thoughts. It was really like magic. Who could be living there? Where was the actual entrance? For, both in the street and in the lane at the side, the whole ground floor was a row of shops; and people could not always be passing through them.

One evening the foreigner sat on his balcony. A light was burning in his own room, just behind him, and thus it was quite natural that his shadow should fall on the wall of the opposite house; yes, there it sat among the flowers on that balcony, and when the foreigner moved, his shadow moved also. For that is the habit of shadows.

"I think my shadow is the only living thing to be seen over there," said the learned man. "Just look how pleasantly it sits amongst the flowers! The door stands half open: my shadow ought to be clever enough to step in and glance about him, and then come back and tell me what he has seen. Thou couldst make thyself useful in this way," said he, jokingly. "Be so good as to step in! Well, art thou going in?" And then he nodded to the shadow, and the shadow nodded in return. "Now go, but don't stay away forever!"

The foreigner rose, and the shadow on the opposite balcony rose also; the foreigner turned round, the shadow turned; and if anyone had paid particular attention he would have noticed that the shadow went straight into the half-opened door of the opposite balcony as the learned man reentered his own room, and let the curtain fall.

The next morning the learned man went out to take his coffee and read the newspapers. "What's that?" he exclaimed, as he stood in the sunshine. "I have lost my shadow! So it really did go away last night and did not return! This is very annoying."

And it certainly did annoy him, not so much because the shadow was gone, but because he knew there was a story of a man without a shadow.[1] All the people at home, in the cold climates, knew this story; therefore, if he should return and relate his adventure, they would say it was only an imitation. And he was not the man to put up with such things being said of him. So he decided not to speak of it at all; and this was wisely thought.

In the evening he went out again on his balcony, taking care to place the light behind him; for he knew that a shadow always wants its master for a screen; but he could not lure it back. He made himself little, he made himself tall; but there was no shadow, and no shadow came. He said, "Hem, hem!" but it was of no use.

It was vexatious; yet in the warm countries everything grows very quickly; and, after a week had passed, he noticed to his great joy that

1. Peter Schlemihl: *The Shadowless Man.*

a new shadow was sprouting out from his feet, when he walked in the sunshine; so that the root must have remained. After three weeks he had quite a respectable shadow, which, when he set out for his home in the northern lands, continued to grow on the journey, and became at last so long and so large that he might very well have done with half of it.

Well, the learned man arrived home, and he wrote books about the True, the Good, and the Beautiful on earth, and in this way days and years passed by—many, many years.

One evening, as he was sitting in his study, there was a gentle knock at the door. "Come in!" said he; but no one entered. He opened the door, and there stood before him a man so extremely lean that he felt uneasy in his presence. The man, however, was very well dressed, and looked like a gentleman. "To whom have I the honor of speaking?" asked the learned man.

"Ah, that is exactly what I expected," said the elegant stranger: "that you would not recognize me. I have become so completely flesh and blood that I even have to wear clothes. You certainly never dreamed of seeing me so well off? Do you not recognize your old shadow? You must have thought that I should never come back again. Things have gone extremely well with me since I was with you last. I have become prosperous, in every respect. If I have to purchase my freedom from service, I can easily do it." And as he spoke, he jingled a bunch of costly trinkets fastened to his watch. And he stuck his hand through the massive gold chain he wore round his neck. How his fingers glittered with diamond rings! And all the gems were pure!

"I cannot recover from my astonishment," said the learned man. "What does all this mean?"

"Well, it is not commonplace," said the Shadow, "but you are not of common stock yourself, and you know that from childhood I have always followed in your footsteps. As soon as you found that I was mature enough to make my way alone in the world, I started out for myself, and am now in the most brilliant circumstances. But I felt a kind of longing to see you once more before you die—for die you must! I also wished to see this place again; one is always attached to his fatherland, you know. I know that you have got another shadow; do I have to pay anything to him, or to you? If so, have the kindness to say what it is!"

"Is it really thou?" said the learned man. "Well, this is most remarkable. I never would have believed that a man's old shadow could return as a human being."

"Just tell me what I owe you," said the Shadow, "for I do not like to be in anybody's debt."

"How canst thou talk that way?" said the learned man. "What question of debt can there be between us? Thou art as free as anyone. I rejoice exceedingly to hear of thy good fortune. Sit down, old friend, and tell me a little of how it all happened, and what thou hast seen in the opposite house, down there in the hot countries."

"Yes, I will tell you all about it," said the Shadow, and took a seat. "But you must promise me never to divulge, in this city, wherever you may meet me, that I have been your shadow. I am thinking of getting married, for I have more than enough to support a family."

"Don't worry," said the learned man, "I will not tell anyone who you really are. Here is my hand—I promise it—and a word is sufficient between man and man."

"Between man and shadow," said the Shadow; for he could not help saying so.

It was really most remarkable how very much he had become a human being in appearance. He was dressed in a suit of the very finest black cloth, polished boots, and an opera hat, which could be collapsed so that nothing could be seen but the crown and the rim; the golden chain and the diamond rings have already been spoken of. The Shadow was, in fact, extraordinarily well dressed, and this was exactly what made a man of him.

"I will now begin my story," he said, placing his feet in their patent leather boots as heavily as possible on the arm of the learned man's new shadow, which lay like a poodle dog at his feet. This was done either out of sheer arrogance or, perhaps, in the hope that the new shadow would stick to his feet. But the prostrate shadow remained quite quiet and all attention; for, no doubt, he also wished to know the way to get away and become his own master.

"Do you know," said the Shadow, "who lived in the house opposite to you? The most magnificent of all creatures—Poetry! I remained there three weeks, but it was more as if it had been three thousand years and as if I had read all that has ever been written in poetry or prose. That's what I say, and it is true. I have seen everything and I know everything!"

"Poetry!" exclaimed the learned man. "Yes, she is accustomed to live in great cities as a recluse. Poetry! Well, I saw her once myself, for a single short moment, but I was half asleep. She stood on the balcony and shone like the Northern Lights amidst flowers like living flames. Go on, go on! Thou wert on the balcony, thou went through the door, and then . . . and then . . ."

"Then I found myself in the ante-room," said the Shadow. "You still sat opposite me and looked over to the ante-room. There was no light, but a sort of twilight, for the doors of a whole suite of halls and rooms stood open, and they were all brilliantly lighted. The blaze of light would have killed me, had I approached too near the maiden herself; but I was cautious and took my time, as everyone should do."

"And what didst thou see then?" asked the learned man.

"I saw everything, as you shall hear. But—it really is not pride on my part—as a freeman and with the knowledge that I possess, not to speak of my position in the world and of my excellent circumstances, I wish you would say 'you' to me, instead of 'thou.'"[2]

"I beg your pardon," said the learned man, "it is an old habit which it is difficult to break. You are quite right; I will try to remember it. But now tell me everything that you saw!"

"Everything," said the Shadow, "for I saw everything and I know everything!"

"How did it look in the inner rooms?" asked the learned man. "Was it like a cool grove, or a holy temple? Were the chambers like the starlit firmament seen from the summit of a high mountain?"

"Everything was there," said the Shadow, "but I did not go all the way in: I remained in the twilight of the ante-room. There I had a very good place: I saw everything and I know everything! I have been in the atrium at the Court of Poetry."

"But what did you see? Did all the gods of antiquity stalk through the large rooms? Did ancient heroes fight their battles over again? Did lovely children play there and narrate their dreams?"

2. It is the custom in Denmark for persons related to each other and for intimate acquaintances to use the second person singular, *du* (thou). Master and mistress say *du* to their servants, but servants and inferiors do not use the same term to their masters or superiors, nor is it ever used when speaking to a stranger, or to anyone with whom they are but slightly acquainted; then they say, as in English, *de* (you).

"I told you that I have been there, and therefore you may be assured that I saw everything that was to be seen. If you had gone there, you would not have remained a human being, whereas I became one; and at the same time I became aware of my inner nature, of my inborn affinity to poetry. It is true, I did not think about it while I was with you, but you will remember that I was always marvelously larger at sunrise and sunset, and in the moonlight even more visible than yourself. I did not then understand my nature. In the ante-room of Poetry it was revealed to me. I became a man; I came out in full maturity. But you were no longer in the hot countries. As a man, I felt ashamed to go about as I was; I was in need of boots, of clothes, of all the varnish that maketh man. I was looking for a shelter—I can confide it to you, for you will not put it in a book. I hid myself under the petticoats of a cake woman; but she little thought of what she concealed. It was not until evening that I ventured out. I ran about the streets in the moonlight. I drew myself up to my full height upon the walls—it refreshes and tickles the back so pleasantly! I ran up and down, peeped through the highest windows into the rooms, and over the roofs. I peeped where no one could peep, and I saw what no one else could see—or, indeed, ought to see. In fact, it is a bad world, and I would not care to be a man, were it not accepted and regarded as something remarkable to be so. I saw the most incredible things going on between husbands and wives, parents and children—oh those so-called 'sweet, [darling]' children! I saw," said the Shadow, "what no one is supposed to know, but everyone would have been only too glad to know—his neighbor's faults. Had I written for a newspaper, how eagerly would it have been read! But instead, I wrote directly to the persons themselves, and there was great alarm in all the towns I visited. They had so much to fear from me that they dearly loved me. The professors made me a professor; the tailors gave me new clothes—I am well provided for; the master of the mint struck coins for me. The women declared that I was handsome, and so I became the man you now see me. And now I must say adieu. Here is my card. I live on the sunny side of the street, and always stay at home in rainy weather." And the Shadow departed.

"This was indeed remarkable," said the learned man.

Years and days passed by, and then the Shadow came again. "How are you doing," he asked.

"Alas," said the learned man, "I am writing about the True, the Beautiful, and the Good; but no one cares to hear about such things. I am quite desperate, for I take it so much to heart."

"That is what I never do," said the Shadow. "I am growing quite fat and stout, and that's what everyone ought to be. You do not understand the world. If you go on like this you will get sick. You ought to travel. I am going on a journey this summer. Will you join me? I should like to have a traveling companion. Will you come with me as my shadow? It would give me great pleasure to take you with me, and I will pay all traveling expenses."

"This is going too far," replied the learned man.

"That is a matter of opinion," said the Shadow. "In any event, a journey will do you good. If you will be my shadow, you shall have everything free on the journey."

"This is ridiculous," exclaimed the learned man.

"Such is the world, and such it will always be," said the Shadow. And away he went.

The learned man had bad luck. Sorrow and trouble pursued him, and what he said about the Good, the Beautiful, and the True was to most people as a rose would be to a cow. At length he fell ill.

"You really look like a shadow," people would say to him, and then a cold shudder would run over him, for he had his own thoughts on the subject.

"You definitely ought to go to some watering place," said the Shadow on his next visit. "There is no other help for you. I will take you with me, for the sake of old acquaintance. I will pay the traveling expenses, and you shall write a description of our journey and shall help me to pass the time. I have to go to a watering place myself, because my beard does not grow as it ought, which is a sickness too. For one has to have a beard. Now do be sensible and accept my offer. We shall travel as comrades."

And so at last they started, the Shadow as master and the master as his shadow. They drove together, they rode together, and they walked together, side by side, or one in front and the other behind, according to the position of the sun. The Shadow always took care to keep on the right side. But the learned man did not pay attention; he was very good-natured, mild, and friendly.

One day he said to the Shadow, "We have grown up together from our childhood, and now that we have become traveling companions, shall we not drink to our good fellowship, and say 'thee' and 'thou' to each other? It sounds more familiar."

"What you say is very straightforward and well meant," said the Shadow, who was now the real master, "so I will be equally well meaning and straightforward. You, as a learned man, certainly know how strange human nature is. There are men who cannot endure the smell of brown paper; it makes them sick. Others will shiver to their very marrow, if a nail is scratched on a pane of glass. I myself have a similar kind of feeling when I hear you say 'thou' to me. I feel humiliated, as if I were back to my former position with you. You see that this is a matter of feeling, not pride. I cannot allow you to say 'thou' to me, but I will gladly say it to you. Then your wish will be at least half fulfilled."

So henceforth the Shadow addressed his former master as "thou."

"This is absurd," the latter thought, "that I am to say 'you' when I speak to him, and he is to say 'thou' to me." However, he had to put up with it.

They arrived at length at the baths, where there were many strangers, and among them a beautiful princess, whose malady was that she was too sharp-sighted, which was highly distressing.

She saw at once that the Shadow was a man quite different from others. "They say," she thought, "that he is here for the growth of his beard, but I see the real reason: he is unable to cast a shadow."

Her curiosity having been stirred, she entered into conversation with the stranger at once, on the promenade. Being the daughter of a king, she was not obliged to stand upon much ceremony. So she said to him without hesitation: "Your illness consists in not being able to cast a shadow."

"Your Royal Highness must be on the high road to recovery," retorted the Shadow. "I know your complaint arose from being too sharp-sighted; but this seems to be over now. You are cured! I just happen to have a very unusual shadow. Have you not seen that person who is always at my side? Other people have a common shadow, but I do not like what is common. Some people often give their servants finer cloth for their liveries than they use for their own garments, and so I had my shadow trimmed up to a man. You may observe that I have even given him a shadow of his own. It is rather expensive, but I like to have about me something peculiar."

"What," thought the Princess, "am I really cured? This must be the best watering place in the world! No doubt, they have developed the powers of water astonishingly nowadays. But I will not leave this place just now, when it promises to become amusing. This foreign prince—for a prince he must be—pleases me tremendously. I only hope his beard won't grow, for then he will leave us."

In the evening the Princess and the Shadow danced together in the large ballroom. She was light, but he was still lighter. Such a partner she had never had. She told him what country she came from, and he knew it and had been there, but not while she was at home. He had peeped through the windows of her father's palace, both the upper and the lower windows; he had seen many things and could therefore converse with the Princess very knowingly and make allusions which quite amazed her. Surely he was the wisest man in the world! She became imbued with the greatest respect for his knowledge.

When she danced with him again, she fell in love with him, which the Shadow could not fail to discover, for she did not take her eyes from him. They danced once more together, and she was about to disclose herself, but she was prudent. She thought of her kingdom and all the people over whom she would one day have to rule. "He is a clever man," she said to herself, "which is a good thing, and he dances admirably, which is also good. But has he also *solid* knowledge? This is the most important thing, and I shall find out." Then she began, by degrees, to question him about the most difficult things she could think of and finally asked him a question she herself could not have answered. The Shadow looked nonplussed.

"You cannot answer that," said the Princess.

"I knew it already as a child," the Shadow replied, "and I am convinced that even my very shadow, standing over there by the door, could answer it."

"Your shadow?" said the Princess. "That would be remarkable, indeed."

"I do not say for a certainty that he can," interjected the Shadow, "but I am almost sure. He has now followed me for so many years, and has heard so much from me, that I have little doubt. But, if your Royal Highness will graciously allow me to make an observation, he is proud and so intent upon passing for a man that he must be treated as such to be kept in good humor, as he must be in order to answer well."

"Oh! I like that," said the Princess. And she walked up to the learned man, who stood in the doorway, and spoke to him of the sun, and of the moon, of the green forests, and of people near home and far off, and the learned man answered with great prudence and pertinence.

"What a wonderful man he must be to have such a clever shadow," thought she. "It would be a real blessing to my country and my people if I chose him for my consort. I will do so!"

So the Princess and the Shadow were soon engaged to each other, but no one was to be told a word about it till she returned to her kingdom.

"No one shall know," said the Shadow, "not even my own shadow!" And he had very special reasons for saying so.

After a time they went to the country where the Princess reigned when she was at home.

"Listen, my friend," said the Shadow to the learned man, "now that I am as fortunate and as powerful as any man can be, I will do something extraordinary for thee! Thou shalt live with me in the palace, drive with me in the royal carriage, and have a hundred thousand dollars a year; but thou must allow everyone to call thee a shadow, and must not say that thou hast ever been a man. And once a year, when I sit on the balcony in the sunshine and show myself to the people, thou must lie at my feet as it behooves a shadow to do; for I must tell thee that I am going to marry the Princess, and the wedding shall be tonight."

"Nay, this is going too far!" said the learned man. "I cannot and will not co-operate in this! That would be deceiving the Princess and her whole country. I shall disclose everything: that I am a man and you only a shadow dressed up in men's clothes."

"No one would believe thee," said the Shadow. "Be sensible, or I will call the guard."

"I shall go straight to the Princess," said the learned man.

"But I shall be there first," replied the Shadow, "and thou wilt go to jail!" And so it turned out, for the guards readily obeyed the Shadow who they now knew was going to marry the king's daughter.

"You tremble," said the Princess, when the Shadow entered her chamber. "Has anything happened? You must not be ill today, when we are to celebrate our nuptials."

"Oh, I have gone through the weirdest experience that anyone can go through," said the Shadow. "Just imagine, my shadow—such a poor shadow skull cannot bear much!—my shadow has gone mad! He fancies that he is a man, and that I—just think!—that I am his shadow."

"This is terrible," cried the Princess, "but I hope he is locked up, isn't he?"

"He is. And I fear he will never recover."

"Poor shadow!" said the Princess. "He is very unfortunate. Wouldn't it be a good deed to deliver him from his frail existence? And, indeed, when I think how often nowadays people take the part of the lower class against the higher, I think it will be necessary to do away with him in all silence."

"This is hard," the Shadow said, "for he was a faithful servant." And he feigned to sigh.

"Yours is a noble character," said the Princess, and bowed to him.

That night the whole town was illuminated; the cannons went off with a boom, and the soldiers presented arms. It was, indeed, a grand wedding! The Princess and the Shadow stepped out on the balcony to show themselves, and to receive one more cheer.

The learned man knew nothing of all these celebrations; he had been put to death.

The Child and the Shadow

By Ursula K. Le Guin

Once upon a time, says Hans Christian Andersen, there was a kind, shy, learned young man from the North, who came south to visit the hot countries, where the sun shines fiercely and all shadows are very black.

Now across the street from the young man's window is a house, where he once glimpsed a beautiful girl tending beautiful flowers on the balcony. The young man longs to go speak to her, but he's too shy. One night, while his candle is burning behind him, casting his shadow onto the balcony across the way, he "jokingly" tells his shadow to go ahead, go on into that house. And it does. It enters the house across the street and leaves him.

The young man's a bit surprised, naturally, but he doesn't do anything about it. He presently grows a new shadow and goes back home. And he grows older, and more learned; but he's not a success. He talks about beauty and goodness, but nobody listens to him.

Then one day when he's a middle-aged man, his shadow comes back to him—very thin and rather swarthy, but elegantly dressed. "Did you go into the house across the street?" the man asks him, first thing; and the shadow says, "Oh, yes, certainly." He claims that he saw everything, but he's just boasting. The man knows what to ask. "Were there rooms like the starry sky when one stands on the mountaintops?" he asks, and all the shadow can say is, "Oh, yes, everything was there." He doesn't know how to answer. He never got in any farther than the anteroom, being, after all, only a shadow. "I should have been annihilated by that flood of light had I penetrated into the room where the maiden lived," he says.

He is, however, good at blackmail and such arts; he is a strong, unscrupulous fellow, and he dominates the man completely. They go traveling, the shadow as the master and the man as servant. They meet a princess who suffers "because she sees too clearly." She sees that the shadow casts no shadow and distrusts him, until he explains that the man is really his shadow, which he allows to walk about by itself. A peculiar arrangement, but logical; the princess accepts it. When she and the shadow engage to marry, the man rebels at last. He tries to tell the princess the truth, but shadow gets there first, with explanations: "The poor fellow is crazy, he thinks he's a man and I'm his shadow!"—"How dreadful," says the princess. A mercy killing is definitely in order. And while the shadow and the princess get married, the man is executed.

Now that is an extraordinarily cruel story. A story about insanity, ending in humiliation and death.

Is it a story for children? Yes, it is. It's a story for anybody who's listening.

If you listen, what do you hear?

The house across the street is the House of Beauty, and the maiden is the Muse of Poetry; the shadow tells us that straight out. And that the princess who sees too clearly is pure, cold reason, is plain enough. But who are the man and the shadow? That's not so plain. They aren't allegorical figures. They are symbolic or archetypal figures, like those in a dream. Their significance is multiple, inexhaustible. I can only hint at the little I'm able to see of it.

The man is all that is civilized—learned, kindly, idealistic, decent. The shadow is all that gets suppressed in the process of becoming a decent, civilized adult. The shadow is the man's thwarted selfishness, his unadmitted desires, the swearwords he never spoke, the murders he didn't commit. The shadow is the dark side of his soul, the unadmitted, the inadmissible.

And what Andersen is saying is that this monster is an integral part of the man and cannot be denied—not if the man wants to enter the House of Poetry.

The man's mistake is in not following his shadow. It goes ahead of him, as he sits there at his window, and he cuts it off from himself, telling it, "jokingly," to go on without him. And it does. It goes on into the House of Poetry, the source of all creativity—leaving him outside, on the surface of reality.

So, good and learned as he is, he can't do any good, can't act, because he has cut himself off at the roots. And the shadow is equally helpless; it can't get past the shadowy anteroom to the light. Neither of them, without the other, can approach the truth.

When the shadow returns to the man in middle life, he has a second chance. But he misses it, too. He confronts his dark self at last, but instead of asserting equality or mastery, he lets it master him. He gives in. He does, in fact, become the shadow's shadow, and his fate then is inevitable. The Princess Reason is cruel in having him executed, and yet she is just.

Part of Andersen's cruelty is the cruelty of reason—of psychological realism, radical honesty, the willingness to see and accept the consequences of an act or a failure to act. There is a sadistic, depressive streak in Andersen also, which is his own shadow; it's there, it's part of him, but not all of him, nor is he ruled by it. His strength, his subtlety, his creative genius, come precisely from his acceptance of and cooperation with the dark side of his own soul. That's why Andersen the fabulist is one of the great realists of literature.

Now I stand here, like the princess herself, and tell you what the story of the shadow means to me at age forty-five. But what did it mean to me when I first read it, at age ten or eleven? What does it mean to children? Do they "understand" it? Is it "good" for them—this bitter, complex study of a moral failure?

I don't know. I hated it when I was a kid. I hated all the Andersen stories with unhappy endings. That didn't stop me from reading them, and rereading them. Or from remembering them . . . so that after a gap of over thirty years, when I was pondering this talk, a little voice suddenly said inside my left ear, "You'd better dig out that Andersen story, you know, about the shadow."

At age ten I certainly wouldn't have gone on about reason and repression and all that. I had no critical equipment, no detachment, and even less power of sustained thought than I have now. I had a somewhat less conscious mind than I have now. But I had as much, or more, of an unconscious mind, and was perhaps in better touch with it than I am now. And it was to that, to the unknown depths in me, that the story spoke; and it was the depths which responded to it and, nonverbally, irrationally, understood it, and learned from it.

The great fantasies, myths, and tales are indeed like dreams: they speak *from* the unconscious *to* the unconscious, in the *language* of the unconscious—symbol and archetype. Though they use words, they work the way music does: they short-circuit verbal reasoning, and go straight to the thoughts that lie too deep to utter. They cannot be translated fully into the language of reason, but only a Logical Positivist, who also finds Beethoven's Ninth Symphony meaningless, would claim that they are therefore meaningless. They are profoundly meaningful, and usable—practical—in terms of ethics; of insight; of growth.

Reduced to the language of daylight, Andersen's story says that a man who will not confront and accept his shadow is a lost soul. It also says something specifically about itself, about art. It says that if you want to enter the House of Poetry, you have to enter it in the flesh, the solid, imperfect, unwieldy body, which has corns and colds and greeds and passions, the body that casts a shadow. It says that if the artist tries to ignore evil, he will never enter into the House of Light.

That's what one great artist said to me about shadows. Now if I may move our candle and throw the shadows in a different direction, I'd like to interrogate a great psychologist on the same subject. Art has spoken, let's hear what science has to say. Since art is the subject, let it be the psychologist whose ideas on art are the most meaningful to most artists, Carl Gustav Jung.

Jung's terminology is notoriously difficult, as he kept changing meanings the way a growing tree changes leaves. I will try to define a few of the key terms in an amateurish way without totally misrepresenting them. Very roughly, then, Jung saw the ego, what we usually call the self, as only a part of the Self, the part of it which we are consciously aware of. The ego "revolves around the Self as the earth around the Sun," he says. The Self is transcendent, much larger than the ego; it is not a private possession, but collective—that is, we share it with all other human beings, and perhaps with all beings. It may indeed be our link with what is called God. Now this sounds mystical, and it is, but it's also exact and practical. All Jung is saying is that we are fundamentally alike; we all have the same general tendencies and configurations in our psyche, just as we all have the same general kind of lungs and bones in our body. Human beings all look roughly alike; they also think and feel alike. And they are all part of the universe.

The ego, the little private individual consciousness, knows this, and it knows that if it's not to be trapped in the hopeless silence of autism it must identify with something outside itself, beyond itself, larger than itself. If it's weak, or if it's offered nothing better, what it does is identify with the "collective consciousness." This is Jung's term for a kind of lowest common denominator of all the little egos added together, the mass mind, which consists of such things as cults, creeds, fads, fashions, status-seeking, conventions, received beliefs, advertising, popcult, all the isms, all the ideologies, all the hollow forms of communication and "togetherness" that lack real communion or real sharing. The ego, accepting these empty forms, becomes a member of the "lonely crowd." To avoid this, to attain real community, it must turn inward, away from the crowd, to the source: it must identify with *its own* deeper regions, the great unexplored regions of the Self. These regions of the psyche Jung calls the "collective unconscious," and it is in them, where we all meet, that he sees the source of true community; of felt religion; of art, grace, spontaneity, and love.

How do you get there? How do you find your own private entrance to the collective unconscious? Well, the first step is often the most important, and Jung says that the first step is to turn around and follow your own shadow.

Jung saw the psyche as populated with a group of fascinating figures, much livelier than Freud's grim trio of Id, Ego, Superego; they're all worth meeting. The one we're concerned with is the shadow.

The shadow is on the other side of our psyche, the dark brother of the conscious mind. It is Cain, Caliban, Frankenstein's monster, Mr. Hyde. It is Vergil who guided Dante through hell, Gilgamesh's friend Enkidu, Frodo's enemy Gollum. It is the Doppelgänger. It is Mowgli's Grey Brother; the werewolf; the wolf, the bear, the tiger of a thousand folktales; it is the serpent, Lucifer. The shadow stands on the threshold between the conscious and the unconscious mind, and we meet it in our dreams, as sister, brother, friend, beast, monster, enemy, guide. It is all we don't want to, can't, admit into our conscious self, all the qualities and tendencies within us which have been repressed, denied, or not used. In describing Jung's psychology, Jolande Jacobi wrote that "the development of the shadow runs parallel to that of the ego; qualities which the ego does not need or cannot make use of are set aside or repressed, and thus they play little or no part in the conscious life of the individual. Accordingly, a child has no real shadow, but his shadow becomes more pronounced as his ego grows in stability and range."[3] Jung himself said, "Everyone carries a shadow, and the less it is embodied in the individual's conscious life, the blacker and denser it is."[4] The less you look at it, in other words, the stronger it grows, until it can become a menace, an intolerable load, a threat within the soul.

Unadmitted to consciousness, the shadow is projected outward, onto others. There's nothing wrong with me—it's *them*. I'm not a monster, other people are monsters. All foreigners are evil. All communists are evil. All capitalists are evil. It was the cat that made me kick him, Mummy.

If the individual wants to live in the real world, he must withdraw his projections; he must admit that the hateful, the evil, exists within himself. This isn't easy. It's very hard not to be able to blame anybody else.

3. Jolande Jacobi, *The Psychology of C. G. Jung* (New Haven: Yale University Press, 1962), p. 107.

4. Carl Gustav Jung, *Psychology and Religion: West and East*, Bollingen Series XX, *The Collected Works of C. G. Jung*, vol. 11 (New York, Pantheon Books, 1958), p. 76

But it may be worth it. Jung says, "If he only learns to deal with his own shadow he has done something real for the world. He has succeeded in shouldering at least an infinitesimal part of the gigantic, unsolved social problems of our day."[5]

Moreover, he has grown toward true community, and self-knowledge, and creativity. For the shadow stands on the threshold. We can let it bar the way to the creative depths of the unconscious, or we can let it lead us to them. For the shadow is not simply evil. It is inferior, primitive, awkward, animal like, childlike; powerful, vital, spontaneous. It's not weak and decent, like the learned young man from the North; it's dark and hairy and unseemly; but, without it, the person is nothing. What is a body that casts no shadow? Nothing, a formlessness, two-dimensional, a comic-strip character. The person who denies his own profound relationship with evil denies his own reality. He cannot do, or make; he can only undo, unmake.

Jung was especially interested in the second half of life, when this conscious confrontation with a shadow that's been growing for thirty or forty years can become imperative—as it did for the poor fellow in the Andersen story. As Jung says, the child's ego and shadow are both still ill defined; a child is likely to find his ego in a ladybug, and his shadow lurking horribly under his bed. But I think that when in pre-adolescence and adolescence the conscious sense of self emerges, often quite overwhelmingly, the shadow darkens right with it. The normal adolescent ceases to project so blithely as the little child did; he realizes that you can't blame everything on the bad guys with the black Stetsons. He begins to take responsibility for his acts and feelings. And with it he often shoulders a terrible load of guilt. He sees his shadow as much blacker, more wholly evil, than it is. The only way for a youngster to get past the paralyzing self-blame and self-disgust of this stage is really to look at that shadow, to face it, warts and fangs and pimples and claws and all— to accept it as himself—as *part* of himself. The ugliest part, but not the weakest. For the shadow is the guide. The guide inward and out again; downward and up again; there, as Bilbo the Hobbit said, and back again. The guide of the journey to self-knowledge, to adulthood, to the light.

"Lucifer" means the one who carries the light.

5. Jung, *Psychology and Religion*, p. 83.

It seems to me that Jung described, as the individual's imperative need and duty, that journey which Andersen's learned young man failed to make.

. . . And it seems to me that the way you can speak absolutely honestly and factually to a child about both good and evil is to talk about himself. Himself, his inner self, his deep, the deepest Self. That is something he can cope with; indeed, his job in growing up is to become himself. He can't do this if he feels the task is hopeless, nor can he if he's led to think there isn't any task. A child's growth will be stunted and perverted if he is forced to despair or if he is encouraged in false hope, if he is terrified or if he is coddled. What he needs to grow up is reality, the wholeness which exceeds all our virtue and all our vice. He needs knowledge; he needs self-knowledge. He needs to see himself and the shadow he casts. That is something he can face, his own shadow; and he can learn to control it and to be guided by it. So that, when he grows up into his strength and responsibility as an adult in society, he will be less inclined, perhaps, either to give up in despair or to deny what he sees, when he must face the evil that is done in the world, and the injustices and grief and suffering that we all must bear, and the final shadow at the end of all.

Fantasy is the language of the inner self. I will claim no more for fantasy than to say that I personally find it the appropriate language in which to tell stories to children—and others. But I say that with some confidence, having behind me the authority of a very great poet, who put it much more boldly. "The great instrument of moral good," Shelly said, "is the imagination."

APPENDIX B

Where to Find Support

Usually the best way to find and select professionals who will support your creativity, your shadow work, and your personal growth is to ask people you know for referrals. Ask your friends who they see for massage or therapy or where they've found interesting classes. Ask co-workers or colleagues if they have a coach or a mentor. Talk to other participants in workshops and classes about what books they like, what stores are great little finds, and what organizations are worth belonging to.

Ask the people who work at stores and service businesses you frequent what they recommend—the clerk at your local art supply store will probably have good recommendations for organizations and individuals who teach watercolor classes. Likewise, the clerk at the store where you buy incense and herbs will know good aroma therapists in your area. The professionals you're already working with probably have names of other professionals who provide related services.

Also, look for alternative press newspapers and magazines to see who's writing the articles as well as who is advertising classes and services. Also check the telephone yellow pages and the Internet. Exercise a little more caution when selecting a potential support person without a recommendation from someone your know and trust. Ask more questions. Request names and phone numbers of satisfied customers and follow up by actually calling those people to see whether they are satisfied. Then ask those people what they were looking for and make sure that fits with what you're looking for. Check with your Better Business Bureau to see if there are any complaints on file. Practice discernment, especially in the first two or three meetings with a person. Remember what kind of support you were looking for and ask yourself if that's the kind of help you're actually getting. If not, clarify your expectations, and if you still don't get what you're looking for, look elsewhere.

Breathwork

If you're intrigued with the idea of using the breath to enhance your ability to move into different states of consciousness (and that's what creativity is, after all, a different state of consciousness), contact any of the following for more information:

HOLOTROPIC BREATHWORK: Using the breath to change consciousness is a spiritual and healing practice in nearly all ancient and native traditions. Dr. Stanislav Grof and Christina Grof have drawn on this awareness and combined it with modern consciousness research and depth psychology to pioneer Holotropic Breathwork. For more information about this powerful method of self-exploration and healing, access www.breathwork.com on the Internet, or contact Grof Transpersonal Training, 20 Sunnyside Avenue, A-314, Mill Valley, CA 94941, 415-383-8779.

INTEGRATIVE BREATHWORK: Jacquelyn Small studied with Dr. Stansilov Grof in the Holotrophic Breathwork method and decided she wanted to incorporate more activities that would help participants integrate the material. Thus Integrative Breathwork was developed and Eupsychia, Inc. was founded to provide workshops, training, and a certification process for Integrative Breathwork facilitators across the country. For more information on Eupsychia's programs and professionals who are certified by Eupsychia to facilitate Integrative Breathwork, call 800-546-2795 or write to P.O. Box 3090, Austin, TX 78764.

SHAMANIC BREATHWORK: Linda Star Wolf combines her training and experience in Integrative Breathwork with the teaching of Native American spiritual leaders and the wisdom she gains from her own inner work into a healing and training program she calls Shamanic Breathwork. Adopted by Seneca Elder and Wolf Clan Grandmother Twylah Nitsch, Linda weaves ancient and contemporary teachings to reflect a working wisdom applicable to modern-day life. Linda is a powerful teacher, as are the guest presenters she works with. For more information, call 415-435-7550 or write Venus Rising, P.O. Box 1174, Fairfax, CA 94978.

DREAMTIME JOURNEY BREATHWORK: Jeremiah Abrams has adapted this breathwork technique to fit the soul-centered psychology workshops he and guest teachers lead at the Mt. Vision Institute. Jeremiah is a Jungian therapist with twenty-seven years of experience, an author, and a tremendously gifted workshop facilitator. For more information, call 415-721-7324 or write to Mt. Vision Institute, P.O. Box 1042, Woodacre, CA 94973.

Coaching

The number of personal and business coaches grows every day. Most coaches have a special niche in the service they provide. For example, as a creativity coach, I work with people who want coaching sessions to include strategies that will encourage and support their creative projects. If you don't have a friend who can recommend a good personal coach or if you have a special interest you want to focus your coaching sessions on, contact any of the following for referrals. Not all coaches will be listed with these organizations, but these are a good second place to look (following asking people you know for referrals, of course):

Coach University, 800-482-6224 (800-48COACH).

The Coaches Training Institute, 415-274-7551 or e-mail: thecoaches@aol.com

International Coach Federation, 888-423-3131 or Internet access at http://www.coachfederation.org

New Ventures West, 800-332-4618.

References

Prologue

p. xiii
Julia Cameron, *The Artist's Way* (New York:
J. P. Tarcher/Putnam, 1992), 18.

p. xiv–xv
Joyce Sequichie Hifler, *A Cherokee Feast of Days*
(Tulsa, OK: Council Oak Books, 1992), 35.

Chapter 1

p. 6
Sandra G. Shuman, *Source Imagery* (New York:
Doubleday, 1989), 37.

Chapter 2

p. 18
John A. Sanford, as quoted in D. Patrick Miller, *The
Sun,* quoted in Connie Zweig and Jeremiah Abrams,
eds., *Meeting the Shadow* (Los Angeles: J. P. Tarcher,
1991), 24.

Chapter 3

p. 32
Robert Bly, *A Little Book on the Human Shadow,* ed.
William Booth (San Francisco: HarperSanFran-
cisco, 1988), 17.

p. 34
Jacquelyn Small, *Awakening in Time* (New York:
Bantam, 1991), 43.

p. 39
Alice Miller, *For Your Own Good: Hidden Cruelty in*

Child-Rearing and the Roots of Violence (New York:
Farrar, Strauss & Giroux, 1983), 166–168.

p. 41
Jeremiah Abrams, personal
communcation/interview, January 1994.

p. 46–47
William A. Miller, *Your Golden Shadow* (San
Francisco: HarperSanFrancisco, 1993), quoted in
Connie Zweig and Jeremiah Abrams, eds., *Meeting
the Shadow* (Los Angeles: J. P. Tarcher, 1991), 39.

Chapter 4

p. 66
M. Scott Peck, *The Road Less Traveled* (New York:
Simon and Schuster, 1978), 15.

p. 71
Brenda Ueland, *If You Want to Write* (St. Paul:
Graywolf, 1987), 32–34.

Chapter 5

p. 90–91
Helen Palmer, *The Enneagram: Understanding Yourself
and Others in Your Life* (San Francisco:
HarperSanFrancisco, 1988), 41–42.

p. 91
Kathy Hurley and Ted Dobson, *The Hurley/Dobson
Professional Training for Enneagram Transformation
Manual* (Lakewood, CO: Enneagram Resources,
1993), 47.

Chapter 7

p. 131
Brenda Ueland, *If You Want to Write* (St. Paul: Graywolf, 1987), 42.

p. 131
Julia Cameron, *The Vein of Gold* (New York: J. P. Tarcher, 1996), 30.

p. 133
SARK, *Inspiration Sandwich* (Berkeley, CA: Celestial Arts, 1992), 16.

Chapter 8

p. 147
Deepak Chopra, *The Seven Spiritual Laws of Success* (San Rafael, CA: New World Library, 1994), 57, 60.

p. 148
Marsha Sinetar, *Do What You Love, the Money Will Follow* (New York: Dell, 1989) 36–38.

p. 159
Trudi Hahn, "With Solitaire, She Lays Her Cards on the Table," *Minneapolis Star Tribune*, 9 November 1994, metro edition, variety section, 1E and 10E.

Chapter 9

p. 165
Anthony Stevens, quoted in Jeremiah Abrams, ed. *Shadow in America* (Novato, CA: Nataraj Publishing, 1994), 7.

p. 166
Jeremiah Abrams, ed. *Shadow in America* (Novato, CA: Nataraj Publishing, 1994), 15–16.

p. 166
Julia Cameron, *The Artist's Way* (New York: J. P. Tarcher/Putnam, 1992), 3.

Chapter 12

p. 215
Betty Edwards, *Drawing on the Artist Within* (New York: Simon and Schuster, 1987), 2–4. 10–14, 41–47.

p. 218
Anna Wise, *The High Performance Mind* (New York: J. P. Tarcher/Putnam, 1995), 1–22.

p. 222
Clarissa Pinkola Estés, *Creative Fire* (Boulder, CO: Sounds True, 1991).

p. 223
Clarissa Pinkola Estés, *Creative Fire* (Boulder, CO: Sounds True, 1991).

Chapter 13

p. 243
Salman Rushdie, quoted in Julia Cameron, *The Vein of Gold: A Journey to Your Creative Heart* (New York: J. P. Tarcher, 1996), 71.

p. 243
Clarissa Pinkola Estés, *Women Who Run With the Wolves* (New York: Ballantine, 1994), p. 15.

p. 244
Clarissa Pinkola Estés, *Women Who Run With the Wolves* (New York: Ballantine, 1994), 15, 16–17.

p. 248
Susan O'Halloran and Susan Delattre, *The Woman Who Found Her Voice: A Tale of Transforming* (Philadelphia: Innisfree Press, 1997), 106.

p. 262–263
Richard Stone, *The Healing Art of Storytelling* (New York: Hyperion, 1996), 173.

Appendix A

p. 269
Hans Christian Andersen, "The Shadow," in *Shocking Tales*, ed. Robert K. Brunner (New York: Current Books, 1946).

p. 280
Ursula K. Le Guin, "The Child and the Shadow," in the *Quarterly Journal of the Library of Congress 32*. Used with permission. See editor's note on copyright page.

Resource Directory

Creativity

Bledsoe, Sara. *The Horse Drawing Club Workbook.* Hugo, CO: Bledsoe Publishing, P.O. Box 521, Hugo, CO 80821. Written for kids, this book is an encouraging guide for anyone who wants to draw horses better. Sara was one of my students and I'm delighted to let people know what a great book she's written and self-published.

Brande, Dorothea. *Becoming a Writer.* New York: J. P. Tarcher, 1981.

Brown, Rita Mae. *Starting From Scratch: A Different Kind of Writer's Manual.* New York: Bantam Books, 1988.

Buzan, Tony. *The Mind Map Book: How to Use Radiant Thinking to Maximize Your Brain's Untapped Potential.* New York: Penquin Books, 1993.

Cameron, Julia. *The Artist's Way: A Spiritual Path to Higher Creativity.* New York: J. P. Tarcher, 1992. One of the finest books ever written on creativity.

Cassou, Michell, and Stewart Cubley. *Life, Paint and Passion: Reclaiming the Magic of Spontaneous Expression.* New York: J. P. Tarcher, 1995. Although the short essays in this marvelous book are addressed primarily toward painters and about painting, they apply equally to any form of spontaneous expression. Excellent!

Cornell, Judith. *Drawing on the Light from Within: Keys to Awaken Your Creative Power.* New York: Prentice Hall, 1990.

Cornell, Judith. *Mandala: Luminous Symbols for Healing.* Wheaton, IL: Quest Books, 1994. Whatever your drawing level, however you regard your drawing talent, I guarantee you will be amazed at the results you will produce following the exercises in this luminous book.

Csikszentmihalyi, Mihaly. *Flow: The Psychology of Optimal Experience.* New York: HarperCollins, 1990. Fascinating discussions.

Diaz, Adriana. *Freeing the Creative Spirit: Drawing on the Power of Art to Tap the Magic & Wisdom Within.* San Francisco: HarperSanFrancisco, 1992.

Edwards, Betty. *Drawing on the Artist Within.* New York: Simon and Schuster, 1986. Even if you don't want to follow the excellent drawing guidance this book offers, the first few chapters are worth reading solely for Edwards' solid insight to the stages of the creative process.

Evershed, Jane. *More Than a Tea Party.* San Francisco: HarperSanFrancisco, 1994. The paintings and poetry in this amazing little book are food and drink for the soul. You'll be glad you found this book and delighted to meet this artist.

Franck, Frederick. *Zen Seeing, Zen Drawing: Meditation in Action.* New York: Bantam, 1993.

Friedman, Bonnie. *Writing Past Dark: Envy, Fear, Distraction, and Other Dilemmas in the Writing Life.* New York: HarperCollins, 1993. Addressed to writers, this book discusses the shadow issues of living a creative life, although Friedman doesn't identify these issues as "shadow" issues.

Goldberg, Natalie. *Writing Down the Bones.* Boston: Shambhala, 1986. A classic. The first book that introduced me to the power of freewriting.

Goldberg, Natalie. *Wild Mind.* New York: Bantam Books, 1990.

Goldberg, Natalie. *Living Color.* New York: Bantam Books, 1997. Particularly delightful to see Goldberg's development as she "crosses" from writing to painting.

Koff-Chapin, Deborah. *Drawing Out Your Soul: The Touch Drawing Handbook.* Langley, WA: The Center for Touch Drawing, 1996; (800-989-6334). A fascinating technique.

Mandali, Monique. *Everyone's Mandala Coloring Book* (multiple volumes). Billings, MT: Mandali Publishing, 1994; (800-347-1223). Great fun! Coloring mandalas is an excellent way to move into a meditative, creative-flow state of mind.

SARK. *A Creative Companion.* Berkeley, CA: Celestisal Arts, 1995. All of SARK's books are fun, playful, and packed with power.

SARK. *SARK's Journal and Play! Book.* Berkeley, CA: Celestial Arts, 1995.

SARK. *Succulent Wild Woman: Dancing With Your Wonder-full Self!* New York: Simon and Schuster, 1997.

Shaughnessy, Susan. *Walking on Alligators.* New York: HarperCollins, 1993.

Shuman, Sandra G. *Source Imagery: Releasing the Power of Your Creativity.* New York: Doubleday, 1989.

Ueland, Brenda. *If You Want to Write: A Book About Art, Independence and Spirit.* St. Paul: Graywolf Press, 1987. The title is a little misleading: this book is excellent for anyone exploring their creativity, not just writers!

Dreamwork

Mellick, Jill. *The Natural Artistry of Dreams: Creative Ways to Bring the Wisdom of Dreams to Waking Life.* Berkeley, CA: Conari Press, 1996. An inspiring book to work with.

Quenk, Alex T., and Naomi L. Quenk. *Dream Thinking: The Logic, Magic and Meaning of Your Dreams.* Palo Alto, CA: Davies-Black Publishing, 1995. Solid. This book doesn't presuppose or try to impose any one theory on your dreams. Instead it helps you ponder your dreams in ways that will be most useful to you.

Enneagram

There are many worthwhile books written on the Enneagram, and I must confess I'm a bit biased in my strong preference for Kathy Hurley and Ted Dobson's books. I have studied with Kathy and Ted and am certified by them to facilitate the Enneagram Experience®. But it's more than just bias; I do think their emphasis on the Repressed Center is a major contribution. Therefore, I recommend you begin with their books.

Hurley, Kathleen, and Theodore Dobson. *What's My Type?* San Francisco: HarperSanFrancisco, 1991.

Hurley, Kathleen, and Theodore Dobson. *My Best Self: Using the Enneagram to Free the Soul.* San Francisco: HarperSanFrancisco, 1993.

Keyes, Margaret Fringes. *Out of the Shadows: Uses of Depression, Anxiety and Anger in the Enneagram.* Sausalito, CA: Molysdatur Publications, 1988; (Box 203 Start Route, Muir Beach, CA 94965). A good look at how the Enneagram clarifies some shadow issues and how you can understand the Enneagram to grow with and beyond those shadow issues.

Meditation and Relaxation

Gawain, Shakti. *Creative Visualization.* San Rafael, CA: New World Library, 1995.

Hanh, Thich Nhat. *The Blooming of a Lotus: Guided Meditation Exercises for Healing and Transformation.* Boston: Beacon Press, 1993. If you bought only one book on meditation, let it be this one. Gentle, powerful, effective.

Hanh, Thich Nhat. *Peace is Every Step: The Path of Mindfulness in Everyday Life.* New York: Bantam Books, 1991. Excellent!

Radcliffe, Rebecca Ruggles. *Dance Naked in Your Living Room.* Minneapolis: EASE Publications, 1997; (800-470-4769). Fun suggestions for relaxing and enjoying your life.

Wise, Anna. *The High Performance Mind: Mastering Brainwaves for Insight, Healing and Creativity.* New York: J. P. Tarcher, 1995. Wise explains how you can benefit from research on brain waves to achieve what she and her mentor C. Maxwell Cade call the Awakened Mind. Also offers some good guided imageries you can use to move into the creative flow.

Fascinating Philosophy, Important Principles and Skills, and Significant Spirituality

Andrews, Ted. *Animal Speak: The Spiritual and Magical Powers of Creatures Great and Small.* St. Paul: Llewellyn Publishers, 1995. A great resource when an animal ally has appeared in your dreams, on a walk, or in your cards (see *The Druid Animal Oracle* and *Medicine Cards* on page 297).

Arrien, Angeles. *The Four-Fold Way.* New York: HarperCollins, 1993. Arrien, a cross-cultural anthropologist, shares the wisdom she has gathered from indigenous people all over the world.

Boldt, Laurence. *Zen and the Art of Making a Living.* New York: Arkana, 1993. If you're contemplating a career change or looking for more meaning in your work, this is an excellent workbook.

Boe, John. *Life Itself: Messiness Is Next to Goddessness and Other Essays.* Wilmette, IL: Chiron Publications, 1994. I particularly recommend the title essay, "Messiness Is Next to Goddessness."

Breathnach, Sarah Ban. *Simple Abundance: A Daybook of Comfort and Joy.* New York: Time Warner Books, 1995.

Chopra, Deepak. *The Seven Spiritual Laws of Success: A Practical Guide to the Fulfillment of Your Dreams.* San Rafael, CA: New World Library, 1994. Fascinating perspective. I reread sections of this book frequently and often use it as a starting point in my meditation.

Covey, Stephen. *The Seven Habits of Highly Effective People.* New York: Simon and Schuster, 1989. My first thought was that this book would be too "business oriented" to be useful to "artists," which only shows some of the prejudices I held in 1989. Most of us need this kind of pragmatic approach to help us make our creative dreams into creative reality.

Frankl, Viktor. *Man's Search for Meaning: An Introduction to Logotherapy.* Boston: Beacon Press, 1962.

Grof, Stanislav, and Christina Grof, eds. *Spiritual Emergency.* Los Angeles: J. P. Tarcher, 1984. Fascinating stuff!

Jeffers, Susan. *Feel the Fear and Do It Anyway.* New York: Fawcett Columbine, 1987. A classic.

Jung, Carl G. *Memories, Dreams, Reflections.* New York: Random House, 1989.

Orsborn, Carol. *Enough Is Enough: Exploding the Myth of Having It All.* New York: G. P. Putnam's Sons, 1986. A book that will at least challenge, if not transform, some of your basic assumptions about work and life.

Peck, M. Scott. *The Road Less Traveled.* New York: Simon and Schuster, 1978. Another classic.

Radcliffe, Rebecca Ruggles. *Enlightened Eating: Understanding and Changing Your Relationship with Food.* Minneapolis: EASE Publications, 1996; (800-470-4769). If your shadow shows up in your eating habits, this gentle book will lead you through a powerful exploration of your relationship to food.

Silber, Lee. *Time Management for the Creative Person.* New York: Three Rivers Press, 1988.

Sinetar, Marsha. *Do What You Love, The Money Will Follow.* Boston: Bantam Books, 1987.

Talbot, Michael. *The Holographic Universe.* New York: HarperCollins, 1991. Absolutely fascinating!

Shadow

Abrams, Jeremiah, ed. *The Shadow in America: Reclaiming the Soul of a Nation.* Novato, CA: Nataraj, 1994. Ten essays about the collective shadow of America, including discussions of race relations, gender, money, sexuality, addiction, love, and politics.

Bly, Robert. *A Little Book on the Human Shadow.* San Francisco: HarperSanFrancisco, 1988.

Johnson, Robert A. *Owning Your Own Shadow: Understanding the Dark Side of the Psyche.* San Francisco: HarperSanFrancisco, 1991. A small, rich book that explores the shadow from a Jungian perspective.

Small, Jacquelyn. *Awakening in Time: From Codependence to Co-Creation.* New York: Bantam Books, 1991.

Small, Jacquelyn. *Embodying Spirit: Coming Alive with Meaning and Purpose.* New York: HarperCollins, 1994.

Zweig, Connie, and Jeremiah Abrams, eds. *Meeting the Shadow: The Hidden Power of the Dark Side of Human Nature.* New York: J. P. Tarcher, 1991. Probably your best first resource, this book includes articles and essays by Carl Jung, Robert Bly, Joseph Campbell, John Bradshaw, Susan Griffin, M. Scott Peck, Rollo May, Sam Keen, Marie-Louise von Franz, Audre Lorde, and others.

Mixed Media—audiocassettes, videocassettes, and other non-book resources

Bane, Rosanne. *Dancing in the Dragon's Den Guided Imageries.* CD. Refer to www.dancinginthedragons-den.com for additional ordering information. Order from www.Amazon.com or bookstores. This collection of the eleven guided imageries provided in this book is recorded by the author. These inner journeys will introduce you to your own deep wisdom and leave you relaxed and refreshed.

Bly, Robert. *A Little Book on the Human Shadow.* Audiocassette. Order from Sounds Horizon at 800-524-8355. Bly has a book by the same title, but I found the tape much more entertaining and approachable.

Bly, Robert, and Marion Woodman. *Facing the Shadow in Men and Women.* Audiocassette. Order from Sounds True at 800-333-9185 or Oral Tradition at 800-779-1116. Bly and Woodman are an excellent team and their telling of the Bear King story is captivating!

Estés, Clarissa Pinkola. *Creative Fire.* Audiocassette. Order from Sounds True at 800-333-9185. Estés is a powerful storyteller and her telling of the Persephone myth shines new light on the creative process. Excellent!

Gawain, Shakti. *Creative Visualization* and *Creative Visualization Meditations.* Audiocassettes. Gawain was one of the first and strongest authors to spread the word about the power of visualization. She'll lead you in some wonderful meditations.

Roth, Gabrielle. *The Wave.* Videocassette. Order from Lightworks Audio and Video at 310-398-4949. A talented musician and healer, Roth combines music from her CDs and a group of non-professional dancers to guide you in a moving meditation consisting of five universal rhythms. Excellent resource for anyone who wants an easy way to deepen awareness of her or his body.

Small, Jacquelyn. *Awakening in Time Series: Healing the Shadow: Our Wounded and Disowned Self.* Audiocassette. Order from Eupsychia Press at 800-546-2795. Includes an explanation of the personal shadow and a guided imagery for meeting your shadow.

Background Music

There is a vast variety of music you can use in the background to help you relax during meditation and guided imageries. I'm listing just a few of my absolute favorites:

Bell, Derek. *The Mystic Harp.* Clarity Sound & Light, 1996, 800-424-1055.

Exchange. *Into the Night.* Paris Productions, 1988, distributed by Rhino Records, Inc.

Merlin's Magic. *Chakra Meditation Music.* Inner Worlds Music, 1996, 800-444-9678.

Soulfood. *Breathe.* Free Schaeffer, 1998, Institute for Integrative Healing Practices, 27306 County Road A, Spooner, WI 54801. Produced by one of my "Breathwork Buddies," this is an inspiring combination of indigenous musical influences with contemporary western approaches. Visit Soulfood at www.netradio.net/soulfood.

Wheater, Tim. *Heartland.* Almo Sounds, Inc., 1995, distributed by Uni Distribution Corp. Wheater's vocal toning is marvelous. I use it during the body relaxation part of every guided imagery I lead. Consider yourself among the blessed if you can find a copy of Wheater's *Heartsteps,* an earlier recording that is exclusively toning and was extremely limited in its distribution.

Cards

There are a number of cards or other oracles you can use to give you focus during meditation or give you questions to ponder. I use the *Druid Animal Oracle* cards and the *Medicine Cards* to contemplate what I can do to draw on the qualities of a synchnronistically selected animal ally. I use the *Soul Cards* as a starting place for freewriting or meditation or other process work. I encourage you to find the cards that your spirit resonates with, and you may want to start by looking at these.

Carr-Gomm, Philip, and Stephanie Carr-Gomm, illustrated by Bill Worthington. *The Druid Animal Oracle.* New York: Simon and Schuster, 1994. The illustrations on the cards are beautiful and rich with detail. These cards and the background information provided in the accompanying book speak to my spirit, perhaps because the Celts are part of my ethnic background.

Koff-Chapin, Deborah. *Soul Cards.* Langley, WA: The Center for Touch Drawing (800-989-6334), 1996. These beautiful cards will almost certainly evoke an emotional response. There is a handbook, but no set interpretations of the cards. Your response, which will vary each time you use the cards, is what is significant. Also take a look at Koff-Chapin's book *Drawing Out Your Soul: The Touch Drawing Handbook* (listed on page 294), which will guide you in using the touch drawing technique to make your own evocative drawings.

Sams, Jamie, and David Carson. *The Medicine Cards.* Sante Fe: Bear and Co., 1988. Jamie Sams shares Native American understanding, wisdom, and interpretations from her experience in diverse Native American traditions. The animals in this deck and book are ones all Americans share the land with and, hence, are animals we all can learn from.

Index

About the Author

ROSANNE BANE, M.A., is a widely-published writer and creativity coach. She has taught creativity classes for over ten years and works with individuals in one-to-one coaching sessions to support them as they explore, expand, and express their creativity. Bane helps her students and clients discover the connections between their creativity and shadows, break through creative blocks, and walk through fear to embrace the gifts hidden inside themselves. She lives in Minneapolis with two dogs, two cats, one human and one invisible dragon.